Foucault's

This b
theor
tion
biogra
'Kant
Gordc
projec
sugges
subjec
ters, ir
menta
Meure
politic
talist s
into n
constr
relatio
(Donz
realitie
nologi
the hu
subjec
critiqu
logical
enable
By
struct
social

1998

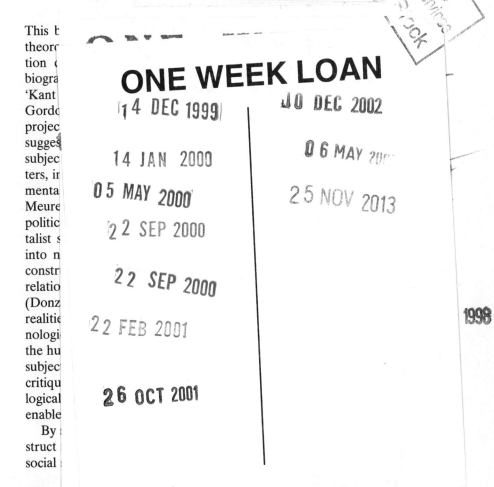

Mike Ga   gy at the University of Lough-
borough and **Terry Johnson** is Professor of Sociology at the University
of Leicester.

Foucault's new domains

Edited by
Mike Gane and Terry Johnson

London and New York

First published 1993
by Routledge
11 New Fetter Lane, London EC4P 4EE

Simultaneously published in the USA and Canada
by Routledge
29 West 35th Street, New York, NY 10001

© 1993 selection and editorial matter, Mike Gane and Terry Johnson;
individual chapters, the contributors

Printed and bound in Great Britain by
T.J. Press (Padstow) Ltd, Padstow, Cornwall

British Library Cataloguing in Publication Data
A catalogue record for this book is available from the British Library

Library of Congress Cataloging in Publication Data
Foucault's new domains / [edited by] Mike Gane and Terry Johnson.
    p.   cm.
    1. Power (Social sciences)   2. Individualism.   3. Critical theory.
    4. Foucault, Michel.   I. Gane, Mike.   II. Johnson, Terry.
    HM136.F68   1993
    303.3′3–dc20   93–7212
                                                               CIP

ISBN 0-415-08660-4
    0-415-08661-2 (pbk)

Contents

Contributors   vi

Acknowledgements   viii

Introduction: the project of Michel Foucault   1
Mike Gane and Terry Johnson

1 **Kant on Enlightenment and revolution**   10
Michel Foucault

·2 **Question, ethos, event: Foucault on Kant and Enlightenment**   19
Colin Gordon

3 **Michel Foucault (1926–84): The Will to Knowledge**   36
Pasquale Pasquino

4 **A political genealogy of political economy**   49
Denis Meuret

·5 **Governing economic life**   75
Peter Miller and Nikolas Rose

6 **The promotion of the social**   106
Jacques Donzelot

·7 **Expertise and the state**   139
Terry Johnson

8 **Personality as a vocation: the political rationality of the humanities**   153
Ian Hunter

·9 **Archaeologizing genealogy: Michel Foucault and the economy of austerity**   193
Phil Bevis, Michèle Cohen and Gavin Kendall

Name index   216

Subject index   219

Notes on contributors

Phil Bevis is presently working on a book, *The Birth and Death of the Author*, concerned with the technologies of the self and the changing positions of the reader of the novel. It examines the accumulated historical series of prefixed biographical sketches of a sixteenth-century Spanish writer who died on the same day as Shakespeare.

Michèle Cohen teaches French and Women's Studies at Richmond College, London. She is working on a poststructuralist history of the learning of French in England in relation to gender subjectivation, and has published several articles on the subject.

Jacques Donzelot is *Maître de Conference* in Political Science and Director of the Centre d'Etudes des Politiques Sociales in Paris.

Mike Gane teaches in the Department of Social Sciences at Lough-borough University. He has recently published two studies on the French writer Jean Baudrillard, published by Routledge.

Colin Gordon works on medical informatics for the Imperial Cancer Research Fund. He has been active as translator, editor and author. He was recently a contributor to and, with Peter Miller, a co-editor of *The Foucault Effect* (Harvester, 1991).

Ian Hunter teaches in the Faculty of Humanities, Griffith University, Brisbane. He is the author of *Culture and Government: Emergence of Literary Education* (Macmillan, 1988) and co-author (with D. Saunders and D. Williamson) of *On Pornography: Literature, Sexuality and Obscenity Law* (Macmillan, 1992). He is currently working on a genealogy of post-Kantian humanism as a spiritual discipline.

Terry Johnson is Professor of Sociology at Leicester University and is currently working on a book on the relationship between expertise and the state.

Gavin Kendall is Lecturer is Psychology at Lancaster University.

Denis Meuret works for the Ministry of National Education in Paris. He is engaged in research on the history of ideas in economics and management.

Peter Miller is a Senior Lecturer in the Department of Accounting and Finance at the London School of Economics and Political Science. He is the author of *Domination and Power* (Routledge, 1987), a comparative study of the work of Michel Faucault and the Frankfurt School. Together with Nikolas Rose he is the author of *The Power of Psychiatry* (Polity Press, 1986), and is also a co-editor, with Colin Gordon, of *The Foucault Effect* (Harvester, 1991). He is Associate Editor of the journal *Accounting, Organizations and Society.*

Pasquale Pasquino, born 1948, working at CNRS (CREA) at Paris, has been Visiting Professor at the Collège de France and published various articles on the constitutional theory of the French Revolution and the Weimar Republic; his current work is on political thought (Machiavelli, Hobbes and the English civil war).

Nikolas Rose is Professor and Head of Department of Sociology at Goldsmiths' College, University of London. He is co-ordinator of the 'History of the Present Network', an international network of researchers whose work has been influenced by the writings of Michel Foucault. He is the author of *The Psychological Complex: Psychology, Politics and Society in England, 1869–1939* (Routledge, 1985) and joint author, with Peter Miller, of *The Power of Psychiatry* (Polity Press, 1986). He is currently writing a social and intellectual history of the Tavistock Clinic and Tavistock Institute of Human Relations (with Peter Miller) and researching changing forms and strategies of political power.

Acknowledgements

All but one of the papers collected here were first published in the journal *Economy and Society*, and we would like to thank the editors of the journal for their permission to publish them in this volume.

Introduction
The project of Michel Foucault

Mike Gane and Terry Johnson

Michel Foucault died in 1984, almost ten years ago. At his death he left a considerable corpus of work, which had already provoked a huge mass of critical commentary for and against. Before his death in 1983 Michael Clark had just published his 'annotated bibliography' on Foucault, subtitled curiously 'Tool Kit for a New Age' – still a useful source book since it summarizes many of Foucault's more inaccessible pieces as well as the principal commentaries available at that date. Today, many items could be added – not merely the last and posthumous works of Foucault, but that enormous explosion of writing responding to, and taking off from, his ideas. However, in some areas, including feminist writing, Foucault's influence has been unevenly developed since his death. This volume is a selection of some recent writing, influenced largely by the dominant interests of Foucault's later period of work. As such it has much in common with the recent collections *The Foucault Effect* (edited by Burchell, Gordon and Miller) and *Michel Foucault: Philosopher* (edited by Armstrong).

This introduction will contextualize the collection in two ways: by indicating the implications of Foucault's later perspective for specific fields of study, but first by providing a brief introduction to Foucault through a review of the recently published biography of him by Didier Eribon (first published in French in 1989).

Michel Foucault was born in 1926. His academic career was extraordinarily rapid and brilliant. By 1962 he was Professor of Philosophy at the University of Clermont-Ferrand, and by 1970 he was elected to the highest institution in French higher education, the Collège de France. Foucault was educated at the Ecole Normale, where he was taught by and became a close friend of Althusser and where he also spent a short time as a member of the PCF (French Communist Party) (1950–3). He had, however, broken with both Marxism and the Communist Party before taking up foreign appointments, beginning in 1955.

In 1952 he had been appointed as assistant in psychology at the

University of Lille (though he never lived in Lille, staying one night a week in a hotel and teaching two or three days). He went to Uppsala in 1955 for three years, where he taught literature and French language at the French Institute. Foucault seems to have been more interested in his research than in teaching, and ex-students reported (to Eribon) that they were still 'angry' that the classes he did take were far too difficult. After Uppsala, Foucault moved on to Warsaw in 1958 for one year, and then to Hamburg for a further year, where he was again based at the French Cultural Institute but giving lectures at the university. By the time he left Poland, Foucault had developed a political position that was markedly anti-Communist and highly critical of Marxism.

In 1960, Foucault joined the staff of the University of Clermont-Ferrand to teach psychology, and in 1962 was promoted to the post of Professor of Philosophy (actually still teaching psychology). Again, typically, he never moved house to Clermont-Ferrand but travelled down by train from Paris each week, staying in a hotel, and teaching for one or two days. Appropriately for the 1960s, Foucault had by this time become quite a dandy, wearing a black corduroy suit, white turtleneck jumpers, and a green cape. His lecturing style had also changed considerably from that reported at Uppsala. His lectures were no longer regarded as too difficult. They became increasingly well organized and precise, and in consequence very popular, and 'during his last year at Clermont, Foucault was applauded at the end of every lecture – something that had never happened before in the Auvergne; nor since' (Eribon 1991: 141). Curiously he divided his class into groups of seven people. The students who remained unattached he called exiles, 'bedouins', and were subject to constant questioning and gibes.

During this period Foucault scandalized the university by appointing Daniel Defert, his lover, to the position of assistant in the department. He said later 'I am living in a state of passion with someone ... [a state] in which I am entirely invested, one running through me. I think there is nothing in the world, nothing, no matter what, that could stop me from going to see him again, or speaking to him' (Eribon 1991: 141–2). Without identifying his source, Eribon reports that when Foucault was asked to explain why he had appointed Defert in preference to a more highly qualified and older woman, he said 'because we don't like old maids (*les vieilles filles*) here' (Eribon 1991: 142).

Foucault's departure from Clermont-Ferrand, initially on 'administrative leave', was influenced by Georges Canguilhem, who advised him not to take up the sociologist Georges Gurvitch's suggestion of a move to the Sorbonne. He was similarly persuaded to turn down offers of posts in Tokyo, Congo-Kinshasa and São Paulo (though he did lecture at the last of these).

In September 1966, he left France again, this time for Tunis, on a three-year contract. He stayed for two-and-a-half years, living on the coast not far from Tunis in a house overlooking the sea. A friend and colleague noted his 'greedy appetite for living and loving in the sun' (Eribon 1991: 188). He lectured to large audiences drawn from the cultured elite of Tunis. His students found Foucault now clearly anti-Marx and pro-Nietzsche in orientation. But it was at Tunis that Foucault entered into a new phase of radical politicization that deepened in subsequent years. He recalled later that it was in Tunis that he was

) NEW
(PHASE

> present for large, violent student riots that preceded by several weeks what happened in May in France. This was March 1968 ... I have to say that I was tremendously impressed by those young men and women who took terrible risks ... It was a political experience for me. (Eribon 1991: 195)

He noted that his previous contacts with political organizations had left him 'with a rather bitter experience of politics, and a thoroughly speculative scepticism'. But, he continued, in Tunis he 'came round to offering some concrete aid to the students' (Eribon 1991: 195). His comments here are important: the students

> all claimed to be inspired by Marxism, with a violence, intensity, and passion that was altogether remarkable. It constituted for them not merely a better analysis of things, but at the same time a kind of moral energy ... It was the evidence that myth is necessary. A political ideology or a political perception of the world ... was absolutely necessary to begin the struggle. The precise theory and its scientific value, on the other hand, were entirely secondary. (Eribon 1991: 195)

On returning to France, Foucault commented that what he saw there 'was exactly the opposite of what he had found interesting in Tunisia' (Eribon 1991: 195). Henceforth, he worked to overcome the division between his theoretical interests and politics; always connecting with what he saw as specific, concrete, limited but effective struggles.

Although in the autumn of 1968 he accepted a position at Nanterre, he resigned in December of the same year to take up the Directorship of the Department of Philosophy at the new University of Vincennes. Members of his new department were mostly Althusserians and included Judith Miller, Alain Badiou, Jacques Rancière, François Regnault and Etienne Balibar, as well as Henri Weber, François Chatelet and Michel Serres. Courses launched in early 1969 were immediately disrupted by campus action in solidarity with events in central Paris. The brand-new equipment was used as barricades, as the 'occupied' campus was invaded by two thousand police officers. Many students were expelled from the university, and Foucault, increasingly drawn into the politics of the university sector, spoke out against such crude repressive action.

The university was highly politicized and Foucault attracted enormous numbers of students – over six hundred enrolled for his lecture-course. His department was, however, immediately singled out by the education minister, Olivier Guichard, who refused state recognition for its degrees. Foucault responded by pointing to the fact that his department was trying to cope with 950 students with a teaching staff of only eight lecturers, and that the remarkable freedom of the new courses was being undermined. Foucault's position was made impossible by the fact that the department did not require students to be examined for their degree. Eribon cites a former secretary as saying that in

> the first year, the professors shut themselves up in a room and the students slipped a little piece of paper, with their names written on it, under the door. They were then listed as having passed. The second year, a list of those who had passed was typed up; it included anyone who asked to be on it. (Eribon 1991: 208)

Whether or not this account is completely accurate is not really important; it suggests something of the anarchic mood and practice in the Philosophy Department at the time.

Foucault's politicization was influenced by Daniel Defert, now a sociology lecturer at Vincennes and active in Maoist groups. While he was joining in demonstrations and writing manifestoes, Foucault also spent a good deal of time away from the university preparing his move to the Collège de France. His politicization was developed primarily at the practical level; in his lectures and published work, he was still writing on Nietzsche and the critique of the subject. It was following his election to the Collège de France in 1970 that his intellectual work – he was required to produce a new course each year – also gradually became radicalized.

While there are a large number of works outlining Foucault's intellectual career, none as yet can be regarded as definitive. Our task in this introduction is to note some of the characteristic links between his life and his work in the period when he was at the Collège de France, particularly those themes and concerns that are taken up in this collection. His retrospective course summaries (published as *Resumé de Cours 1970–1982* (Foucault 1989)) indicate the range of his interests in these years. In one of the lectures given during this period, published below (see Chapter 1, p. 10 'Kant on Enlightenment and revolution') he speaks of a 'critical thought which has the form of an ontology of ourselves'. Certainly this idea is indicative of Foucault's emergent desire to combine engagement and theory in a complex web which would ensure that theory could never be simply academic. He insisted that engagement should be effective and that such effectiveness could only arise out of a new relation of theory to action: an 'ontology of the present'.

In 1971–2, following his move to the Collège de France, Foucault took a leading role in the Groupe d'Information sur les Prisons (GIP). A year later he became a member of the Djellali committee. These engagements involved action on behalf of prisoners and those subject to racialist attacks and injustice. Foucault organized questionnaires and surveys and researched widely into the treatment of prisoners. Pamphlets were published on police brutality, prison suicides, and deaths in prison custody. In November 1971, there were widespread revolts in the French prisons, culminating in the prison fire at Toul in December. Foucault initiated public discussion and led a protest demonstration to the Ministry of Justice. The GIP extended its organization and operations throughout France, its membership growing to about 3000. However, once prisoners established their own organization in 1972, the GIP, still run from Foucault's apartment, was dissolved. These practical involvements led up not only to the publication of Foucault's *Discipline and Punish* but also to the projects on justice, and the 'analytic of truth' discussed in this collection by Pasquino (Chapter 3). This latter concern with the strategic importance of information and 'truth' led Foucault to support an important new daily newspaper, *Libération*, which grew out of the already established networks for gathering information associated with GIP; the Agence de Presse-Libération (APL). It was becoming increasingly clear to Foucault that effective engagement depended on the capacity to speak the 'truth' (*véridiction*: see Erbon 1991: 254). This self-same issue was raised and developed in a completely different language and style in the lectures at the Collège de France at the same time as Foucault was providing practical support to the founding of *Libération*.

In 1976, Foucault took action over human rights in Iran in association with the Iranian activist Ahmed Salamatian. Foucault visited Iran just as the Shah's repression was intensifying. After talking to people from all shades of the political spectrum, he concluded that for Iran secularization and modernization were already archaic. Opposing the 'illusions' of Western analysts, he argued that modernity was experienced by Iranians not as progressive but as old and corrupt. His articles on Iran created a storm of controversy, particularly when he argued that wearing the veil had become an impressive political gesture. Following the revolution, however, the situation changed rapidly, and Salamatian was forced to flee fundamentalist repression in 1981. Today we can only speculate about whether Foucault would have thought that on balance he had misjudged the possibilities of the revolution. We do know that he admitted elsewhere in his work a fundamental ambivalence about the nature of modernization and secularization; an ambivalence not represented or discussed in the collection presented here.

In the early 1980s, a new socialist government came to power in France and new repression emerged in Poland. The evident inactivity of the French government prompted Foucault (with Bourdieu) to write to *Libération* with an appeal for decisive support for the popular movement in Poland. In September 1982, Foucault drove to Poland with Bernard Kouchner and Médecins du Monde in a gesture of solidarity. Again, an object of the visit was an attempt to establish information centres, and liaisons between intellectuals and unions.

This period turned out to be a critical moment in the development of Foucault's assessment of the governing process. In particular, he came to the conclusion that the French socialists lacked an 'art of government' and he began to consider writing something on the possibility of 'governing in a different way' (Eribon 1991: 306). Clearly this idea, arising out of practical concerns, was also linked to Foucault's emerging intellectual project for a study of governmentality, raised in his short but influential paper 'On governmentality' (published in Italian in 1978, and in English in 1979). In this volume, there are a number of chapters which flow from this theme: Miller and Rose on 'Governing economic life' (Chapter 5), Johnson's analysis of governmentality and the professions (Chapter 7), and Hunter's consideration of political rationality (Chapter 8).

Foucault's developing intellectual concerns also included a reflection on the self – on self-discipline and the 'care of the self'. These themes connect in complex ways with his sexual ontology, discussed in this collection by Pasquino (Chapter 3) and, very critically, by Bevis, Cohen and Kendall (Chapter 9). Foucault seemed to have relished the relative freedoms in sexuality and drug use existing in New York and California. Eribon speculates that drug use may have been a factor in the car collision in which Foucault was involved in 1978. It is clear also that sexual experimentation was a factor leading up to the AIDS-related illness that was the cause of Foucault's death. Deeply interested in marginality and homosexuality, Foucault speculated on why homosexuality had become a problem in Western cultures. This was, however, only one strand in a vast programme of work on the genealogy of sexuality in the West, much of which has now been published. This work has stimulated a number of wide-ranging parallel enquiries. Meuret's essay in this collection (Chapter 4) investigates the genealogy of political economy, and Donzelot's (Chapter 6) the genealogy of the formation of 'the social' itself. All of these projects, apparently disparate, are in fact linked. At the epistemological level they seem to be on the point of providing a synthesis of the field of the new domains. However, in departing from the idea of the ontology of the self, the project seems after Foucault's death to have become detached from its original strategic and practical matrix and to have become, perhaps inevitably, abstract and academic.

In this final section, we will turn to an assessment of the nature of the importance of Foucault's intervention in social thought and analysis. Rather than attempting to summarize all the chapters which follow, we will take one key domain – the analysis of the professions and expert knowledge. What is different and decisive in Foucault's approach is that his concept of government rejects the notion of the state as a coherent, calculating subject whose political power grows in concert with its insertions into civil society. Rather, the state is viewed quite differently, as an ensemble of institutions, procedures, tactics, calculations, knowledges and technologies, which together comprise the particular form of government – the outcome, in a sense, of governing. Governmentality, Foucault argues, is a novel capacity of governing that gradually emerged in Europe from the sixteenth century, in association with the invention, operationalization and institutionalization of such knowledges, tactics and technologies. Foucault is not attempting to present an alternative theory of the state; he seeks to identify a particular way of governing, which is associated with the parallel crystalization of new forms of expertise and state institution.

The implication of expertise in this process, particularly from the eighteenth and nineteenth centuries, has meant that the professions became as much a condition for the exercise of political power as were the formal bureaucratic instruments of government. A major implication of the argument is to displace the terms of a long-standing controversy in sociology, the alternatives of professional autonomy and state intervention. This controversy arises only insofar as the relationship between state and professions is misconceived as existing between two differently acting subject, with all the possible grounds of disputation this makes possible: the degree of autonomy of profession, the degree of intervention of state, type of subordination of the profession to the state, proletarianization, and so on. But much of this argument is clearly circular and simply repeats the premises of the division already established.

The dominant view of the relationship is again one-dimensional; that is, it comprises only one set of possible alternatives – externally imposed control or internally generated autonomy. Eliot Freidson was the first sociologist to provide a more systematic and sophisticated view of the relationship. He confronted the issue by asking how it is possible to acknowledge the extent to which a profession is subject to state regulation, even state control, while at the same time retaining the idea that these occupations are fundamentally characterized by their autonomy. His answer has been seminal. Medicine, he argued, emerged by the 'grace of powerful protectors' (Freidson 1970: xii), and it was from such a protected 'shelter' in the nineteenth century that it was able to achieve autonomy both from the ideological dominance of such protective elites and, subsequently, from the constraining effects of all external evaluation, including that exercised by governments. Freidson asked the question: 'Can an occupation be truly autonomous, a profession free, when it must submit to the protective custody of the state' (1970: 24). His answer was that while a profession may be entirely subordinated to the state when it comes to the 'social and economic organisation of work', modern states, nevertheless, whatever their ideological leanings, 'uniformly' leave in the hands of professionals control over the technical. aspect of their work. In the United States for example, doctors retain control over the 'quality and the terms of medical practice' (Freidson 1970: 33). State intervention does not, he argued, undermine the autonomy of technical judgment so much as establish the social and moral premises on which the judgment of illness is based (Freidson 1970: 43). Freidson then resolves his initial paradox by way of the claim that the autonomy of a profession depends on its dependence on the state. The paradox is resolved once we distinguish between the types of autonomy (technical against socio-economic), and forms of dependence (absolute and relative).

Despite his achievements, Freidson retains a conception of the state as external, as exerting control over the socio-economic terms of professional work, leaving matters of technical evaluation in the hands of professionals. It is this conception which leads to an incoherence in Freidson's position, an incoherence which Foucault's conception of governmentality allows us to eliminate. The relevance of Foucault for this domain is best approached from his view of history, in particular his rejection of history as the unfolding of essence, or as a search for pure origins. As is clear in Freidson, there is a strong tradition in sociology that locates the essence of professionalism in a body of esoteric knowledge, the process of professionalization being in effect the unfolding of this essence to the end state – the pure profession. In the telling of this story, state intervention is often viewed as a pathological inhibition of the process. In the search for origins, sociologists of the professions have usually identified a mythical original state of separation roughly located during the *laissez-faire* period, and written the history of the professions as the history of state intervention. In this perspective all that remains of Freidson's question is: does intervention always mean less autonomy?

Foucault's position would be to reject any attempt to present these accounts of professionalization or state intervention as histories. According to Foucault, they constitute inadmissible alternatives to genealogy. Equally, they tend to assume that power is an attribute of the subjects in the process, the profession and the government. Foucault's conception implies that power cannot be reduced to an act of domination or intervention; rather, the relationship of power peculiar to modern liberal democracies emerged with the shift from divine to popular legitimacy. That is to say, in the modern era the legitimate political power has resided in the obedience of subjects, and it is Foucault's central concern with formation of the obedient subject that explains his focus on the role of discipline (disciplines/knowledges) in his analysis of modernity.

Foucault's concern with governmentality is crucially linked to the process of what he calls normalization, the establishment or institution-alization of those disciplines, knowledges and technologies that lay the ground for the emergence of the autonomous, self-regulating subject. This conception of government focuses our attention on the mechanisms through which the political programmes and objectives of governments have been aligned to the personal and collective conduct of subjects. Governmentality is, in short, all those procedures, techniques, institutions and knowledges that as an ensemble empower these political programmes. Important here is the notion that expertise was crucial to the development of such an ensemble, and that the modern professions were the institutionalized form such expertise took. This change in the way that questions are posed has had important ramifications throughout the social sciences.

In conclusion, it is now possible to see more clearly the scope of Foucault's influence. Much recent work, including the essays here, is still exploratory, and as yet the full extent of Foucault's influence cannot be determined. The essays contained in this collection indicate, both positively and in critique, the growing significance and consolidation of the social research provoked by a remarkable thinker who aspired both to the construction of new specialisms and to the exposure of new unities in social analysis.

References

Armstrong, T. (ed.) (1992) *Michel Foucault: Philosopher*, London, Harvester.

Burchell, G., Gordon, C. and Miller, P. (eds) (1991) *The Foucault Effect*, London, Harvester.

Clark, M. (1983) *Michel Foucault: An Annotated Bibliography*, New York, Garland.

Eribon, D. (1991) *Michel Foucault*, Cambridge, MA, Harvard University Press.

Foucault, M. (1989) *Resumé des Cours 1970–1982*, Paris, Jullard.

Freidson, E. (1970) *The Profession of Medicine: A Study of the Sociology of Applied Knowledge*, New York, Dodd, Mead.

Gane, M. (ed.) (1986) *Toward a Critique of Foucault*, London, Routledge.

1 Kant on Enlightenment and revolution*

Michel Foucault
Translated by Colin Gordon

Kant's essay, 'What is Enlightenment?' seems to me to introduce a new type of question into the field of philosophical reflexion. Of course it is certainly not the first text in the history of philosophy, nor indeed the only one of Kant's writings, which takes as its theme a question concerning history. One finds texts by Kant which address to history a question of origin: the essay on the beginnings of history itself, the essay on the definition of the concept of race; other pieces address to history the question of its fulfilment: thus, in this same year of 1784, 'The Idea of a Universal History from a Cosmopolitan Point of View'. Lastly there are other writings which consider the inner finality which organises historical processes, such as the text concerning the use of teleological principles. All these questions, which are moreover closely interrelated, can be found running through Kant's analyses concerning history. It seems to me that the text on *Aufklärung* is rather different; at any rate, it does not directly pose any of these questions, neither that of origin nor, despite appearances, that of completion, and it poses only in a relatively discreet, almost lateral manner the question of the teleology immanent in the very process of history.

The question which seems to me to appear for the first time in this text by Kant is the question of the present, of the contemporary moment. What is happening today? What is happening now? And what is this 'now' which we all inhabit, and which defines the moment in which I am writing? This is not the first time in philosophical reflexion that one finds references to the present, at least as a determinate historical situation regarded as having a value for philosophical reflexion. After all, when at the beginning of the *Discourse on Method* Descartes tells the story of his own personal itinerary and all the philosophical choices which he has made, at once on his own behalf and on that of philosophy, he does make reference in an explicit manner to what might be termed a historical situation in the realm of knowledge and of the sciences of his time. But this sort of reference always has to do with the possibility of adducing within this configuration designated as present

Published in *Economy and Society Volume 15 Number 1 February 1986*

a motive for a philosophical decision; you will not find in Descartes a question of the order of: 'What then is the precise character of this present to which I belong?' Now it seems to me that the question Kant answers, and which he comes to answer because he has been asked it, is of a different kind. It is not simply: what is there in the present situation which can determine such and such a decision in philosophy? The question has to do with what this present is; it centres on the determination of a certain element of the present which has to be identified, distinguished, deciphered from among all the other material which surrounds it. The question is: what is there in the present which can have contemporary meaning for philosophical reflexion?

Kant's response aims to show in what sense this meaningful element in the present manifests itself as the bearer and sign of a process which concerns thought, knowledge, philosophy; but it is also and more particularly concerned with determining how and in what respect someone who speaks as a thinker, as a savant, as a philosopher forms a part of this same process, and (furthermore) how he has a certain role to play in this process, figuring in it that is to say at once as an element and as an actor.

It seems to me in short that one sees the appearance in this text by Kant of the question of the present as a philosophical event incorporating within it the philosopher who speaks of it. If one cares to think of philosophy as a form of discursive practice with its own history, it seems to me that with this text on *Aufklärung* one sees philosophy — and I think I am not overstretching the facts by saying that this is for the first time — problematising its own discursive present-ness: a present-ness which it interrogates as an event, an event whose meaning, value and philosophical singularity it is required to state, and in which it is to elicit at once its own *raison d'être* and the foundation of what it has to say. And thereby one can see that for the philosopher to pose the question of his own inclusion in this present will no longer be a question of his adherence to a doctrine or a tradition; it will no longer even simply be the question of his belonging to a human community in general, but rather that of his membership of a certain 'we', a we corresponding to a cultural ensemble characteristic of his own contemporaneity.

The philosopher's own singular state of adherence to this 'we' now begins to become an indispensable theme of reflection for the philosopher himself. Philosophy as the problematisation of a present-ness, the interrogation by philosophy of this present-ness of which it is part and relative to which it is obliged to locate itself: this may well be the characteristic trait of philosophy as a discourse of and upon modernity.

To put it very schematically: the question of modernity had been posed in classical culture according to an axis with two poles, antiquity and modernity; it had been formulated either in terms of an authority to be accepted or rejected (what authority should be accepted? what model followed? etc.), or else in the form (which was actually a correlate of the first alternative) of a comparative evaluation: are the Ancients superior to the Moderns? are we living in a period of decadence? and so forth. There now appears a new way of posing the question of modernity, no longer within a longitudinal relationship to the Ancients, but rather in what one might call a 'sagital' relation to one's own present-ness. Discourse has to take account of its own present-ness, in order to find its own place, to pronounce its meaning, and to specify the mode of action which it is capable of exercising within this present.

What is my present? What is the meaning of this present? And what am I doing when I speak of this present? Such is, it seems to me, the substance of this new interrogation on modernity.

All the foregoing remarks are meant as no more than a sketch: a possible path which would need exploring in greater detail. One would need to attempt a genealogy, not so much of the notion of modernity as of modernity as a question. And in any case, even if I am taking Kant's text as marking the point of emergence of this question, this essay itself obviously forms part of a wider historical process whose scope needs to be assessed in its own right. Certainly it would be an interesting line of enquiry for the study of the Eighteenth century in general, and more particularly for that of the *Aufklärung*, to consider the fact that it was the *Aufklärung* itself which named itself the *Aufklärung*: a cultural process of indubitably a very singular character, which came to self-awareness through the act of naming itself, situating itself in relation to its past and its future, and prescribing the operation which it was itself required to effect within its own present.

Is not the *Aufklärung*, after all, the first epoch which names its own self and which, instead of simply characterising itself, according to old custom, as a period of decadence or prosperity, splendour or misery, names itself by the invocation of an event in the general history of thought, reason and knowledge, an event in which it has its own special role to play?

The *Aufklärung* is a period which formulates its own motto, its own precept, a period which defines its own task in relation both to the general history of thought and to its own present and the forms of knowledge, ignorance, illusion in terms of which it identifies its historical situation.

It seems to me that in this question of the *Aufklärung* we see one of the first manifestations of a way of philosophising which was to have a long history over the following two centuries. One of the great functions of what is called modern philosophy, that philosophy whose starting-point lies in the last years of the Eighteenth century, is that of questioning itself about its own present-ness.

It would be possible to follow the trajectory of this modality of philosophy down through the Nineteenth century to the present day. For the moment, the only point which I would like to stress is that this question treated by Kant in 1784 in response to a question put to him by an outside enquirer was not one which Kant himself was destined subsequently to forget. He was to pose it again and seek to answer it in connection with another event which, like the *Aufklärung*, has never ceased from questioning itself about itself. That event was, of course, the French Revolution.

In 1798, Kant produced a kind of sequel to the text of 1784. In 1784 he tried to answer the question put to him, 'What is this *Aufklärung* of which we are a part?', and in 1798 he answered a question which contemporary reality posed for him, but which had also already been raised since 1794 by the whole of philosophical discussion in Germany. This question was 'What is the Revolution?'

As you know, 'The Conflict between the Faculties' is a set of three dissertations concerning the relations between the different Faculties which compose the University. The second dissertation concerns the conflict between the Faculties of Philosophy and Law. Now the whole field of relations between philosophy and law is taken up here by the question: 'Is there a constant progress of the human race?' And it is in order to answer this question that Kant puts forward, in Section V of this dissertation, the following reasoning: if one wants to answer the question, 'Is there a constant progress of the human race?', one needs to determine whether there exists a possible cause for this progress; but having once established this possibility, one needs then to show that this cause does actually operate, and for that purpose to identify an event which shows that cause in action. The designation of such a cause can never do more than determine possible effects, or more exactly the possibility of effect; but the reality of the effect can only ever be established except by the existence of an event.

Thus it does not suffice to follow the threads of a teleological fabric which would make progress possible; it is necessary to isolate, within history, an event which will have value as a sign.

A sign of what? A sign of the existence of a cause, a permanent cause which throughout history has guided men in the way of progress. A constant cause, one which it must be possible to prove has acted in the past, is acting in the present, and will act in the future. Hence the event which will enable us to decide if there is progress will be a sign which is '*rememorativum, demonstrativum, prognosticon*'. It must be a sign which shows that things have indeed always been thus (the rememorative sign), a sign which shows that things are at present happening thus (the demonstrative sign), a sign finally which shows that things will always be thus (the prognostic sign). We will be then be sure that the cause which makes progress possible has not been operative only at a particular moment, but that it guarantees a general tendency of the whole human race to advance in the direction of progress. This then is the question: Is there an event taking place around us which is be rememorative, demonstrative and prognostic of a permanent progress embracing the human race in its totality?

You will have guessed Kant's answer; but I would like to read to you the passage in which he introduces the Revolution as the event which has this signifying value. 'Do not expect', he writes at the start of Section VI, 'that this event will consist either in momentous deeds or crimes committed by men whereby what was great among men is made small or what was small made great, or in ancient and splendid edifices which vanish as if by magic while others come forth in their place as if from the depths of the earth. No, nothing of the sort.'

Kant is evidently alluding here to traditional arguments which adduce proofs of the progress or non-progress of the human species from the overthrow of empires, the catastrophes in which the most firmly established states disappear, the shifts of fortune which cast down existing powers and set up new ones in their place. Take heed, Kant tells his readers, it is not among such great events that one should seek the rememorative, demonstrative, prognostic sign of progress, but rather among events which are far less grandiose, far less readily noticeable. One can analyse these elements of meaning in our present only through a reckoning which reveals crucial significance and value in things which are apparently neither significant nor valuable. What, then, is this event which is decisive without being 'great'? Of course it would be paradoxical to suggest that the Revolution is not a noisy, spectacular occurrence: is it not indeed the very model of an event which overturns everything, whereby what had been great is made small and what had been small is made great, an event which swallows up the apparently solid structures of society and State? But for Kant it is precisely not this aspect of the Revolution which counts. The rememorative, demonstrative, prognostic event is not the exploits of the revolutionary drama itself or their accompanying gesticulation. What is significant is the way the Revolution operates as spectacle, the way it is generally received by spectators who do not take part in it but watch it, witness it and, for better or worse, allow themselves to be swept along by it. It is not the revolutionary upheaval as such which in Kant's view offers proof of progress: no doubt because, in the first place, it does no more than turn things upside down, and, furthermore, if one were in a position to make such a revolution over again, one would not wish to do so. There is an extremely interesting passage on this latter point: 'Small matter whether the revolution of a gifted people, which we have seen taking place in our own day (so it is the French Revolution which Kant has in mind), succeed or miscarry, small matter whether it pile up misery and atrocity to a point where a sensible man, even if he could hope to carry it through success-fully at a second attempt, would still resolve never to make the trial at such a cost.' So it is not the revolutionary process itself which is important. Never mind whether it succeed or fail, that is nothing to do with progress, or at least with the sign of progress which we are looking for. The success or failure of the revolution are not signs of progress or a sign that there is no progress. Even indeed if it were possible for someone to understand the Revolu-tion and its process and furthermore to be capable of bringing it to a successful outcome, even then, reckoning up the inevitable price to be paid for such a revolution, a rational being would decide against making it. So, considered as an 'upheaval', as an enterprise which may succeed or fail, or as an unacceptably heavy price, the Revolution cannot in itself be taken as the sign of a cause capable of sustaining throughout the course of history a constant progress of humanity.

What, on the contrary, does have meaning and constitutes the sign of progress is the fact that, as Kant expresses it, the Revolu-tion is surrounded by 'a wishful participation that borders closely on enthusiasm'. What matters in the Revolution is not the Revolu-tion itself, it is what takes place in the heads of the people who do not make it or in any case are not its principal actors, it is the relation they themselves experience with this Revolution of which they are not themselves the active agents. Enthusiasm for the Revolution is, according to Kant, the sign of a moral disposition of humanity; this disposition manifests itself in two permanent ways: the right of every people to provide itself with the political consti-tution which appears good to the people itself, and the lawful and moral principle of a constitution framed in such a way as to avoid, by its very principles, all possibility of offensive war. Now it is precisely the disposition leading humanity towards such a consti-tution which is attested by the enthusiasm for the Revolution. The Revolution as spectacle and not as gesticulation, the Revolution as

a focus of enthusiasm for its witnesses and not as a principle of upheaval for its participants, is a '*signum rememorativum*', since it
reveals the disposition as having been present in men from the
beginning; it is a '*signum demonstrativum*', since it shows the present efficacy of this disposition; and it is also a '*signum prognosticon*', since while there are indeed results of the Revolution whose
value can be questioned, it will never be possible to forget the disposition which has been revealed through it.

It is clear moreover that it is precisely these two elements, a
political constitution decided by the free choice of men and a
political constitution which avoids war, which comprise the process
of *Aufklärung*; that is, the Revolution does indeed complete and
continue the process of *Aufklärung*, and it is to this extent that
both *Aufklärung* and Revolution are events which can never be
forgotten. 'I maintain,' Kant writes, 'that, even without partaking
of a spirit of prophesy, I can predict for the human race, on the
basis of the appearances and precursive signs of our time, that it
will reach this end (that is to say arrive at a state such that men
will be able to give themselves the constitution they wish and a
constitution which will prevent offensive war), and that thence-
forth these advances will never again be put in question. Such a
phenomenon in the history of humanity can never be forgotten,
since it has revealed in human nature a disposition, a faculty for
betterment such that not even the subtlest politician could have
elicited it from the previous course of events, and which only
nature and liberty united in the human species according to the
inner principles of right would have been capable of foretelling,
and even then only in an indeterminate manner and as something
in the character of a contingent event. But even should the goal
foreshadowed by this event still remain yet to be reached, in
case of the final failure of the Revolution or reform of a people's
constitution, or even if, after a certain lapse of time, everything
should relapse into its former rut, as politicians now predict, this
philosophical prophecy would lose none of its force. For this event
is too important, too much interwoven with the interests of
humanity and of too widespread an influence on every part of the
globe not to be recalled to memory by the peoples at the occasion
of each favourable circumstance, so that they would then be
aroused to a repetition of new attempts of this kind, for in an
affair of such importance for the human race it must needs be that
sooner or later the intended constitution shall finally attain to that
solidity which the lessons of repeated experience could not fail
to give it in the minds of all.'

The Revolution will in any event always be at risk of relapsing
into the former rut, but, seen from a viewpoint where its specific

content becomes unimportant, its existence attests to a permanent virtuality which cannot be ignored: it is the guarantee for future history of the continuity of progress.

I have been seeking here only to situate this text of Kant's on *Aufklärung* for you; I will try in a moment to offer a closer reading of its content. I wanted also to indicate how, some fifteen years later, Kant reflected on that other, distinctly more dramatic event, the French Revolution. With these two texts we are in a sense at the place of origin, the point of departure of a whole dynasty of philosophical questions. These two questions, 'what is *Aufklärung*?', 'what is the Revolution? , are the two forms in which Kant posed the question of his own present. They are also, I believe, the two questions which have continued to haunt, if not all modern philosophy since the Nineteenth century, at least a great part of it. After all, it does seem to me that the *Aufklärung*, understood at once as a singular event inaugurating European modernity and as a permanent process manifesting itself in the history of reason, the development and establishment of forms of rationality and technique, the autonomy and authority of knowledge, represents something more for us than a mere episode in the history of ideas. It is a philosophical question, inscribed in our thought since the Eighteenth century. Let us leave to their piety those who wish us to preserve alive and intact the heritage of *Aufklärung*. Such piety is doubtless the most touching of treasons. It is not the legacy of *Aufklärung* which it is our business to conserve, but rather the very question of this event and its meaning, the question of the historicity of the thought of the universal, which ought to kept present and retained in mind as that which has to be thought.

The question of *Aufklärung* or of reason considered as historic problems runs through the whole of philosophical thought since Kant in a more or less occluded fashion. The other aspect of the present Kant encountered is the Revolution: the revolution as at once event, rupture and historic upheaval, as failure, but also as value, as the sign of a disposition which operates in history and the progress of mankind. Here again, as with *Aufklärung*, the question for philosophy is not that of determining what part of the Revolution should be retained and set up as a model. It is rather one of what is to be made of this will to revolution, this 'enthusiasm' for revolution which is something distinct from the revolutionary enterprise itself. The two questions: 'What is *Aufklärung*?' and 'What is to be made of the will to revolution?' together define the field of philosophical questioning which bears on what we are in our present-ness.

Kant seems to me to have founded the two great critical traditions between which modern philosophy has been divided. We can say that in his great work of critique Kant laid down and founded that critical tradition of philosophy which defines the conditions under which a true knowledge is possible; and one can say that a whole area of modern philosophy since the nineteenth century has been presented and developed on that basis as an analytic of truth.

But there also exists in modern and contemporary philosophy another kind of questioning, another mode of critical interrogation: this is the one whose beginning can be seen precisely in the question of *Aufklärung* or in Kant's text on the Revolution; this other critical tradition asks: what is our present? What is the contemporary field of possible experience? Here it is not a question of an analytic of truth, but of what one might call an ontology of the present, an ontology of ourselves, and it seems to me that the philosophical choice which today confronts us is the following: one can opt for a critical philosophy which is framed as an analytical philosophy of truth in general, or one can opt for a critical thought which has the form of an ontology of ourselves, an ontology of the present; it is this latter form of philosophy which, from Hegel to the Frankfurt School by way of Nietzsche and Max Weber, has founded a form of reflection within which I have tried to work.

Note

* 'Un cours inédit', *Magazine littéraire* no. 207, Paris May 1984, pp. 35–39. This is an excerpt, revised by the author, from the first lecture in Foucault's 1983 course at the Collège de France. Translations by Lewis White Beck and Robert E. Anchor of the essays by Immanuel Kant, 'What is Enlightenment?' and 'An Old Question Raised Again: Is The Human Race Constantly Progressing?' may be found in I. Kant, *On History*, ed. L. W. Beck, Bobbs-Merrill 1963. I have consulted, and usually followed Robert Anchor's version of the passages quoted by Foucault from the latter piece.

I am most grateful to George Salemohammed for his help in revising and correcting this translation. (C.G.)

2 Question, ethos, event
Foucault on Kant and Enlightenment

Colin Gordon

This was one of the last pieces which Foucault published; it was also the first time since his inaugural lecture given in 1970 that an excerpt from one of his Collège de France lectures appeared in print in France.[1] The place of publication was in a dossier of articles edited for the *Magazine littéraire* by Foucault's former assistant François Ewald, on the occasion of the appearance of the two further volumes of Foucault's *History of Sexuality*. The topic of the lecture was one which Foucault had long felt to be close to the heart of his work. The published transcript is itself only a fragment. The closer reading of Kant's essay on Enlightenment which Foucault promises is missing here; the gap is filled, however, by another related essay by Foucault entitled 'What is Enlightenment?', in Paul Rabinow's American *Foucault Reader*.[2] These two pieces are best read together.

Foucault had discussed Kant's 'What is Enlightenment?' on more than one previous occasion: among these were his Prefaces to *L'Ere des ruptures*, a book of memoirs by Jean Daniel, the editor of *Le Nouvel Observateur*, and to the English translation of Georges Canguilhem's *The Normal and the Pathological*.[3] The theme reappears in some interesting later texts published in America: the essay 'The Subject and Power'[4], and an interview with Gérard Raulet (notable for some fresh and stimulating remarks on the course of twentieth-century philosophy and the intellectual antecedents of his own work), published in *Telos* under the inappropriate title 'Structuralism and Post-structuralism'.[5] A point which emerges in several of these discussions is Foucault's recognition that the affiliation on his own work to the theme of Kant's historic question has been shared by a group of contemporary thinkers with whom he feels a paradoxical kinship: the Frankfurt School. Foucault expressed a lively regret that their work had been ignored or unknown in France during the earlier part of his career. In his later years of teaching in America he undoubtedly became forcibly aware of the unfavourable view taken of his own

Published in *Economy and Society Volume 15 Number 1 February 1986*

work by later Frankfurt thinkers such as Jürgen Habermas. A number of his later occasional essays and interviews document Foucault's desire to explain himself in such a way as to dissipate these misunderstandings and to facilitate a more open philosophical dialogue with his American colleagues; this effort of explanation converges, in turn, with the later evolution of his own studies and preoccupations. The present piece became, within a few weeks of its publication, the principal theme of an obituary article by Habermas which showed an unaccustomed sympathy and (within certain limitations) understanding for the intentions of Foucault's thought.

Foucault remarks that Kant's reflections on the philosophy of the present centre on two objects: Reason or Enlightenment, and Revolution. Foucault's own developments on Kant's theme share this double focus, even if the meaning of each, of their connection, and of the respective resonances of Kant's originating insights are altered — and this not only or mainly through an effect of ironic distancing, but with a sense of tellingly apposite recurrence. In his preface to Canguilhem, Foucault views the differing repercussions of Kant's question of Enlightenment as developing along diverging paths in German and French philosophy: in the former, as dialectical philosophy, sociology and Marxism, and in the latter through positivism and the philosophy of science; but these trajectories issue in a parallel preoccupation of the Critical Theory of the Frankfurt School and the epistemology of Bachelard and Canguilhem with 'examining a reason, the autonomy of whose structures carries with it a history of dogmatism and despotism — a reason, consequently, which can have an effect of emancipation on condition that it manages to liberate itself from itself'. Reflection on the impact of technology, the fate of revolutions and the twilight of colonialism prompt converging doubts on the meaning of Western rationality. 'Two centuries later, the Enlightenment returns: but now not at all as a way for the West to take cognizance of its present possibilities and of the liberties to which it can accede, but as a way of interrogating it on its limits and on the powers which it has abused. Reason as despotic enlightenment.'[6] Foucault writes here of Kant and Mendelssohn as inaugurating by their articles on Enlightenment a modern genre of 'philosophical journalism'. In his preface to Jean Daniel's book, he comments on the experiences of a political journalist of the independent Left encountering the events and upheavals of the last two decades and the changes of thinking, opinion or attachment which these have inspired. The generational experience which Foucault singles out most strikingly is not that of the floridly histrionic spectacle of doctrinal conversions and deconversions, but rather a mutation in the problem of political identity as such. The independent Left made up of those who had left the Communist Party, whose dissenting convictions needed to be defined and sustained without effective recourse to a bureaucratic or doctrinal apparatus, represented in the 1950s a choice inseparable from the imperative of struggle for a basis of collective existence and expression. By the 1970s, Foucault suggests, the imperatives had changed: the pressing question was no longer 'how can we exist?', but 'who are we?' 'The heroism of political identity has had its day. What one is has now become a question one poses, moment by moment, to the problems one encounters. Experiments with, rather than engagement in.'[7]

The moral issue which Foucault is raising here is not that of whether we should change or remain unchanged, but rather that of how it is possible for us to hold on to liberty and truth in our ways of changing and not changing. The point is surely well taken. What is more ethically debilitating in the habitus of the orthodox left that the ways real change is covered up by a show of perpetual consistency, or (what is more frequent) immobility face-lifted by a noisy charade of fundamental critique and iconoclasm. Foucault's interests in the linkages between thought, conduct and event posed in Kant's essays are, among other things, a way of continuing this reflection. The ways in which he reads the Kantian texts presents them as speaking, explicitly or implicitly, to the political experiences of our recent past. Around 1970 Foucault was involved in discussion of what a desirable revolution could be like and how it might be possible. This already signified an awareness — to put it in the terms Foucault cites here from Kant — that some revolutions have not been worth repeating; and a sense of the contradictory nature of the will to a revolution which would only be a repetition. Around 1980 he seems — in common with many of his contemporaries — to have reached a profound scepticism as to whether any possible revolution could, at least in our own societies, be a desirable one. Publicly laconic or reticent though Foucault generally preferred to remain about these matters, to ignore them entirely would surely be to deprive the present lecture of a good part of its point. Take the passages in Kant which Foucault singles out for quotation: never mind whether the revolution succeeds or fails, never mind if a sane person would never try to repeat it, what matters about the revolution is something other than the revolution itself, namely the 'wishful participation bordering closely on enthusiasm' of its audience: their enthusiasm, and not the gesticulations of the revolutionaries; and the question which, for Foucault, becomes thus bound up for a part of modern philosophy with the question of Enlightenment: what is to be made of the enthusiasm for revolution; what is to be made of it, more particularly, if the revolution itself is not desirable? This latter question can be read as stating a constant, rather than a variable factor of recent political experience. The political consciousness which announced itself in 1968 — that of what one might call a free Left, something not quite to be identified with the New Left — and for which in France Foucault became, in effect, the representative philosopher, amounted in its essence to nothing more or less than a confronting of that question. The euphoric paradox of May 1968 was, precisely, that of a 'revolution' consisting ultimately in nothing beyond or other than 'enthusiasm for revolution'. All the struggles of the following decade were, in so far as they escaped the Leninist or Maoist mould, attempted liberations of the energy of revolution from revolution as plan, general staff, strategic totalisation: signs, if one may thus borrow Foucault's paraphrase of Kant, of a 'disposition' towards liberty unguessed at by politicians. 'No matter whether all this was Utopian; what we have seen has been a very real process of struggle; life as a political object was in a sense taken at its face value and turned back against the system which was bent on controlling it.'[8] The question concerning these experiences which Foucault's last discussions continue to address, with due prudence and sobriety, at a time when much may seem to have 'fallen back into the former rut', is: can they still provide the basis of a consistent political rationality which is distinct from — even, in a sense, the opposite of — the traditional ethos of revolution?

Kant's own answers to his question about Enlightenment command Foucault's attentive interest and respect, but it is in the question itself that Foucault finds the most precious clue for his own thinking. The pertinence today of the question of Enlightenment follows, in part, from a questioning of a hope of Revolution which had itself been 'borne by a rationalism of which one is entitled to ask what part it may have played in the effects of despotism in which that hope lost itself'.[9] Hence the Enlightenment, considered as a decisive event, choice or tendency in human history, becomes for us, as did the Revolution for Kant, an ambiguous undertaking, liable to succeed or to miscarry, or to succeed at unacceptable cost. Kant distinguishes between revolution as event and the enthusiasm for revolution which is the true and sure sign of progress. Foucault distinguishes between an Enlightenment of sure identity, conviction and destiny, and an Enlightenment which is question and questioning, which is commitment to uncertainty. Foucault reads in Kant's original formulation of what Enlightenment is a permanent possibility of questioning what subsequently comes of Enlightenment: conversely, he discards from Kant's inaugural perception of specific philosophical meaning in the content of the present moment the decisive valorising judgement of that content as portentous of a definitive and unambiguous event in the history of humanity, man's release from his self-incurred tutelage. What Foucault recognises and retains in this perception is something rather different: a reflexivity of the contingent and the inessential in the time and in ourselves.

Nearly two decades ago Foucault published a laudatory review of Ernst Cassirer's *The Philosophy of Enlightenment* in which he wrote that all modern thought is, in a sense, neo-Kantian.[10] In *The Order of Things*, the special significance attributed to Kant's philosophy is its coordination of critique with anthropology.[11] The critical philosophy is designed as an education of reason towards enlightenment and release from its self-incurred tutelage. The questions addressed in his Critiques lead, Kant tells us, to a further question which recapitulates them: What is Man? 'What is our present? Who are we, as beings in and of our present?' 'What is man?' Must the former questions still lead us to the latter one? May they modify the meaning we accord it? It would be a gross simplification to represent Foucault's attitude to the configuration of these questions in Kant's thought as a pure polemical refusal. Foucault objects to the identification of Enlightenment — in general, and so by implication in Kant — with humanism. He sees in Kant's 'pragmatic' anthropology a hint of possibilities beyond what had been dreamt of in the critical philosophy and quite different from the paths followed after Kant by the human sciences.[12] Foucault himself remained profoundly attached throughout his career to the development of a certain notion of critique: some of his last comments on this theme formulate his agreement and disagreement with Kant in a way which also clarifies his attitude to the questions of anthropology. 'Criticism indeed consists of analysing and reflecting upon limits. But if the Kantian question was that of knowing what limits knowledge must abstain from transgressing, it seems to me that the critical question today has to be turned back into a positive one: in what is given to us as universal, necessary, obligatory, what part is taken up by things which are actually singular, contingent, the product of arbitrary constraints? The point, in brief, is to transform critique conducted in the form of necessary limitation into a practical critique that takes the form of a possible transgression . . . criticism is no longer going to be practiced in the pursuit of formal structures with universal value, but rather as a historical investigation into the events that have led us to constitute ourselves and recognise ourselves as subjects of what we do, think and say.'[13] Such a critique 'will be genealogical in the sense that it will not deduce, from the form of what we are, what it is possible for us to do and to know; but it will separate out, from the contingency that has made us what we are, the possibility of no longer being, doing or thinking what we are, or do, or think. It is not seeking to make possible a metaphysics that has finally become a science; it is seeking to give new impetus, as far and as wide as possible, to the undefined work of freedom.'[14] Or, as Foucault puts it in 'The Subject and Power', 'maybe the point nowadays is not to discover what we are but to refuse what we are.'[15]

So large a part of the New Left generation has become accustomed over the years to support its positions by reference to a discourse of identity — whether in a recovered memory of class, a Freudian 'theory of the subject', or a pure parade of doctrinal conformity — that it is advisable to emphasise the otherwise obvious point that an ethic of 'refusing what we are' does not mean a mere leap into the void, an immoralism of the gratuitous act. In the first place, the form of freedom which Foucault envisages requires a form of knowledge obtainable only by means of exacting historical and political investigation: tasks to which Foucault himself devoted a certain effort. To interpret the relation between freedom and knowledge in Foucault as antinomic is a symptom of anorexic thought. 'What we are' nearly always connotes in Foucault's discussion the component of the taken-for-granted in our thoughts, actions and selves: the questioning of 'what we are' in the name of a principle of permanent contingency demands that vigorous appetite for facts which Ian Hacking so justly recognises in Foucault.[16]

In the second place, the question of 'what we are' enfolds within its apparently naive simplicity a rich complex of historico-political issues, a vast knot of recurrences and relativisations. The passage quoted above reminds us of the mutual implication in Foucault's thinking of the question of the present and the 'history of the present', the term which he employs in *Discipline and Punish* to describe his own *démarche* and which has sufficiently often been seen as the motto-theme of his work for scholarly trouble to have been taken to document instances of its prior use by others. And these latter findings are themselves of more than anecdotal interest because, firstly, the history of the question of the present (or, to use Nietzsche's word, of 'genealogy') is itself a significant element in the history of the present, and secondly, the investigation of what we are by recourse to a history of the present has become itself one of the traditions of modernity, a significant institution of our culture. The history of the genealogical genre has yet to be written. Without Foucault we might not even have become aware of its lack; this blind spot of our intellectual culture may be one of the reasons why so much difficulty is still being found in placing Foucault's work relative to other, more familiar landmarks. This problem cannot be adequately dealt with here; but the topic of the present note demands that it be paid at least a cursory glance. The genealogical connection considerably intensifies the paradoxes entailed in Foucault's ability to recognise his own problems in Kant's question. At the same time, the content of that recognition only becomes evident in its full singularity when note is taken of Foucault's highly distinctive relationship to the genealogical tradition.

The relationship between the practice of genealogy and the question of Enlightenment has of course always been charged with polemic. The genealogical attitude is almost synonymous with mistrust of Enlightenment; genealogical narration is an inverse, a post-mortem, a satire of the Enlightenment's prospectuses of progress. Moreover, in contrast to what Foucault remarks on as an element of novelty in Kant's mode of reflection on the meaning of the present time, it has the effect of replacing the theme of Enlightenment within a style of historical questioning which the question of Enlightenment had thought to supplant: Augustinian exegeses of the time for signs of an impending event, or of the end of all things; debates on the ruin of empires; disputes on the meaning of modernity as prosperity or decadence. On the whole it may be said that the specific genre of genealogy, of a question of the present linked to a history of the present, seldom coexists with revolutionary thought. Its representatives tend, where politically classifiable at all, to belong within a broadly liberal tradition or, if of the Left, to represent a heterodox minority standpoint. In their different ways both Foucault and the Frankfurt School are exceptions who confirm this rule. By far the most brilliant and concentrated outburst of genealogical thought in the present century would seem to have been due to the German and Austrian emigration of 1933 and after. The history of the present here assumes the most compelling of all its modern forms as reflection on the causes of present catastrophe. Cassirer in Gothenburg with *The Myth of the State*, Hayek in London with *The Road to Serfdom*, Adorno and Horkheimer in America with *Dialectic of Enlightenment*, Karl Polanyi in England and America with *The Great Transformation*, Benjamin in Paris with the 'Theses' and the *Passagenarbeit*, Rüstow in Istanbul with *Ortsbestimmung der Gegenwart* are among the lastingly significant thinkers for whom the German disaster compels, on the one hand a new forensic edge in the interrogation of the past for evidence of the negation of progress, and on the other a harsher judgement on present, undiagnosed trends and propensities, even within the surviving democracies, which prepare or facilitate the totalitarian *débacle*.

But at the same time it must be noted that, especially within the liberal tradition, this semiology of catastrophe (linked, as its preventative counterpart, to a prophylactic fundamentalism) is not the sole or overriding version of all genealogical thought. Alongside it and sometimes overlapping with it is the different and more classical mode represented by Tocqueville, Weber or Schumpeter, which might instead be called a permanent pragmatics of survival, oriented to the longer-term identification of historic trends which may be irreversible in character and may impose inescapable costs and intrinsic, though finite risks. The difference, not so much in political partisanship as in ideological tonality, between the conclusions adduced by a Weber or Schumpeter on the one side, and a Hayek on the other, may be related, at least in part, to this difference in genealogical style. Weber, for all the ethical and polemical vehemence of his contemporary diagnoses, writes within an overall perspective such that the probable future of capitalist bureaucracy promises to be only marginally more appealing than that of a socialist bureaucracy. The later Schumpeter judges that the requirement for the survival of a rational economic system imposes the grave but, in the last analysis, bearable necessity of a transition to socialism. In either case, the analysis addresses the endogenous hazards and necessities of a system, not the unrecognised incursions of an alien, pathological mutation. The neo-liberal Friedrich Hayek performs, on the other hand, a tour de force in the paradoxical-prophetic genre by warning the British that their wartime recourse to a kind of state-socialism may eventually lead them involuntarily to repeat the political fate of Germany and Austria.

This (doubtless partial and oversimplified) contrast may help us to specify the particular style of genealogy practiced by Foucault. What has just been said may already indicate one obvious singularity of Foucault's work, namely that it is one of the relatively few contributions to genealogical thinking to have been produced since the great generation of the German-Austrian exiles. It may well be that the sceptical view often taken of genealogical discourse in recent decades has to do with the sense that it has been too exclusively bound up with the experience of political catastrophe, itself symptomatic as well as diagnostic of the cultural traumas of totalitarianism and exile, too lurid or unbalanced in its conclusions to minister acceptably to the concerns of more stable polities. Some of the English-speaking critical response to Foucault's work may be a reflection of these views. Another contributory factor which cannot be explored here is the coincidence of Foucault's later work with the curiously delayed peak of impact on Western thinking of the testimony of exiled witnesses of another great political catastrophe of the twentieth century: the Soviet and East European dissidents. The description of a seventeenth-century 'Great Internment' in his *Histoire de la Folie* (1961) seems likely to have evoked undesirable modern associations for Foucault's French Communist readers. *The Gulag Archipelago* began to appear in 1973; Foucault's *Discipline and Punish* coined the term 'carceral archipelago' to characterise certain institutions of nineteenth-century French society. But Foucault himself was always both scrupulous and lucid in circumscribing the proper ways in which the (re)discovery of the facts of Soviet history can and should be a proper object of moral and political reflection in the West.[17] Despite the violent counter-literature which his own diagnostic conclusions have provoked from some quarters, it needs to be emphasised that they actually issue from a genealogical approach which is in many ways closer (if I may once again be permitted for a moment to abstract from these thinkers' respective political commitments) to that of a Weber or Schumpeter than to that of a Hayek. Foucault is not a Cassandra; his works do not warn of an impending catastrophe or the repetition of an accomplished catastrophe. Foucault is not writing in external or internal exile but, at worst, in conditions of limited political adversity. The potential point of issue in reality for his analyses is not constrained to the vast detours of ethical conversion and reconstruction prescribed by the reflections of the German exiles, but lies in the possibility of existing and proximate forms of political action: specifically, the 'local struggles' current during the 1970s. One can see here how Foucault's celebrated 'microphysical' method of analysis goes hand in hand with a modification of previous genealogical approaches: the possibility of focussing powerful analytical resources on detailed, localised problems demands an ability to interrogate the present without recourse to apocalyptic meta-narratives, a more sophisticated and discriminating means of dissecting the contradictions of rationality than traditional dialectic has generally allowed. In this respect, and more particularly in terms of our understanding of his interest in Kant's question of Enlightenment and his attitude to philosophical anthropology, Foucault's sense of affinity with Weber may, as Pasquale Pasquino has recently suggested, reward further scrutiny.[18]

One of Foucault's few direct comments on Weber was made in the course of an exceptionally interesting series of lectures in 1979 on the history of liberalism and neoliberalism.[19] Weber's decisive contribution to twentieth-century thinking is seen here as the creation, in place of the Marxian theme of a contradictory logic of capital, of the problematic of an 'irrational rationality of capitalist society'. The present condition of society and its prospects of future survival are, that is to say, evaluated in the light of a historical analysis of processes of rationalisation which are multiple, specific and potentially discordant. Foucault departs from many received views of recent intellectual history by tracing a parallel filiation with Weber's ideas of two opposed schools of thinkers in subsequent German intellectual history: the Frankfurt School (whose basic concern is, according to Foucault's avowedly over-schematic formula, with the possibility of constructing a new social rationality capable of eliminating the irrationalities of the capitalist economy) and the neoliberal economists and jurists of the Freiburg school, also active in Germany during the Weimar period, mostly exiled during the Third Reich and profoundly influential in the early years of the Federal Republic, whose objective was, on the contrary, to establish or recover a (capitalist) economic rationality capable of eliminating the social irrationalities hitherto known to capitalism. This double destiny, as Foucault puts it, of Weberianism in Germany ends with the street battles of 1968 in which the last disciples of the Frankfurt School confront the police of a government inspired by the teachings of the Freiburg school.[20]

Foucault's main reason for drawing attention to the rather neglected contribution of the Freiburg school (called in the postwar years, after the title of the journal in which they collaborated, the *Ordoliberalen*) was undoubtedly the desire to contribute towards a more informed reflection on the recent, impressive and disconcerting political successes scored in both Germany and France by neoliberal methods of government. For our present purposes, two features of the German neoliberals' version of Weberianism are worth briefly singling out because of the respectful and even — allowances being made for a degree of Weberian irony on his part — sympathetic treatment accorded them by Foucault. The first feature is a Weberianism turned militantly against the conclusions of the later Schumpeter; the second, a Weberianism purged of the contamination of certain ideas propagated by Sombart.

The *Ordoliberalen* take sides against Schumpeter for what they regard as an invalid historical deduction of the inevitable failure of liberalism. They argue that the disasters of German history are not proofs of the consequences of a market economy, but consequences of the consistent frustration in modern Germany of liberal economic policies. The market system has not been tried and found wanting, it has been denied a trial. This contention is

linked to what foucault describes (attributing it in part to a Husser-
lian influence on some members of the Freiburg school) as a rigorously antinaturalistic conception of the market itself, which is
considered not as a quasi-autonomous given of developed economies but rather as a reality which can exist and be maintained in
existence only by virtue of activist policies of political intervention: by legal measures designed to safeguard the game of free
competition, and by socio-legal measures designed to propagate
and diffuse throughout the social body, and not only within the
narrowly conceived limits of strictly economic activity, an ethos
of enterprise. Alexander Rüstow gave this latter set of objectives
the significant title of *Vitalpolitik*. On this view, a capitalist system
is by no means inherently doomed to destruction but its survival
depends on a capacity for inventive responses to the more or less
aleatory structural hazards and blockages to which is it inevitably
liable.

The *Ordoliberalen* take issue, secondly, with what Foucault
terms Sombart's thesis: the idea, developed in his sociological
writings on *Gesellschaft* and *Gemeinschaft*, of an ineluctable tendency of the modern economy to produce a 'mass society' which
impoverishes human relations and replaces true community with
the false gratifications of, as Foucault phrases it, 'signs, speed and
spectacles'. The neoliberals' answer to this is that it is not so
much the market economy as such which is at the root of these
evils as, on the one hand the methods of planning and bureaucracy which have been adopted by enemies of the market system
(the National Socialist experience providing the definitive object-
lesson of a regime, conceived as a Sombartian restitution of
national community, which evolves into the most avid exponent
in modern times of the culture of 'signs and spectacles'), and on
the other hand by the narrow and over-abstract conception adopted
by an older, 'palaeo-liberal' political economy, of the nature and
meaning of economy and enterprise.

Foucault shows no sign of endorsing the neoliberals' doctrines
but he quite clearly shows a degree of temperamental affinity
(albeit for slightly different motives) for these parts of their
approach: anti-naturalism; the stress on history as the analysis of
contingent hazards, not ineluctable destinies; the taste for a politics of invention; the interest in the Weberian theme of the ethical
conduct of life; the suspicion of a certain genre of cultural criticism.
These themes are developed in an interesting manner in the
interview with Gérard Raulet. Foucault distinguishes here between
the analysis of the formation and mutation of a plurality of different forms of rationality and the prognosis – which he repudiates
– of an impending or actual collapse of rationality in general.

'Here, I think, we are touching on one of the forms — perhaps we should call them habits — one of the most harmful habits in contemporary thought, in modern thought even; at any rate, in post-Hegelian thought: the analysis of the present as being precisely, in history, a present of rupture, of high point, of completion or of a returning dawn, etc. The solemnity with which everyone who engages in philosophical discourse reflects on his own time strikes me as a flaw. I can say so all the more firmly since it is something I have done myself; and since, in someone like Nietzsche, we find this incessantly — or, at least, insistently enough. I think we should have the modesty to say to ourselves that, on the one hand, the time we live in is not *the* unique or fundamental irruptive point in history where everything is completed and begun again. We must also have the modesty to say, on the other hand, that — even without this solemnity — the time we live in is very interesting; it needs to be analysed and broken down, and that we would do well to ask ourselves, "What is the nature of our present?" I wonder if one of the great roles of philosophical thought since the Kantian "Was ist Aufklarung?" might not be characterised by saying that the task of philosophy is to describe the nature of the present, and of "ourselves in the present". With the proviso that we do not allow ourselves the facile, rather theatrical declaration that this moment in which we exist is one of total perdition, in the abyss of darkness, or a triumphant daybreak, etc. It is a time like any other, or rather, a time which is never quite like any other.'[21]

Thus it is as much necessary to be nominalist about the present as about power. Foucault's approach further implies a carefully defined way of posing questions about 'modernity'. He indeed remarks in this same interview that he has 'never clearly understood what was meant in France by the word "modernity" ', and confesses to being 'not up to date' on what is meant by 'postmodernity'. His own views are stated most fully in the essay 'What is Enlightenment?' Foucault proposes here an understanding of modernity as meaning not an epoch but an attitude (a distinction which may correspond obliquely with one made by Kant: we are not living in an *enlightened age*, but only in an *age of enlightenment*). By 'attitude' Foucault means here 'a mode of relating to contemporary reality', a 'voluntary choice made by certain people', a way of thinking and feeling, of acting and behaving: an ethos. Foucault gives a gloss on Baudelaire's celebrated writings on this theme.[22] Modernity is not a quality in the course of things, but a specific attitude to their process, 'a difficult interplay between the truth of what is real and the exercise of freedom'. Modernity is a discipline, an asceticism, a specific culture of the self: 'modern man, for Baudelaire, is not the man who goes off to discover himself, his secrets and his hidden truth; he is the man who tries to invent himself'. But all these modern options are limited, in Baudelaire's thought, to the life and the world of art.

There is certainly a note of sympathy in Foucault's citation of the Baudelairian precept: 'You have no right to despise the present.' Cultural critique and genealogy have often been allied pursuits. Nietzsche is, after all, the patron saint of both genres in our century. In Foucault's case the association is, by and large, a misleading one. Foucault is a genealogist but not a cultural critic. He does not lament a loss of human values, a decay of community; he is not impressed by the Sombartian bogies of mass consumption, signs, speed, spectacles (a set of codewords aptly suited, of course, to evoke the more recent French neo-Sombartian exponents of situationism and post-modern prophesy: Baudrillard, Virilio, de Bord). 'I do not believe in the old dirges about decadence, the lack of good writers, the sterility of thought, the bleak and foreboding horizons ahead of us. I believe, on the contrary, that our problem is one of overabundance; not that we are suffering from an emptiness, but that we lack adequate means to think all that is happening.'[23]

In some ways the themes of Foucault's last books appear, despite the historical remoteness of their material, wholly in tune with a prevailing contemporary mood. The interviews in which he discusses their objectives centre on the idea that the sphere of personal life and relations is ceasing in our societies to be regulated through a morality of imperative or prohibitive codes and that the space thus being vacated can be filled only by a different kind of ethical practice, that of what he calls 'an aesthetic of existence'. 'Why should not each individual be able to make of his life a work of art?'[24] Foucault sees one of the uses of his last books as being to document forgotten options of this kind (which is not to say that the particular practices described are presented as worthy of admiration and imitation; on the contrary[25]). Meanwhile, in the years Foucault spent writing these books, the idea of a promotion of new 'lifestyles' has increasingly found its way, in a similar sense if not in identical terms, into some orthodox political agendas.

Foucault's brief discussion of Baudelaire's views on the modern 'way of life' acquires an added interest when one notes his reference in his last books to Walter Benjamin's study of Baudelaire as one of the few analyses of the modern history of the practice of the self.[26] Benjamin's recent political popularity seems to owe less to these explorations than to his more readily digestible pronouncements such as the dictum, quoted with platitudinous frequency by New Left writers, on the contrast between the politicised aesthetics of communism and the aestheticised politics of fascism. It is not clear that this particular distinction suffices to unravel the issues which Foucault has posed. On the one hand, the very idea of an 'aesthetics of existence' may entail that (as Foucault has argued) the relations between ethical and political practices are variable and contingent[27]: there may thus be some reason for doubting the *political* value of the idea of making one's life into a *political* work of art, a reincarnation of the militant ideal in the form of a 'lifestyle'. A different option would be to regard the possibility of a space of indetermination in personal existence as a value and a necessity: an idea which it is certainly possible to translate into practical political terms. Foucault has described this question as standing at the centre of the current so-called crisis of the Welfare State: in the initial period of welfare institutions it proved necessary and acceptable to sacrifice a degree of individual autonomy for the sake of individual security; in recent years this quidproquo has become an object of massive dissatisfaction, creating a new demand for a system capable of simultaneously maximising security *and* autonomy. Foucault emphasises that this objective can be achieved only by a major new effort of collective and institutional invention, reform, negotiation and compromise, involving the confrontation of difficult ethical choices.[28] One may be reminded here of Foucault's remark on Kant's account of Enlightenment as the coincidence of the free and public uses of reason, that it does not explain the political means whereby that use of reason can be assured.[29] But no doubt Foucault would also think that problem too narrowly stated: it would have to be enlarged at least so as to include the means of ensuring adequate scope for the free *private* use of practical reason.

One may be reminded also of an aspect of Weber's thought which has been brought to attention by the valuable recent articles of Wilhelm Hennis: the sociological appraisal and evaluation of collective powers, and the practical evaluation of existing conditions and choices in terms of their impact on *Lebensstil* and *Lebensfuhrung*, the style and conduct of individual life (a theme later to be vigorously developed in the neoliberals' ideas on *Vitalpolitik*).[30] Weber also sometimes refers to this preoccupation as a 'characterological' criterion. One may well wonder whether Weber would have viewed the modern success of the idea of lifestyle (or the American-led subsumption of the notion of 'way of life' by ideological propaganda) with unalloyed favour, any more than he did the hunts after *Erlebnis* which he saw as the cultural vice of his own day. One of his harshest 'characterological' studies of Wilhelmine Germany ends with the reflection that it is difficult to invent a value or a style.[31] Foucault might not have disagreed. One would have liked, as well, to have heard his comment on another passage from Weber cited by Hennis, on 'the perception that a *human* science, and that is what political economy is, investigates above all else the *quality of the human beings* who are brought up in those economic and social conditions of existence'.[32] It has been suggested of late that Foucault may have come to change his views about the merits of philosophical anthropology or the 'theory of the subject'. This seems to indicate a misunderstanding of what his later work is about. There is no ground for supposing that Foucault would have wanted to embrace, either as a means or an outcome of an ethic of 'changing what we are', an 'anthropological' criterion of Weber's kind. On the other hand, in order for his question of 'what we are' actually to be a question at all, it may be vital to retain a margin of uncertainty or underdetermination regarding the ethical status of anthropological categories, or whatever terms occupy their place: a possibility of knowing that we do not know what we are: 'L'histoire des hommes est la longue succession des synonymes d'une même vocable. Y contredire est un devoir.'[33]

Notes

1 Foucault had previously authorised publication of three lectures in translation: Foucault (1980a) and (1979b). See also note (19) below.
2 Foucault (1980c), p. 32–50.
3 Canguilhem (1980); Daniel (1979).
4 Foucault (1984a).
5 Foucault (1983a).
6 Foucault (1980c), p. 54.
7 Daniel (1979), p. 12.
8 Foucault (1979c), p. 145.
9 Foucault (1980c), p. 54.
10 Foucault (1966).
11 Foucault (1970), Chapter 9.
12 These themes are developed in the unpublished commentary on Kant's *Anthropology* which formed, together with his (published) translation of that work, Foucault's *thèse complémentaire* for the *doctorat ès lettres*. See also Foucault (1970).
13 Foucault (1984a), p. 45–6.
14 Ibid. p. 46.
15 Foucault (1982), p. 785.
16 Hacking (1981), p. 32.
17 Cf. especially Foucault (1980b).
18 Cf. Pasquino (1984).
19 Regrettably, none of this material has been published, except for a short extract in an obituary number of *Libération* (Foucault 1984e). The Collège de France has an archive of recordings and transcripts of Foucault's courses. For a

general introductory survey of this research and a series of essays on related themes by other authors, see Burchell *et al.* (1986).

20 These and the following points are drawn chiefly from Foucault's lectures of 29 March 1979 and 4 April 1979.

21 Foucault (1983a), p. 206.

22 Foucault (1984a), p. 39–42.

23 Foucault (1980d), p. 16–17.

24 Foucault (1984b), p. 90.

25 Foucault (1984c), p. 38.

26 Foucault (1984d), p. 17.

27 Cf. Note (24).

28 Foucault (16: 1983b), p. 41.

29 Foucault (4: 1984), p. 37.

30 Hennis (1983), Hennis (1984). My (1986) paper discusses Hennis's views and their bearing on some points of connection between the thought of Weber and Foucault.

31 Weber (1948), p. 437.

32 Weber (1980), cited in Hennis (1983), p. 164.

33 René Char, cited by Foucault (1984d).

References

Burchell, G., Gordon, C. and Miller, P. eds. (1986), *The Foucault Effect: Essays on Governmental Rationality*, Brighton.

Canguilhem, G. (1980) *The Normal and the pathological*, with a preface by Michel Foucault: cf. Foucault (1980c).

Daniel, J. (1979) *L'Ere des Ruptures*, Paris, with a Preface by Michel Foucault (also published as 'Pour une morale de l'inconfort', *Le Nouvel Observateur* 23/4/1979).

Foucault, M. (1966) Review of French translation of E. Cassirer's *The Philosophy of the Enlightenment, Quinzaine littéraire* 1/7/1966, Paris. (Reprinted in *ibid.*, July 1984.)

Foucault, M. (1970) *The Order of Things*, London.

Foucault, M. (1979a) *The History of Sexuality, Volume 1: An Introduction*, London.

Foucault, M. (1979b) 'On Governmentality', *I&C* 6, 1979; 'La "Governmentalita"', *Aut/Aut* 167–8, Sept.–Dec. 1978.

Foucault, M. (1980a) 'Two Lectures', in *Power/Knowledge*, Brighton.

Foucault, M. (1980b) 'Powers and strategies', in *Power/Knowledge*.

Foucault, M. (1980c) 'Georges Canguilhem: philosopher of error', *I&C* 7.

Foucault, M. (1980d). 'Le philosophe masqué', (anonymous) interview with C. Delacampagne, *Le Monde 6/4/1980*; translation in M. Foucault, *Von der Freundschaft als Lebensweise*, Berlin 1984 (reference above is to this edition).

Foucault, M. (1982) 'The Subject and Power', *Critical Inquiry* 8, p. 777–795;

also in H. Dreyfus and P. Rabinow, *Michel Foucault- Beyond Structuralism and Hermeneutics*, Brighton 1983.

Foucault, M. (1983a) 'Structuralism and Post-Structuralism: An Interview with Michel Foucault' (with G. Raulet) *Telos* 55 p. 195–211.

Foucault M. (1983b) 'Un système fini face à une demande infinie', interview with a R Bono in *Securitè Sociale: l'Enjeu* p. 39–63, editions TEN-Syros, Paris.

Foucault, M. (1984a) *A Foucault Reader*, ed. P. Rabinow, New York.

Foucault, M. (1984b) 'Le sexe comme une morale' (interview with H. Dreyfus and P. Rabinow), *Le Nouvel Observateur* no. 1021, Paris June 1984.

Foucault, M. (1984c) 'Le retour de la morale' (interview with Gilles Barbedette and André Scala), *Les Nouvelles*, Paris 28 June 1984.

Foucault, M. (1984d) *L'Usage des Plaisirs*, Paris.

Foucault, M. (1984e) 'La phobie d'Etat' (excerpt from a lecture given at the College de France, 31 January 1979). *Libéra-tion* 30 June 1984, p21.

Gordon, C. (1986) 'The Soul of the citizen: Max Weber and Michel Foucault on Rationality and Government', in Lash S. and Whimster S. eds. *Max Weber, Rationality and Modernity*, London.

Habermas, J. (1984) 'Taking Aim at the Heart of the Present', *University Publishing* 13 p. 5–6, Berkeley.

Hacking, I. (1981) review of M. Foucault, *Power/Knowledge, New York Review of Books* Vol XXVIII No 8 p 32–7, 14/5/1981.

Hennis, W. (1983) 'Max Weber's "Central Question" ', *Economy and Society* Vol 12 No. 2.

Hennis, W. (1984) 'Max Weber's Thema' *Zeitschrift fur Politik* Jg 31 p 11–52 (translation forthcoming in Lash S. and Whimster S. eds, *Max Weber, Rationality and Modernity*).

Pasquino, P. (1984) 'De la modernité', *Magazine litteraire* no. 207, June 1984.

Weber, M. (1984) *From Max Weber*, Gerth and Mills eds.

Weber, M. (1980) 'The National State and Economic Policy', *Economy and Society* Vol 9 p. 428–49.

3 Michel Foucault (1926–84)
The Will to Knowledge*

Pasquale Pasquino

Translated by Chloe Chard

For Paul Veyne

I The 'disciplines' and the problem of modernity

Re-reading *Discipline and Punish* today, the reader feels some surprise at the slightly reductive character of the sub-title. The 'birth of the prison' is, in fact, a concern somewhat different from the true object of the book — and perhaps less important. The birth of the prison emerges, rather, as the pretext for the analysis of a problem which, in a situation very different from that of ten years ago, now appears to be one of great theoretical relevance — a problem which Foucault himself defines in a note at the end of the book as that of 'the power of normalization and the formation of knowledge in modern society'.**

Discipline and Punish is deceptive in another way, too. The book initially appears easy to read, and the style in which it is written does in fact make it possible to read the whole work right through to the end without a break. Nevertheless, it is a difficult text, which raises more questions than it resolves. Its central group of problems, moreover, revolves, in the end, around one question in particular: the question of what constitutes the specific character of modernity in the west. Indeed, even this is not generally realized — as we can see from the fact that it is often claimed that the author attempts to reduce the figure of modernity to that of the prison. We need, rather, to ask ourselves — as Foucault actually does — what are the elements of modernity which might help us to understand the emergence and consolidation of the system of punishment by imprisonment? We should not, therefore, endeavour to explain modern society by way of the prison, but should attempt instead to see in what ways the prison is consistent with modern society, without then reducing this consistency to an identity. We need, in fact, to find our way out of a labyrinth of mirrors, to escape from the vain exercise of *reductio ad unum*, and so to rediscover a series of questions which still, quite certainly, demand our attention.

Published in *Economy and Society Volume 15 Number 1 February 1986*

In his attempt to explain the birth of the prison — which is one of the problems which his research puts forward, and at the same time the pretext and the point of departure of this research — Foucault encounters the 'disciplines', the real theme of his book. These in turn refer back to 'the power of normalization in modern society', that is, to the theoretical question to which *Discipline and Punish* provides a fragment of a reply. A question which can also be formulated in terms of the problematic of 'social control'. It is towards this perhaps less visible part of his discourse that it seems to me important to direct our attention.

Over almost the same years in which Foucault was working on the 'disciplines' and on the theme of 'government', a German historian little known outside academic circles, Gerhard Oestreich, who had worked on Justus Lipsius, on the organization of modern armies, on the 'police', in the earlier sense of the term,*** and on other aspects of the European societies of the *ancien règime*,[1] at the same time devoted a certain amount of his attention to an age-old process which he termed 'social disciplining'. In this process, both for Foucault and Oestreich, the figure of the soldier assumes a prominent role. Whilst the French philosopher cites Louis de Montgommery's *La Milice française* (1603), the German historian refers to *Trillerey oder exercitia militaria Frederici IV* (1594). But here too we must not be misled: the essential focus of such research is not the organization of the army (*disciplina militaris*) or the identity of the soldier with the prisoner, who would in turn be seen as identical with the schoolboy. The problem under consideration is, rather, that of the conditions of possibility of modern society. Foucault and Oestreich take up, in fact, more or less explicitly, one of the fundamental and insistent questions put forward by Max Weber, from *The Protestant Ethic* up until his last writings on the sociology of religion: what is the mode of conduct of life (*Lebensführung*) compatible with and specific to the modern West?

If it is true that the juridico-political discourse of the seventeenth century was constructed around the idea of 'contract', which presupposes rational individuals as constitutive elements within the contract, Foucault's problem is that of interrogating modernity around the very construction of the subject. Hobbes was perfectly aware of this aspect of the issue. In order to grasp this, we need only reflect on his affirmation of the spontaneously asocial nature of man, and of the fact that men can only become political subjects *ex disciplina* (*De Cive*, I, 1). It even seems to me that, in the end, there is no contradiction between the juridical individual entitled to liberty and to certain rights and the docile subject 'constructed' by the disciplines, and that, on the contrary, the first presupposes the existence of the second. The essential character of a theory of the state, organized like that of Hobbes around the idea of contract, lies not so much in the initial assumption of the existence of abstract juridicial individuals, authors of a contract which was to produce the power of the state — this reading simply confuses the sound of the words with the sense of the discourse — but, rather, in the idea of an immanent principle of the legitimation of power, the principle expressed by Spinoza in the formula *oboedientia facit imperantem*; the idea, in other words, of *omnis potestas a populo*, as opposed to that of *omnis potestas a deo*. This displacement of the site of the legitimation of power towards the governed, produced by the theories of contract, has consequences of which the importance can hardly be overestimated. At the moment when political power seeks to find for itself an autonomous and immanent foundation, to be derived from the obedience of its subjects, it introduces into its own mechanism an element of fragility which changes its very nature and leads it to develop a whole collection of governmental practices. Before they become holders of inalienable rights, the individuals, or rather their forms of behaviour, appear as the instance which proclaims the legitimacy of power. So that, if they are presented in an abstract sense acting out a contract, in a concrete sense they are — and they therefore come to be recognized as — objects of social discipline. Insofar as it is the obedience of the subjects which founds, produces and renders visible the legitimacy of power, these same subjects, their bodies and the range of ways in which they behave towards themselves and others are to become, increasingly, the site of a new production of knowledge and the point of application of rules governing the conduct of life, objects of 'government' or, to adopt a term in use from the seventeenth century onwards, problems of the State.

Max Weber grasped one of the central features of this civilizing process. In reflecting on the specificity of the West, he encountered, and placed great emphasis on, a form of life which could be termed the 'self-discipline' of the subject: the Protestant work ethic, understood as a form of conduct of life which produces a conformity in modes of behaviour, since earthly existence is nothing but the reduction of life itself to a pure and simple instrument, to a means by which salvation is to be achieved. The search for an 'other' life which characterizes Christian spirituality throughout the Middle Ages is replaced by a simple acceptance of existence, or, rather, by the widest possible rationalization and functionalization of existence.

The specific character of this Protestant ethic or mode of conduct of life seems to me to lie in the fact that the conformity of behaviour is derived from inner religious belief and from the straining for salvation. So that one might say that the preoccupation with salvation produces obedience, and obedience produces salvation, and both produce a form of 'social control' which is generated from the very interior of the subject's behaviour.[2] But, from the moment when the preoccupation with the relation between 'government' (*Herrschaft*) and conformity of behaviour first appeared in his work, Weber did not stop at this inner and 'ascetic' aspect of obedience. In *Economy and Society* (1968; Vol. 1, p. 53) he wrote, in fact: ' "Discipline" is the probability that by virtue of habituation a command will receive prompt and automatic obedience in stereotyped forms, on the part of a given group of persons.'

The analysis of the 'construction' of these automatic forms of behaviour — the power of normalization — constitutes, in fact, the central object of Foucault's book on the disciplines. The open space of his analysis, a space already indicated by Weber, certainly merits further investigation. Perhaps we should ask ourselves whether the disciplines, on the one hand, and the Protestant work ethic, on the other, might not represent something like the two faces of our modernity, and if it is not around their articulation that the form of political association and exercise of power that we call the state, or, as I believe we should call it, the statalization of 'government'[3] has assumed a concrete existence.

We might also ask ourselves whether, in the research in which Foucault engaged over the last few years on ethics and on the diverse forms of life in classical antiquity,[4] he did not continue, in some sense, to follow in the footsteps of an intellectual enterprise which we still fail to comprehend in its full significance: that of Max Weber.[5]

II The sexual 'conduct of life' in classical antiquity

On reading the two volumes of the *Histoire de la sexualité* which appeared shortly before Foucault's death, the reader's reaction is, above all, one of astonishment at the gigantic body of work which is condensed into the six hundred-or-so pages of the text — a body of work which occupied, almost exclusively, the last eight years of the author's life.[6] For those familiar with his previous works one of the first questions which springs to mind is, without doubt: what in the world can have driven a specialist in the *âge classique*, in the seventeenth and eighteenth centuries, to become embroiled in research which is situated entirely within the field of Greco-Roman antiquity?

There are, first of all, reasons for this choice which may be described as personal ones. Foucault had little patience with the way in which he was often viewed, above all in Germany and in the Anglo-Saxon countries, as a Parisian Left-Bank intellectual. Throughout his life he always conceived and carried out his work as that of an academic or a scholar, even if he never addressed himself specifically to an academic public — with what academic discipline could he, in fact, have aligned himself? — and even if he always strove to write in a style which would be comprehensible even to non-specialists — a strategy which did not prevent a certain number of misunderstandings arising over the course of the years. His style and language are those of a writer rather than of a university lecturer, in a tradition which has always existed in France, at least from the Enlightenment onwards. This tradition is one which is also manifested in the writings of historians such as Marc Bloch and Lucien Febvre, and Foucault has never, in fact, abandoned the kind of Cartesian conceptual rigour which characterizes the works of his masters Georges Canguilhem and Georges Dumézil. He has tried, in these last two books, to provide an incontrovertible endorsement both of this style of work and of this rigour. The judgment now lies with the readers and with the classical scholars.

Above all, however, there are theoretical reasons for this chronological displacement — which is also, to a certain degree, a thematic one. It is these reasons which I should now like to discuss. They are reasons which provoke some reflection as to the questions to which Foucault had begun, in these two books, to supply the answers. First of all: what, precisely, does his *Histoire de la sexualité* attempt to tell the history of?

Even if the 'why' of the project has to be seen in the will to 'contradict' a 'long succession of synonyms' (René Char, quoted on the back of the book); even if its more general objective consists explicitly in the attempt 'to discover to what extent the work of thinking its own history can free thought from that which it silently thinks and allow it to think otherwise' (*L'Usage des plaisirs*, p. 15) — in reframing, therefore, the horizons of the possible[7] — this problem still remains an unavoidable one. A careful reading of Foucault's last two books brings to light some fragments of replies, which I should now like to illustrate.

Foucault, like Paul Veyne, has always thought, since his study of madness, that 'natural objects' do not exist. 'Sexuality' is not an 'invariable' (ibid., p. 10). This does not mean, moreover, that it is nothing, but only that, in order to say what it is, it is necessary to recount its history. A history which is neither the unfolding of a substance, that is, its 'epiphany', nor the search for an origin or for a natural condition which might be set up as a positive value, in contrast to a state of decadence. Its history consists, rather, in going beyond that which is assumed as a given or a 'presupposed', and in reflecting on the modality in which Western society, in the course of its history, has thought of that field of relations between subjects (women and/or men) which has been known, from the nineteenth century onwards, by the name of 'sexuality'. A procedure of enquiry which in itself contains nothing astonishing, if one compared it, for example, with that of the medievalist who reflects, like Jacques Le Goff, on the conception of *travail* in the Middle Ages, even though the word and the concept did not in fact exist in feudal society. We need only think of how Foucault writes in the methodological introduction to *L'Usage des plaisirs* about the way in which his history of sexuality refers back to and even presents itself as a chapter in a history of ethics. Such a history is conceived neither as a history of 'forms of behaviour' nor as a history of 'moral codes' — that is, of that 'assemblage of values and rules of action which are proposed to individuals and to groups through the mediation of prescriptive apparatuses' (ibid., pp. 32ff.). A history of ethics is understood, rather, as an enquiry into the 'forms of relation to oneself' which 'have been defined, modified, re-elaborated and diversified over the course of our Western civilization' (ibid., pp. 38–9).

The point which seems to me the most important one to emphasize is that this history of ethics or of the conduct of sexual life is presented as a history of *the problematizations of subjectivity*: that is, as a reconstruction of the forms of self-reflection of behaviour which are at the origin of the modes of conduct of life, considered here in the perspective of 'self-government' rather than as 'disciplines'. Subjectivity no longer appears as the given or the presupposed instance of the inquiry, but as its object.

Looking from now on at the work of Foucault as a whole, from *Madness and Civilization* onwards, I believe that one might argue that he has produced a radical shift in the ways in which we reflect on three concepts central to our history of thought: the concepts of truth, of subjectivity and of power.

Truth, first of all, no longer appears as the progressive manifestation of contents which it is necessary to apportion correctly either to ideology or to science. It presents itself, rather, as the product of discursive practices — or, more precisely of the component of discursive practices which we may call practices of *veridiction*. Let us take, for example, on the side of the history of the sciences, the case of classical political economy. The question to put to political economy is concerned not so much with the relative

degrees of truth and error which must be assigned to the theories
of value of Smith, Ricardo or Marx — keeping in mind, naturally,
the present state of the discipline of economics, as J. A. Schumpeter does in his *History of Economic Analysis*. The problem is,
rather, to understand how and why there developed, from the
end of the eighteenth century onwards, a domain of knowledge
and at the same time an academic discipline, which considered it
essential that it should display a 'true' discourse around concepts
such as that of 'value'.[8] From this there results a more general
consequence: the breaking of a privileged link which has always
been considered constitutive of the relation between the philosopher and truth. The philosopher will no longer be able to claim
the privileges of a *maître de vérité*, but, rather, will have to demonstrate 'the requisite degree of care, patience, modesty and attention' (ibid., p. 13, note 1), in a work which will consist above all
in the reconstruction of the practices and models which are employed in order to 'tell the truth'. To the question last reformula-
ted by Heidegger on the nature of truth, Foucault replies by proposing a history of *véridiction*.

The subject is, in turn, as indicated, the category to which
Foucault devotes the most important theoretical effort in his
last two books. In fact, whilst in *Discipline and Punish* the subject
appears essentially as the 'docile body' produced by the disciplines
in the *Histoire de la sexualité* it comes to be considered, rather, as
the site of a problematization, the object of an unease, the axis
about which a whole process of reflection on the relation to the
self and to others will be concentrated, a process of reflection constitutive of the conduct of life. It is, then, this question or this
field of enquiry — which we may call 'anthropological' in the
sense in which the term is used in the *Nicomachean Ethics* (1181
b 14) — which Foucault, following the example of Weber, opposes
to the phenomenological, existential and individualist philosophy
of the subject. The problematization of subjectivity and the constitution of *Lebensführung* in place of 'consciousness', of 'the lived',
or of 'interests'.[9]

We come, finally, to the concept of *power*. This is not conceived of as something to be possessed, the attribute of a subject, but
as a relation, the site of a constant tension which sometimes assumes the form of a collision. This last assertion needs to be defined more precisely, because otherwise it runs the risk of appear-
ing both banal and at the same time devoid of any exact theoretical content. Foucault defines the polemical framework within
which his reflection inscribes itself as follows: it was necessary for
him to reject 'the alternative between a power conceived as domination or denounced as a simulacrum' (ibid., p. 11), even though at

the same time he took the political dimension seriously, never conceiving of it, like the Marxists, as a mere 'superstructure'. The very fact of posing the problem of power in terms of a relation had driven him for ten years — as those who have followed his lecture-courses at the Collège de France know well — to concentrate his researches on the theme of 'government'.[10] If power is neither reduced to the exercise of a domination which it would be necessary in turn to control, to reduce, to divide, or simply to do away with, nor dissolved away into the empty appearances of a simulacrum, or even of a reflex alone, it is therefore necessary to re-think it in terms of the relation of 'government', a relation to be understood in the classical sense — that is, the pre-Rousseauistic one. (It was in fact only from *The Social Contract* onwards (see Book III, Chapter 1) that the word came to be used, in a more narrow and somewhat vague sense, to signify 'executive power'.) Since Aristotle, politics has been considered as the relation between the governed and the governing. This starting-point is one which Foucault accepts, provided that it is agreed that 'the governed' and 'the governing' are not, in their turn, natural objects which refer back to a trans-historical substance or condition, but, rather, the names which are given to the terms of a relation which is established within every exercise of power and which, in fact, constitutes that exercise of power. It would therefore be possible to give the name of archaeology (from *archē*: 'rule', 'government') to this general theory of authority.

In classical Greece, at least as it appears in the *prescriptive* texts which Foucault analyses, 'political' reflection — reflection, that is, which is concerned with the relation between governing and governed — is not limited to consideration of the specific space of the government of the *polis* (characterized by a relation of authority between free and equal citizens),[11] but is situated, rather, at the centre of 'practical philosophy', the crucial problem of which is that of the 'conduct of life'. This problem is posed as much on the individual level, the object of ethics (self-government) as on the 'economic' level (the government of the house), or the political level, in the literal sense of the term (the government of the city).[12] It is in this way that, starting out with the history of sexual ethics in antiquity, we come across the problem of the government of the self and of others. A characteristic element in this practical philosophy of Greece and, up to a certain point, of Rome too — the element which gives it its specificity in relation to the modern problematics of government, as this problematics is constituted from the sixteenth and seventeenth centuries onwards, is that the entirety of this doctrine of *Lebensführung* revolves around the concept of *maîtrise de soi*, or self-mastery (*enkrateia*). (See ibid., pp. 74ff..) To the point that, on the one hand, 'economics' and 'politics' present themselves as spaces of application, under different modalities, of a single principle, regulating the ethical life — that of government of the lower order by the higher, of the inferior realm by the superior — and, on the other hand, political power, even in maintaining its singularity, comes to form part of the extension of the exercise of *maîtrise de soi*. In other words, if a criterion of self-government (*Sōphrosunē*) regulates the relation of the subject to himself — as Diogenes Laertius writes: 'It is best to dominate our pleasures without letting ourselves be conquered by them' — a self-government which, simply, produces a free subject or, what comes to the same thing, a virtuous citizen, this same criterion regulates the conduct of the husband, the head of the household. To the government of the self and of the pleasures of the self, then, is linked 'economic' reflection, that is, reflection concerned with the government of the wife, the sons and daughters and the slaves. Finally, it is this *maitrise de soi* which founds, legitimates and makes possible the exercise of public power, whether it is that of King Nicocles, of which Isocrates speaks (see ibid., p. 193), or that of the citizens, who, in the Athenian democracy, take turns in governing the city, according to a system of rotation (ibid., p. 197).[13] 'In the name of his own virtues, [the king] is able to demand the submission of his subjects' (ibid., p. 189); here we have a model destined to a long period of survival, as demonstrated by the German literature of *Fürstenspiegel* and the various French treatises on the education of the prince.

Why, then, as we asked before, this displacement of Foucault's research towards classical antiquity? We may now attempt to provide a reply to this question. 'It was, in fact,' Foucault writes (ibid., p. 10), 'a matter of seeing how, in *the societies of the modern West* [my italics], a particular "experience" was constituted. . .' : that of the individual and of his or her 'sexuality'. This was the theme announced to the reader in 1976 in the Introduction to *The History of Sexuality* — a theme which had already appeared, alongside various others, in the inaugural lecture of 1970 on *The Order of Discourse*. In the course of his work, the author soon realized that he would have to place the Christian hermeneutics of the 'subject of desire' (a theme which constitutes the contents of the fourth volume) at the point of departure of the modern experience of sexuality. But why go further back? It seems to me, in fact, that a study of the *specificity* of the relation to the self which is governed by the modern form of the sexual conduct of life cannot avoid undertaking the task of a comparative analysis which testifies to this specific character and renders it visible. Specificity is, in fact, like many other concepts, a relative one, which forces us to face the question: if an experience is 'specific', what other experience, then, does it differ from?

Max Weber, in attempting to find an answer to the problem of the specific character of the modern Western world, was driven to embroil himself in a comparative study of economic ethics, the results of which may be found in his writings on the sociology of religion. Foucault, for his part, was driven to go back a lot further in his investigation into the constitution of the 'subject of desire' which was effected by Christianity. In the Introduction to *L'Usage des plaisirs* he himself surveys the risks and the benefits of this long *détournement*. It is perhaps worth pointing out that behind the monotonous historical schema according to which 'the same things return', he produces, in these two books, something like an 'inventory of differences'. The same prohibitions, or rather the same contents, repetitive and not very numerous, of the moral codes, whether these are concerned with the fear attached to the loss of semen or with conjugal fidelity, are in turn specific to the 'subject of desire' or to the citizen capable of controlling his own passions. It is on the basis of this inventory that the object appears — modern subjectivity and its ethics — of which Foucault had started to write the history.

'If it were true, we would know.' With these words, twenty-five years ago, Georges Canguilhem offered his commentary on the manuscript of *Madness and Civilization*.[14] Rejected as a doctoral thesis at the University of Uppsala, where Foucault had worked for four years making use of the archives of the Bastille which had finished up in Sweden during the Napoleonic period, the book, which was turned down by several publishing houses, including Gallimard itself, and which seemed unpublishable, was finally accepted by Plon, thanks to the insistence of Philippe Ariès. Perhaps the same words will be applied to the publication of the last two books.

'An inventory of differences,' I said just now, taking up an expression of Paul Veyne's. But, one might object, does Foucault, the philosopher of 'discontinuity' and of the 'epistemological break', not return, in these two books, to a form of history based on continuity, or, what is worse, to a history of ideas, in the most traditional sense of the term? We must come to some understanding. If it is true, on the one hand, that the substantialist type of philosophy of history has always been one of the polemical targets of his work, I must nevertheless confess, on the other hand, that I always perfectly understood the burst of laughter with which Foucault reacted to the label of 'philosopher of discontinuity' which was often attached to him. This label was employed in order to pass off as a solution, or even as a philosophy, the *problem* — the event or the rupture, if you like — which he posed to philosophical reflection. This theme of discontinuity was never the last word in his writings. It represented, rather, a point of departure, a challenge — the will to contradict a long succession of synonyms — to which it was the task of his research to respond. A challenge that lies at the centre of his *Histoire de la Sexualité*. We need only read the remarks which he makes on fidelity in marriage (ibid., pp. 200–3). Here the procedure adopted in his other works is completely reversed. The starting-point is not, as in *Discipline and Punish*, a point of difference — the disappearance of torture and the general adoption of imprisonment as a method of punishment — but the posing of a continuity: the precept of conjugal fidelity, which recurs with a greater or lesser insistence from Xenophon's *Oeconomicus* to Christian pastoral. Yet this precept does not refer back to the same problematization of the subject in Xenophon, in Pliny or in the Church Fathers. In Athens, fidelity has to demonstrate the capacity of the husband (the citizen and head of household) to govern his own passions, in bearing witness, so to speak, to the 'economic' (domestic) aspect of his own virtue. In the Christian West, on the other hand, fidelity signifies the liberation of the subject from the scourges of the flesh and of sin.

Perhaps this constitutes a history of ideas? — this study which, retracing the path of our culture, goes back to Musonius Rufus and Aristotle, to the relics of antiquity, to which a long line of scholars have devoted their attention for centuries past. Foucault prefers to speak of a 'history of thought' (ibid., p. 16),[15] which he defines as the history of 'problematizations' — a history which differs both from social history and from the history of ideas or representations. What was the essential concern of *Madness and Civilization*? Not representations of madness or of the mad, but the event of the great *enfermement*, and, beyond this, that other event which was the precondition of the *enfermement*, and which accompanied the process of putting it into practice: the emergence of a possibility of *thinking* the limit between reason and madness.

Truth, subject, power — or, as we ought to say, 'government'. It is on the basis of his analysis of these three pivotal points of our culture, and of the concrete historical forms which the relations between them have assumed — exercises of government which accompany the production of discourses of truth and are founded on forms of conduct of life — that Foucault's work must be assessed. The day when all the lecture courses which he gave at the Collège de France are published, the dimensions and importance of his work will receive their due recognition. His 'will to knowledge' has not produced a system — a feature which will be a source of reproach to some and will be seen as a sign of merit by others. The problem, in my opinion, does not lie here. We should be concerned, rather, with gauging how great a displacement he has forced reflection on truth, on the subject and on power to undergo, and of assessing the space which opens us, as a result of this displacement, for philosophic, historical and political thought.

Foucault did not like talking about himself. 'All that I have to say', he would often declare, 'is in my books and in my lectures.' He wrote of himself, however: 'What would the relentless pursuit of knowledge be worth if it had only to secure the acquisition of information, and not, in some way, and as far as is possible, the displacement of he who knows?' (ibid., p. 14).

Faculty of Political Science
University of Turin

Notes

* The first part of the observations which follow was written in April 1984, and appeared, in a slightly abbreviated version, in *Le Magazine littéraire* (no. 202, May 1984). The contents of this section of the article owes a great deal to an exchange of ideas with Alessandro Pizzorno, in the context of a seminar organized by him in the Faculty of Political Sciences at the University of Milan, in Spring 1983. The second part contains comments provoked by reading the two volumes of the *Histoire de la sexualité*: *L'Usage des plaisirs* and *Le Souci de soi* (1984). These pages are intended, quite simply, as a testimony to the ten years of friendship which I have shared with Foucault the man, the teacher and the scholar, and as a testimony, too, to the regret which I feel for the research projects and the reflections on common intellectual concerns planned together for the future.

** (Translator's note: In the original, French text of *Surveiller et Punir* (1975, p. 315), this definition is put forward in a footnote. In the English edition *Discipline and Punish*, translated by Alan Sheridan, 1979, p 308, this note is incorporated in the main body of the text.)

*** (Translator's note: i.e. 'the regulation, discipline and control of a community; civil administration' (*OED*). This same meaning was attached both to the Italian term *polizia* and to the English *police*, which is used to translate it here.)

1 See the collection of Oestreich's essays published in English (1982); the writings in this volume are drawn, in large part, from Oestreich (1969).

2 It was on these themes that Foucault was working during the last months of his life.

3 This point is developed, at least in part, in my article (Pasquino 1982).

4 In mentioning this research, I was thinking, in particular, of Foucault's final course of lectures, at the Collège de France, on the ancient Cynic school of philosophy.

5 For a discussion of Max Weber and the problem of *Lebensführung*, see W. Hennis, 'Max Weber's Problematic', in *E&S* (1983).

6 The manuscript of the fourth volume, *Les Aveux de la chair*, dedicated to the Church Fathers and to Christian pastoral, was practically ready at the beginning of June, 1984, the last time I saw Foucault. There is a hope that Paul Veyne may take upon himself the task of seeing to the publication of this volume.

7 'What is, at this particular moment, the space of possible experiences?' — this is the question and the problem which Foucault uses to define his own 'philosophical choice', a choice to which he gives the name of 'ontology of actuality', and which he sets in opposition to the alternative choice, that of 'a critical philosophy which presents itself as an analytical philosophy of truth *in general*' (see the lecture on Kant published in *Le Magazine Littéraire*, May 1984, p. 39). In a comment on this lecture (*Die Tageezeitung*, 7/7/1984) Jürgen Habermas indicates that he fails to understand Foucault — which is itself a step forward from the time when he presented him, unhesitatingly, as a reactionary thinker — when he considers this choice as one which is in contradiction to his analyses of the 'disciplines' or of the human sciences in modern society.

8 See Tribe (1981 ch. 4).

9 On the two points which are only indicated here very briefly, see Michel Foucault, preface to Georges Canguilhem.

10 The summaries of these courses, from 1971 to 1984, will be published in an edition prepared by the author of this article, under the title *Il governo di sè e degli altri*.

11 See Meier, (1980, pp. 27—47).

12 On the concept of continuity and on the links between ethics and politics in classical Greek thought, see J. Ritter (1977, pp. 106 ff.).

13 See, on this point, Finley, (1983, pp. 73ff.).

14 It is a matter of common knowledge that Canguilhem soon changed his mind, to the extent that Foucault was able to take his *doctorat d'état* under his direction — a doctorate awarded on the basis of this manuscript, and also on the basis of Foucault's French translation of Kant's *Anthropologie in pragmatischer Hinsicht* (Paris, Vrin, 1964).

15 *Histoire des systèmes de pensée* (*History of Systems of Thought*) was the name of the course of lectures which Foucault gave for fourteen years at the Collège de France.

References

Finley, M. (1983), *Politics in the Ancient World*, Cambridge.

Foucault, M. (1975), *Surveiller et Punir*, Paris.

Foucault, M. (1978) Preface to Canguilhem, G., *On the Normal and the Pathological*, Boston.

Foucault, M. (1979), *Discipline and Punish*, trans. Sheridan, A., Harmondsworth.

Foucault, M. (1984), *Histoire de la Sexualité*, vol. I: *L'Usage des plaisirs*; vol. II: *Le Souci de soi* (Paris).

Mejer, C. (1980), *Die Entstehung des Politischen bei den Griechen*, Frankfurt.

Oestreich, G. (1969), *Geist und Gestalt des frühmodernen Staates*, Berlin.

Oestreich, G. (1982), *Neostoicism and the Early Modern State*, Cambridge.

Pasquino, P. (1982), 'Polizia celeste e polizia terrena', *Annali dell' Istituto storico italo-germanico in Trento*, 8, pp. 325—55.

Ritter, J. (1977) ' "Politik und Ethik" in der praktischen Philosophie des Aristoteles', in *Metaphysik und Politik*, Frankfurt.

Tribe, K. (1981), *Genealogies of Capitalism*, London.

Weber, M. (1968), *Economy and Society*, ed. Roth, G., and Wittich, C., New York.

4 A political genealogy of political economy

Denis Meuret
Translated by Graham Burchell

Abstract

If, at the end of the eighteenth century, political economy became the prevailing representation of economic phenomena, this was due to the fact that, better than other economic or political discourses, it constructed a political framework in which three forces could co-exist. These forces were those that all the authors of this century tried to articulate: the state, capitalism, and those who tried to protect themselves from their power.

To do the genealogy, rather than the history, of political economy involves attempting to understand how, at a given moment, it succeeded in organising the production of truth, rather than recounting its progress towards scientific rigour or the way in which it followed the development of the economy itself.

To what Michel Foucault called a *savoir* and what Paul Veyne calls a 'programme of truth' (Veyne, 1983), genealogy does not pose the question of the truthfulness of what it says. By rediscovering how, against what other discourses, it succeeded in imposing itself, it addresses the question of the pertinence of the truth it constructs.

To speak of political genealogy is to say that the reasons for the emergence of political economy are to be found in the field of the political. It is to say that this new way of describing economic phenomena organises according to new forms the coexistence of those forces whose combination defines the form of the political.

It is from this perspective that we will present the genesis of political economy, through authors – political theoreticians and economists – who, from Montchrétien (1615) to Smith (1776), dealt with the economy. First of all though, we will set out the problematic which has led us to believe that this approach might have some relevance.[1]

Published in *Economy and Society Volume 17 Number 2 May 1988*

I For a political approach to economic representations

1. The form of government of modern societies owes more to Adam Smith than to the more strictly political authors of the Enlightenment, than to Locke, Montesquieu or Rousseau. It is defined by a certain aim assigned to the State, by a stake in political debate and by a particular framework fixed for that debate.

An aim for the state: to further the growth of national wealth and to see to its optimal utilisation.

A stake in political debate: parties compete to persuade citizens that each is the best party for achieving this aim. Poverty and unemployment become factors of political crisis which previously they were not.

A framework for this debate: it is in the name of productivity that, on the one hand, one criticises the excessive influence supposedly wielded by the state or denounces the people's unreasonable demands and, on the other, one criticizes the obstacles that private ownership of the means of production, or the archaism of property owners, put in the way of the development of the productive forces.

Starting from this observation we can advance the hypothesis that the success of political economy is due to the fact that its representation of the economy and the political was better than others in that it provided an image of reality on which its government could be based.

2. If we accept what Fernand Braudel says (1985), between the sixteenth and eighteenth centuries capitalism is a considerable force, a factor of progress but also of disorder, that must be distinguished from a market economy governed by competition and multiple regulations.

This leads one to suspect that when political economy brings together under the same concept what Braudel distinguishes under the names of capitalism and economy, it is not a matter of the registration of an observed fact but of an utterance which aims to produce as its effect what it describes as existing.

On this view political economy is not a simple representation of the real economy. For, although not restricted to being a transcription of reality, the function of a representation nevertheless is only to express its unperceived coherence (an order or process). Its sole capacity is to complete a virtuality hidden in things. Now, unless one professes an historical determinism of some kind or other, one must suppose that the economy, at any instant, is able to evolve in several directions, and that the direction corresponding to the then prevailing representation acquires from this fact an additional chance of being realised. In this sense political economy would not so much express as institute what today we call the economy.

Nonetheless, it is neither a utopia (which would require the range of potentialities to be infinite and reality to offer no resistance), nor an ideology (which would require there to exist another discourse dealing with the same object which could be taken as true). It is, as we have said, a *savoir*, a 'programme of truth'.

3. If political economy is the governmental discourse of the modern world, if, moreover, it can be argued that it is an account with programmatic value more than a description of reality, then one might also take the view that this account was constructed precisely in order to make this government possible or, alternatively, one might focus on the characteristics by which it found itself able to fulfill this function.

This leads one to consider the political field in which economic representations take effect. From the sixteenth to the eighteenth century this can be reduced to three terms: capitalism, the state, and the public.

Following Braudel, by capitalism we designate the 'superior, sophisticated' economy in which 'the rules of the market economy regarding, for instance, free competition as described in classical economics . . . operated far less frequently' (Braudel, 1985: 22). This capitalism is what eighteenth century texts call 'Commerce' (trade in England). Two lines intersect in the definition of commerce: it is international rather than local *and/or* it bears on the superfluous rather than the necessary.

It is defined in opposition to the indispensable exchange of necessary products, but also by its capacity to contaminate the routine economy with that 'thirst for profit' that it is supposed to ignore. 'Capitalism', then, will not be used here with its contemporary meaning (the particular form of social organisation which allows private ownership of the means of production) precisely because it is a question of studying the process of this meaning's emergence, i.e., the identification of capitalism with a free economy society.

For this reason capitalism can also designate the set of actors – merchants, industrialists, landowners – who conduct themselves according to its rules, who play its game. In contrast, 'economy' will be employed to designate, in a way that the context will make clear, sometimes all the exchanges of a given society, sometimes that part of the economy which remains outside the capitalist game.

According to Braudel, between the sixteenth and eighteenth centuries the state, 'by turns help or hindrance', is capitalism's only genuine interlocutor. The idea that the state is only a superstructure of society is modern. This is what legitimates it today. We will trace the genesis of this idea and so define the State, beyond this modern definition, as an autonomous actor.

By 'the public' is understood all citizens with the power to repudiate the state to the extent that they exercise this power. The public can refuse a form of government and has the task of proposing one that is acceptable. It is not a sociological but a political reality: a set of opinions, attitudes and propositions, of tacit resistances and acceptances which do or do not allow a governmental apparatus to function. The emergence of political economy is inseparable from the movement by which, in the eighteenth century, the public, which in the seventeenth century was still only an object of discourse, begins to intervene as an explicit actor in an intellectual debate for which it was, at the same time, the stage.

The genealogy of political economy advanced here consists in saying that this representation of economic phenomena succeeded in imposing itself because it offered, through a redefinition of the economy and the state, new rules of the game to its players – the state, capitalism and the public.

We should think of it as a diplomatic treaty, a compromise that each player agrees to because its nature appears such as to protect each of them from the other two. This treaty has effects on what the real economy and the real state will become to the extent that it favours those potentialities which are in accordance with the nature of each of the players.

It is not therefore a question of, in the name of the political, subjecting economic discourse to the kind of treatment that political discourse has been subjected to in the name of the economy: of looking for hidden interests behind manifest declarations. Such a way of proceeding would presuppose that changing forms of representations of the economy can be interpreted as a function of a political field which itself remains immutable. Rather, it is a question of seeing how the reciprocal determinations linking theories of the State and economic representations mark out the site of a fundamental operation by which men agree on a way of perceiving the world in order to inhabit it together, economically and politically. Of course, this operation must be called political, but not in the sense that it treats of the forms of coexistence between different forces. Rather, it is a question of the moment when these forces are themselves named, delineated and, consequently, constructed.

It is the peculiar characteristic of political philosophy, says Claude Lefort, to deem there to be no 'elementary components or structures, no entities (classes or segments of classes), no social relations . . . which pre-exist their forming' (Lefort, 1986: 20), a forming which is, he goes on to say, 'at once an endowing with meaning and a staging'. It is indeed as such – as a forming, endowing with meaning and staging (*mise en forme, mise en sens, mise en scène*) – that political economy interests us.

4. What shall we call political economy? Solely the work of Adam Smith. Not because Smith 'founded Political Economy' in the sense that this has sometimes been claimed in the history of economic ideas. In that sense one knows that precursors to Smith (Boisguilbert, Cantillon) or his inspirers (Hume, Quesnay) have been found. One knows as well that there are differing views on his importance as an economist. Blaug is much less severe than Schumpeter for example. But because, at least this is what we want to show, Smith founded a city, our own, in which this science is possible and necessary. Political economy is the story on which this city is founded, its 'myth of origins' if you like, except that it is called upon to help our society hold up in a completely different way than a primitive society does this by summoning up the story of its foundation.

To defend myself against the accusation of arbitrarily manipulating definitions I can plead that the habitual use of the term political economy designates Smith as a kind of radiating core. The term has two meanings today. Those invoking Political Economy rather than economic science recognise that their discipline 'combines striving for objectivity with doctrinal references' (Lallement, 1984: 62). For them, political economy is what is written about the economy starting from the moment it is treated as an autonomous object, that is to say, starting from Smith or his precursors. Inversely, for those who lay claim to economic science, political economy designates that period where it is no longer a matter for 'advice to the Prince' or of 'system builders', but where normative claims have still not yet been wholly abandoned. This double usage evokes the effect of a force: political economy, by turns pushing what preceded it back into the indistinct or serving as a foil to offset the clarity of what follows it. And, in turn, this force evokes an inaugurating gesture, a founding operation, rather than a slow maturation. Now Smith is the only author whom all consider, in one or the other sense, as belonging to the set 'Political Economy'. In the first, precursors have been found without it ever being claimed that he was one of them. In the second, no-one has been able to subject the whole of *The Wealth of Nations* to the kind of operation that Sraffa suceeded in carrying out with Ricardo: annexing it to science through formalisation, taking Smith out of 'Political Economy'.

5. The genealogy offered here clearly goes in the opposite direction of what one could call, borrowing from psychoanalysis,

the 'family romance' of political economy, its retrospectively dreamt birth and infancy.

There are two versions of this romance. The first asserts the gradual discovery of the unity hidden behind the multiple forms assumed by relations of production and exchange in history. In short, the object is unchanging and was progressively discovered. The second considers the evolution of representations to be wedded to changes in the economy. A good example of this is the distinction suggested by M. Luftfalla between the economy of the *ancien régime* and the modern economy. To the first corresponds the idea of a circuit with its origin in agriculture (Quesnay, Cantillon, Steuart). To the second corresponds the idea of the primacy of demand affirmed by Walras and Leontieff (Luftfalla, 1981: 10–18). Midway between these two versions is the idea that the progress of economic knowledge reproduces that of the economy itself. Thus M. Hasbach (1893) advances the view that 'it is only in Smith's time that the economy was sufficiently developed' for it to be possible to see its mechanism in its full extent.

Putting aside the 'family romance' we will be lead to share Louis Dumont's idea that 'the particular discipline which constructs the economy as its object cannot give us . . . the basic presuppositions on which it is itself constructed'. (Dumont, 1976: 34) However, taking this idea as our point of departure, we will suggest an interpretation of the birth of Political Economy which differs from his.

One knows that Dumont sees in political economy (Mandeville, Quesnay, Smith, Marx) the privileged vector of modern individualism, through its assertion of the primacy of men-things relations over men-men relations. According to Dumont, this acts by transforming 'common sense', by impregnating consciousness in some way (p. 133). This leads him to think that, once established, a politics which deviates by however little from this common sense, Keynesian 'artificiality' for instance, can only engender monstrous regimes. (pp. 132–3)[2]

According to the perspective we develop here, Dumont's mistake lies in thinking that modern societies are individualistic in the same way as ancient societies were holistic. Political economy is seen as having developed not a common sense but rather a blueprint for individualistic government. It has come about not that men's consciousness has become individualistic, but that one has set about governing in the name of economic individualism. Now if individualism is less a characteristic of societies than a principle and aim of their government (the happiness and liberty of individuals), one can better understand how 'artificial' policies have been able to favour and not destroy the democratic life of modern societies. In

other words, one must contrast holistic societies not with individualistic but with political societies and, within this framework,
consider political economy's contribution to the political conceived
of as the common management of societies the principle of which is
no longer stability but change.

II The invention of the economy

Our aim is to understand why, at the end of the eighteenth century,
Smithian political economy supplanted other representations of the
economy, those of other schools of economists as well as those
conveyed by different political thinkers.

Our hypothesis is that Smith, through a new representation of
the economy, also offers a new definition of the state's legitimacy,
of its role and of its relations with citizens – in short, of the political
system – and that this account was at that time best placed to be
accepted by the three interested parties – citizens, state and
capitalism – as the principle for organising their coexistence.

This hypothesis is based on the idea that there is a link between
the pertinence of a representation of the economy and its
congruence with the political system of the time. If one focusses on
this congruence a periodisation in four phases is suggested.

1. The economics of absolutism

To the golden age of absolutism (until about 1680) corresponds an
economic thought (Montchrétien, Petty) in which the state is
responsible for making commerce contribute to the people's
happiness and the nation's strength.

2. The eighteenth century turning point: the crisis

What Paul Hazard called the 'crisis of European consciousness' is
translated in politics by the calling into question of absolutism.
Henceforth, the state no longer figures as organiser but as accused
in discourses on the economy (Boisguilbert, Vauban . . .).

Whereas before the state was called upon to domesticate
commerce, it is now declared that they have entered into an alliance
with each other which is pernicious from both an economic and
political point of view. This confronts authors with what will be the
eighteenth century's problem: to keep both the state *and* commerce
in check.

3. The eighteenth century: the search

Throughout the eighteenth century a solution will be sought through a redefinition of the state. In two ways: either one tries to base the state on a principle which excludes its contamination by commerce thereby enabling the state to keep it in check (this principle can be found in the nobility in Montesquieu or in the people's frugality in Mably and Rousseau), or one looks for a way in which society functions which can found and limit the state at the same time (property, interest, *l'Evidence*; Locke, Helvetius, the Physiocrats). One either protects political society from commerce or civil society from the state. One deals with either one or the other of the two questions bequeathed by the crisis.

4. Smith: the solution

Smith replies to the two questions by redefining the economy. He goes beyond the opposition between an ordered static economy and a destabilising, dynamic commerce by declaring that commerce *is* the economy and that the economy is a dynamic order. The economy, as he defines it, will be the instrument for the domestication of commerce and the State.

We examine below the first two moments of this history (II.1 and II.2) before trying to show in what respects Smith's solution is superior to those of the other authors confronted by the crisis (II.3).

II.1 The economics of absolutism

Absolutism has neither the same duration nor the same history in France and England. With reservations one can go along with certain historians and say that in France absolutism lasts from 1572 (St Bartholomew's Day Massacre) to 1789, and in England, only from 1629 (the break between Charles I and Parliament) to 1688 (the seizure of power from James II by William of Orange).

In France, however, absolutism is on the ideological defensive from the end of the seventeenth century. No doubt its critics do not lay claim to another system nor consider suggesting reforms unacceptable to it, but if solutions are sought which respect its principles, they no longer spring from these principles.

The period of absolutism's ideological ascendancy, if one can call it that, goes from Bodin (1574) to Spinoza (1670) passing through, among others, l'Argenis de Barclay (1621) and Hobbes (1651).

In France and England the economic works of this period exhibit absolute political conformity. No doubt they bring to the fore certain connections and automatisms which impose themselves on all, including the state, and that for that reason Mun and Petty, for example, call 'natural laws'. But they do not establish the existence of a general mechanism of equilibrium able to serve as the paradigm for the social order and so permit society to be thought independently of the state. To consider economic phenomena is thus to indicate on what conditions they can be inserted into a general order of which they do not provide the matrix. In this sense, Montchrétien (1615), Savary (1675, Le Parfait Négociant), Petty (1662) and Mun (1621, 1650) write not so much economic treatises as treatises on public and private management.

That these texts treat the (internal) economy and (international) commerce differently is indicative of how types of exchange, which to modern ideas have the same nature, were seen then as being differentiated by the conditions of their government and the characteristics of the order into which they must be inserted.

The internal economy is hardly analysed.[3] Not because it automatically tends towards equilibrium but because, operating in the space where royal authority is exercised, it is naturally subordinate to that authority. For Montchrétien, 'manual occupations, through the skill of those exercising them, contribute to the work of the nation in which they are fixed and confined, wholly under the management of the public administration which directs them to their end'.[4] Knowing in whose hands wealth is held, for example, is of little importance since 'it is as if one held two vases in one's hands and poured liquid from one into the other' (p. 156).

Of course, there is concern for the well-being of the people but, in Mun as much as in Montchrétien, it is a question of guaranteeing them work and not of raising their standard of living. We are close here to the medieval idea that the King (the Seigneur) is guarantor of his people's subsistence and so must see that the providential order which assures it is not disturbed by the ventures of private individuals. We are a long way from Smith's 'natural effort of every individual to better his own condition', as from the idea of a continuous growth of wealth, as, finally, from the idea that the social process is a competition where all have the same wish to make their fortune.

The principal object of discourse at this time is not the economy therefore but commerce. And one can only be struck that we needed to wait for Braudel (1985) for the conceptualisation of an economy/capitalism distinction clearly legible in the texts but which liberal and marxist traditions have taught us was only the effect of a self-serving or clumsy consciousness.[5] Commerce is the object of discourse because it poses a problem precisely since there is no equivalent, at the international level, of that just providential order to which, within frontiers, it suffices to assign exchanges. It is interstate rivalry that takes the place of this order and that is why 'economists' present the problem in terms of the state's might. Commerce poses a specific question not because it prefigures a free economy, but because the political space into which it must be fitted is itself specific.

Montchrétien wants to defend France from foreign merchant enterprises. Mun and Savary praise the contribution Commerce makes to the realm's wealth and strength. Montchrétien is defensive and somewhat distrustful vis-a-vis commerce. Mun is offensive and concerned for merchants' interests. But whether it is a question of curbing foreign merchants or of encouraging one's own, neither doubts the State's ability to do so judiciously,[6] nor that a well-managed Commerce is beneficial to the realm. Savary's work is only a manual for merchants' use which opens with a list of the benefits of commerce, but it is dedicated to Colbert in recognition of the 'fine regulations' he made for commerce: thirty years later Colbert, for the same reason, will be Boisguilbert's pet hate.

In the same period, Petty thinks of England as an enterprise in which the state is responsible for promoting productivity. Therefore he develops for the State's uses a double-sided knowledge. On the one hand it is a matter of an entrepreneur's cunning and organizing *savoir*. Among other things, the number of traders will be limited to what is necessary (Petty, 1905: 23). On the other hand, it is a question of having access to the very value of things in order to allocate taxes justly, and so of indexing them not only on the real value – of lands above all – but on what one might call their potential value.

If Petty doesn't invent political economy it is because he lacks the mechanism able to draw these two types of knowledge together. He jubilantly identifies innumerable mechanisms and local automatisms that he presents as so many levers for improving the country's management. But he has no idea of a general equilibrium which would give consistency to what came to be called the economy.[7]

To summarise, what characterises representations of the economy in this period is, first of all, that commerce and the routine economy are not treated in the same way, secondly the idea that commerce must be governed by the state, and finally the confidence put in the state in this respect.

II.2 The crisis

At the turn of the century (roughly from 1680 to 1720) this confidence disappears for mainly political reasons. If we follow Koselleck (1973), while the absolute monarch in France holds his legitimacy to be above the parties brought to light by the religious wars,[8] and so considers himself able to bring about peace, with the revocation of the Edict of Nantes in 1685 it is Louis XIV himself who involves his people in endless wars. In England, William of Orange puts an end to absolutism but creates an uncertain regime pulled between rival oligarchic groups preoccupied after William's death with the dream of a Stuart restoration (Plumb, 1981: 50ff). Without making this crisis of confidence the sole cause of the shift detectable in economic discourse at this time, it is difficult not to attribute an important role to it in this respect.

In fact this reorientation manifests itself through the appearance of two very different currents, both of which call into question the direction of commerce by the state.

With variations, both currents appear in France and England. The first is a criticism of the harmful political effects of absolutist management. In England this is made by 'country' authors (Fletcher and Davenant, for example) and in France by Vauban and Boulainvilliers. The second could be called the 'first liberalism'. Boisguilbert in France and Barbon, North, Martyn, Gardiner and others in England, lay down the virtues of the total freedom of economic actors.

The 'country' authors say that progress is beneficial but that it is also pernicious for political organisation and the liberty of citizens. One of them, the economist Davenant, develops a complex but revealing position. He acknowledges that free exchange is favourable to the development of commerce. From a purely economic point of view he is therefore in favour of it. But, from a political point of view, can one envisage the totality of social relations being founded on a 'credit' or reputation which moralises commerce? Davenant toys with the idea but abandons it. The growth of national might is, then, commerce's only indisputably beneficial effect – if, however, it exists. In fact, Davenant, in contrast to Thomas Mun, doesn't consider this effect to be certain: 'if trade cannot be made subservient to the nation's safety, it ought to be no more encouraged here than it was in Sparta' (cited in Pocock, 1975: 443).

For Boulainvilliers (1658–1722), progress and commerce have political drawbacks only because the state and the nobility have each in their way betrayed their true nature. The development of commerce forces the nobility to become corrupt by allying itself with commoners 'through need of money'. But it could avoid this if it engaged in commerce itself rather than considering it, wrongly, as in conflict with the principles on which the nobility's role within the state is founded. Commerce corrupts the state, but only because the latter abandons its alliance with the nobility so that it no longer has any link with the people except through 'financiers and *Intendants*'. These are upstarts who 'ruin the old economy of the State and destroy the sacred bonds of society'. Society itself now only serves to produce wealth for the state. Logically, Boulainvilliers adds to this critique of the state some very modernistic, semi-interventionist projects for the regulation and supervision of commerce by a regenerated state. He is in favour of a regulation of external commerce and, in the sixth *mémoire* to the Duc d'Orléans (Boulainvilliers, 1727), he suggests the creation of 'Directions Générales du Commerce'. These concern societies of private capitals, established right in every parish, which encourage and control the trade in goods, collect economic statistics and offer a system of sickness assurance to the 'humble people'.

In France as in England, this current calls therefore for the return to a form of state capable of domesticating commerce in order to replace the corrupting alliance that state and commerce have entered into with each other above and to the detriment of political society.

Boisguilbert (1646–1714) is Boulainvilliers' contemporary. His works appear between 1691 and 1707. He too reviles the financiers and, through them, the whole of the absolutist system for collecting and setting taxes.

But he also criticizes the nature of the nobility. Through 'politeness', the 'idle class' shatters the transparency necessary to the right order of exchanges. Through its 'cupidity' it contributes to making money the 'tyrant of Commerce' when it should be its 'valet'. The existence of the idle class, the dictatorship of financiers, and the regulation of the economy, form a series of factors likely to lead to economic equilibrium being upset and to its complete destruction through a mechanism of crisis propagation that Boisguilbert subjects to a closely-argued analysis. The solution will not be another type of action by the state but 'that it cease to act'. Then one will see that providence, by assuring a 'well-balanced competition' between buyers and sellers, has provided all the conditions of economic equilibrium. G. Facarello (1986) has recently demonstrated the rigour and coherence of Boisguilbert's theory of this equilibrium.

J. O. Appleby has shown the remarkable liveliness of the English liberalism of the same period which has a different tone from the French liberalism. In place of the resentment that Boisguilbert expresses towards an organisation of society which creates poverty and crises where there should be wealth and equilibrium, there is a kind of annoyance with the stupidity of protectionist politics which shackle the enormous potential for growth and prevent there being greater wealth and more exchanges.

But the break with old discourses is no less fundamental. For these, says Appleby, 'members of society did not compete with one another, but rather participated in the collective enterprise of selling surplus goods abroad' (Appleby, 1978: 164). For their part, the liberals considered England even in this period 'not as a giant workhouse but rather as a giant market whose individual members had differing needs' (*ibid.*, p. 168).

To the protectionist system the liberals opposed a completely different conception of wealth and economic activity. It is no longer the 'surplus' which matters but the total amount of exchanges. The activity of merchants is always the cause of wealth but, in this conception, because it brings in attractive goods which stimulate wants and, thereby, the encouragement to work. The protectionist alliance of the State with manufacturers and landowners prevents this dynamic process from producing all its felicitous effects.

The idea that national wealth is not a surplus but the total amount of exchanges is common to the English liberals and Boisguilbert who defines it as a 'continual blending' of men with men, occupations with occupations. This idea contradicts absolutist economic management. Indeed, the idea that wealth is a surplus extracted from other nations or achieved by commerce with them is in keeping with the practice of a state levy in the service of national might. In the framework of the other, liberal definition, the same levy is akin to a misappropriation of funds or to a breakdown of the mechanism. This definition does not completely exclude such a levy but implies that a stronger justification be given for it.

In this period criticism of absolutism thus spins off into contradictory paths. Moreover, this shows that it is a matter of a crisis and not of a resolution within a new system. It is all the more remarkable that all the critics had a point in common which is the relation of the state to wealth. Criticism of financiers by Boulainvilliers and Boisguilbert and criticism of the public debt in England bear on the same point: the means by which the state obtains resources for itself upsets the equilibrium of society and/or of political society. The new concept of wealth introduced by the liberals reinforces this criticism, even if in England it is the product of a different point of view from that of the 'country' authors.

Nonetheless, the representation of the economy advanced by the liberal current proved unable at this time to establish the basis of an answer to the question of the separation between state and society posed by the first current. From our point of view it is indeed the failure of the liberal current that must be explained. These authors were underestimated by their successors when they are not still ignored today.[9] They were not understood by the political powers of their respective countries. They have not even been able to prevent these they combatted coming back to the fore, sometimes much later.[10]

The failure of the English liberals at the beginning of the eighteenth century, confronted by a resurgence of the theory of the balance of trade, is explained by Appleby in this way: the theory of the balance of trade allowed a protectionist politics and, thereby, avoidance of the social unrest that a liberal politics would have induced, but without justifying it in terms of that objective. For it was necessary to avoid that type of justification, too similar to the discourse used, before 1688, by the monarchy ousted in the name of a natural right to which, on the other hand, *laisser faire* as much as the theory of the balance of trade could lay claim.

This interpretation raises a question: why didn't an equivalent process follow Smith's version of liberalism? It seems to me that there are two reasons for this that will be developed a little further. On the one hand, the seventeenth century liberals want the economy to rediscover a nature from which it has deviated, whereas Smith will require that it be left to obey a nature towards which it has always obstinately tended. Consequently, Smith offers the prospect of a less violent and provoking process than did his predecessors. On the other hand, Smith will be careful to show that exchanges made between individuals concerned with 'bettering their condition' are equitable, and that this productive society is also a just society. In this way he brings together natural law and economic liberalism. Locke's enlistment alongside the supporters of protectionism shows that the seventeenth century liberals failed to present this link as an exclusive one. It seems to me that Smith's modification goes much further than a simple 'correction' of liberalism by themes taken from the mercantilists (cf. Appleby, 1978: 272).

Among these corrections Appleby includes the fact that Smith 'created a model with balances and mechanical adjustments' whereas his predecessors were content to 'probe the dynamic elements in economic life'. This difference surely does not exist between Boisguilbert and Smith. What other difference, then, explains that the second and not the first author was able to found the governmental discourse of modern societies? Both have conceptions of economic equilibrium and its conditions which are close to each other, but the place of equilibrium in the general structure of their discourse is not the same. Resentment against a situation in which the State's action prevents nature from establishing equilibrium dominates in Boisguilbert. And no doubt this resentment is justified since, from the moment that nature, conceived in terms of providence, is not allowed to act, 'the least departure . . . immediately ruins everything' (Boisguilbert, 1966: 992); 'from the moment someone tries to go against this rule of justice . . . defiance occurs, and private individuals who no longer find their subsistence are forced to provide it by exceptional measures' (*ibid.*, p. 1010). Inversely, for Smith, nature is first of all 'men's natural effort to better their condition', and this effort, although hampered by the organisation of the economy, leads all the same to bringing equilibrium closer (cf. infra. Smith's criticism of Quesnay). What is important here is not a divergence between Smith and Boisguilbert on the respective probabilities of a state of equilibrium and a state of crisis. Boisguilbert thinks that crises only occur 'under violent and repeated shocks' and one therefore must suppose that he too thought the system capable of absorbing slight or episodic shocks. Nor is it a greater or lesser confidence in the capacity of the market to correct disequilibria. According to Boisguilbert, in a regime of perfect competition the rational expectations of agents also restore equilibrium (cf. 1966, Ch. VIII). What matters is that, in the radical opposition between the functioning of a free economy and of a regulated economy described by Boisguilbert, it is the state alone which determines order or disorder. In other words, it is the state which decides whether the natural rules are or are not observed. In contrast, in Smith it is the public, the mass of men who have responsibility for nature: it is the public, as a collection of individuals, which restores it and also, as a set of social groups defending their interests against the interest of others, which produces deviations from it.

In this sense, Boisguilbert like the physiocrats, is a prisoner of an adhesion to the absolutism whose management of the economy he severely criticises. In demanding of the state that it cease acting both Boisguilbert and the physiocrats take to absurd lengths the claim of the absolutist state to be able to install the order intended by providence on earth. They are the last 'givers of advice' in the sense that they are the last to furnish the state with an immediately applicable *savoir* which presupposes the state's direct command over things. Smith's text, for its part, takes shape in a completely different space. The public and no longer the state will be its addressee and subject. It will only have an indirect relation to the state because the state is supposed to act only indirectly on things themselves. The principle of the state's legitimacy will be reversed: it won't be a question of bringing to the public an order shown by knowledge to be possible, but of allowing the completion of a movement shown by knowledge to be real. It is this overturning which allows political economy to become the discourse of government. The failure of the first liberalism shows in any case that something other than merely the discovery of the virtues of demand and of *laisser faire* was required to provide a complete alternative to mercantilism.

II.3 Smith's solution

Until Smith, commerce was studied in its concrete existence and one enquired how it could be got to contribute to the people's prosperity, to the nation's greatness, and to the good conduct of the body politic.

Smith himself doesn't start from commerce but from men's desire to better their material condition. A fundamental even if indirect desire he says in *The theory of moral sentiments*: one only desires to be rich in order to benefit from the admiration directed towards the wealthy (Smith, 1976: 50–1). This desire is illusory since the wealthy are not objectively happier than the poor. But it is extraordinarily fruitful since, on the one hand, nothing else gets people to work and, on the other, it is anchored, through the mediation of envy, on the primordial sentiment binding men together: sympathy, the capacity to feel what others feel. Thus, for Smith it is a question of seeing if this progress, this desire for enrichment, can function in an equitable way.[11] The positive answer is given in *The Wealth of Nations*. With equal individuals linked only by a certain 'propensity to exchange' at the outset of the model, one obtains, on leaving it, and thanks to the division of labour, an enrichment which profits everyone without betraying equality since it has arisen only from free and equitable exchanges.

The detour taken by Smith in order to broach the question of commerce can be read in the very plan of *The Wealth of Nations*. In the first two books he invents the economy: the movement and exchanges into which men are launched through their desire to improve their condition. He shows that this movement is effective and just. He then goes on to show, in Book III, that his invention is not just a mental construct but that it is already really at work in history and can therefore be used as a principle of historical explanation. Only then does he use his invention to do what his predecessors did at the outset: in Book IV he makes his pronouncement on economic politics – in other words, he shows how to domesticate commerce – and in Book V, on the role of the state, he shows how to contain and found it.[12]

How does this detour enable him to resolve the two questions bequeathed by the crisis of the beginning of the century in a way acceptable to the three participants in the debate: capitalism, the state, and the public? We will take each question in turn.

a) The domestication of commerce

For the political authors of the eighteenth century the natural economy (moderate profit, small property) is thought to be the bringer of order. For them commerce brings progress but also disorder. Smith brings progress and order together under the aegis of the market economy. According to whether commerce is or is not fitted into the market economy, it will either share its virtues or assume once again its old figure as bringer of disorder. Assigning commerce to the market guarantees that it will remain within the framework of the economy, that is to say, of exchanges which are equitable and the most productive possible. In other words, the market is the means of its domestication.

Smith's liberal precursors held the state responsible for infringements of market laws. Smith innovates by showing that these infringements are only prompted by the pressures of merchants and manufacturers who have an objective interest in bending the rules (Smith, 1976, Book One, Ch.9). Now these infringements not only prejudice the allocation of capital and so the quantity of wealth produced, but also the equity of its distribution (*ibid*. Book Four, Ch. 8). The obscurity necessary to 'leagues and monopolies' prevents equality between individuals and the transparency of their relations.

What Smith calls the capitalists' 'rapacious greed' is beneficial only if, according to J. R. Lingren's formula, they exercise it 'by competing with one another in the observance of the moral sentiments of the larger society – which condition is fulfilled by a completely decentralised pricing procedure' (Lingren, 1975: 130). It is therefore the traders themselves who are responsible for the pernicious effects of commerce, not the state or the idle class.

In Smith the latter are accused only of keeping people unproductive instead of constructing roads and castles, not with destroying a fragile equilibrium beyond repair.

In Smith's rhetoric, merchants and manufacturers are at once good (as individuals acting to improve their condition on the market) and wicked (as a class or, to take up the expression of *The theory of moral sentiments*, 'rank').

It would be tempting to reutilise an economic language in order to claim that between the advantages and disadvantages for capitalism of being described in either mercantilist or market economy terms, there came a moment in its development when the balance tipped in favour of the second. But this would ignore the fact that capitalism is not alone on the stage: this moment was also determined by the evolution of the other actors – the State and the public.

Rather, therefore, we must note that Smith offers an account in conformity with the dominant current of the political thought of the period (natural right, individualism), that is to say, reconcilable with representations of the state then possible. And we must show that, among all the forms of controlling capitalism then proposed, Smith's is the most favourable to the development of capitalism whilst offering to the public a credible protection from it.

An account acceptable to capitalism

Some of the systems then in the lists ignored the question of commerce – Locke's for example. In the *Second Treatise* (1963) merchants leave the stage to the advantage of the 'property owner' surrounded by his family and servants. This is consistent with the protectionist positions, favourable to manufacturers and land-owners, that Locke subsequently takes up.

The other systems profoundly misjudge the nature of capitalism by attempting to impose limits on its development rather than accompanying it with regulations in harmony with its nature. Rousseau wants commerce to die; Montesquieu wants to keep it on the periphery of the great monarchies by restricting transit commerce to the merchant cities; Quesnay wants to put it in tow behind agricultural development; numerous authors rail against luxury and elaborate political systems on the basis of an economy of small landowners, contenting themselves with re-cognising that, sadly, it is not possible to return to the past (Helvetius, Mably).

In a general way Smith is the only one who assigns commerce to an order the existence of which is already perceptible and in which it participates, even if in other respects it seeks to subvert it. In this sense he is the only political author who assigns commerce to what he declares is its profound and virtuous nature, and not to an order external to it (Rousseau, Montesquieu). And he is the only economist for whom a liberal economic politics derives from rather than institutes the economic order.

This singularity can be read in the aside on Quesnay in *The Wealth of Nations* (Smith, 1976: 674), an aside which is no doubt one of the principal keys to Smith's work, its theme being repeated three times in Book II Ch. 3

> Mr. Quesnai . . . seems to . . . have imagined that [the political body] would thrive and prosper only under a certain precise regimen, the exact regimen of perfect liberty and perfect justice. He seems not to have considered that, in the political body, the natural effort which every man is continually making to better his own condition is a principle of preservation capable of preventing and correcting, in many respects, the bad effects of a political economy, in some degree, both partial and oppressive.

It seems to me that Michel Foucault bases himself on this idea when he emphasises that Smith was the first to conceive the time of the economy as 'the interior time of an organic structure which grows in accordance with its own necessity' (Foucault, 1970: 226). This conversion in the form of knowledge confers an eminent place on history, since it is now history which attests an order the mark of which is no longer the mechanics of perfect equilibrium, but the continual and 'natural effort' of men to make this order manifest by overcoming the obstacles put in their way. This difference has little heuristic value, at least if one follows Schumpeter concerning the weakness of Smith's distinctive contribution to economic analysis. But the political content of Smith's approach differs profoundly from that of Boisguilbert and Quesnay. These latter are on Hobbes' side, just as Smith is on Locke's. Admittedly, for Hobbes the sovereign's action brings an end to natural disorder whereas, for Quesnay, deciding not to act puts an end to a disorder which has an artificial origin. But, in both cases, order is instituted from the starting point of a decision taken by the state to remedy a radical disorder.

Locke constructs a state of nature against Hobbes which is no longer conflictual but peaceful, occasionally disturbed by 'covetousness' just as Smith's economic order is by merchants' combines. The figure of the State is softened for society itself, but also for the capitalists: in fact, in the *laisser faire* version of Quesnay and Boisguilbert, what matters is that capitalism is indebted to the state for the institution of conditions favourable to its development, whereas in Smith's version the state is indebted to capitalism to the extent that the latter realises the progress towards opulence on which the former bases its *raison d'être*. This is so even if the State is responsible for seeing to it that capitalism respects the rules of the economy.[13]

An account acceptable to the public

When Smith holds up to society the mirror of the economy he gives it a distorted image of itself: it was not true then that everyone sought first of all the improvement of their material condition, and it is still not true. Moreover, the question is one of knowing why the public thought that this fiction, better than another, domesticated capitalism to its advantage.

First of all, we must note that it is only if one accepts that the economy is the organising principle of the social that the latter acquires enough 'weight' for capitalism to be governable in its name.

Next, we must understand Smith's 'happy' account as so many criteria for judging capitalism. That for Smith capitalism is only one of the forms of all men's activity to improve their condition means also that capitalism is only legitimate if it increases productivity for the benefit of all. That it is only a sophisticated version of barter means that it is only legitimate to the extent that the equity of exchanges is assured by the market.

Henceforth it matters little that political economy gives a truncated vision of men and their society. It is not required, least of all by Smith, to be a general discourse on the being of man, but rather that it provide a framework for the social management of capitalism. And this is why it is so easy to criticise political economy for everything in human society which it ignores (symbolic exchanges, spending, social status . . .).

b) Domestication of the state

To the couple capitalism/economy corresponds, in the political order, that which opposes the state insofar as it is doing battle with the 'ranks' of society, and the state insofar as it represents the interests of individuals.

The first is powerless insofar as it is a question of doing good (it never transpires that the state gets any rank to sacrifice itself to the general interest). But it is powerful when it comes to doing harm, whether this be through prodigality ('Great nations are never impoverished by private, though they sometimes are by public prodigality' writes Smith before noting that 'however . . . upon most occasions' the mechanism described in the aside on Quesnay is at work (Smith, 1976: 342–3)) or weakness (the laws which 'the clamour of our merchants and manufacturers has extorted from the legislature . . . may be said to be all written in blood' (*ibid.* p. 648)).

The second is not the liberals' minimum state. In the first chapter of Book V of *The Wealth of Nations* Smith proposes a technician-state, the provider of services, charged with encouraging the advance of productivity by taking responsibility for collective investments. Among the latter, some are intended to reinforce the 'active principle' of commercial society, others to compensate for its harmful effects. Where 'commercial society' worsens people's conditions it is necessary to provide remedies. Smith is then close to Fletcher who demanded that 'suitable remedies' be found for the risks of progress. This is the case for 'the gross ignorance and stupidity which, in a civilised society, seem so frequently to benumb the understandings of all the inferior ranks of people' (*ibid.* p. 788) and which will be mitigated by schools intended for these people. It is not a question then of producing a 'good' but of 'the prevention of so great a public evil' (*ibid*). Where, by contrast, commercial society improves conditions, the state must reinforce that action: here it is a matter of investments, and even protections, for promoting productivity through commerce. That it is a question of productivity in the final resort is shown by the criterion Smith uses: the person who pays the tax must gain 'by the application more than he loses by the payment of it' (*ibid*. p. 725).

Not only does Smith not think that all investments can be left to the initiative of private individuals, but he also distances himself from *laisser faire* by demanding that tolls be higher for the luxury carriages of the rich (p. 725) and that management of investments not be ceded back to private individuals when their interest doesn't absolutely oblige them to manage them appropriately (pp. 725–6). To promote progress and repair its damages: one has here a very modern figure of the state far removed from any liberal dogmatism.

In what way was this figure more acceptable than others, both to the state itself and to a public concerned with controlling its action? Just as capitalism could not accept being attenuated or contained as Rousseau or Montesquieu proposed, so the state could not accept being required to 'cease acting' in the manner of Quesnay or Boisguilbert. As he did for commerce, Smith traced a route for the state's development, a route which, as we know, has been followed with perserverance and success.

But above all Smith offers the state a principle of legitimacy, that of being the representative of the historical movement of societies towards opulence. In doing this he founds the necessity for a particular form of the state on a description of a society that the state's only task is to represent. In this respect Smith is in Locke's line of descent and is as far removed from Rousseau as he is from Montesquieu. Both Rousseau and Montesquieu produce discourses on the state that the state cannot adopt as its own. How could it find support in Montesquieu who established essentially that no one form of state is necessary and that, on the contrary, each is answerable in terms of its adequacy to the world which supports them and to the particular characteristics of the people they govern? And how can it get support from Rousseau? The latter looks for the conditions of individual autonomy and finds them in a political order either by men making a collective somersault (*The Social Contract*) or through a prior draconian legislation (*Project for a constitution for Corsica* and *Considerations on the government of Poland*). In both cases there is a discourse that cannot be used by the state. In the first, the state is realised and abolished at the same time in the manifestation of the general will. In the second, the state takes on a monstrous shape since, on the grounds that the chaos of 'civilization' cannot in any case be represented, it fabricates the social instead of representing it.

On the one hand, Smith offers the public a 'soft version' of the state and, on the other, a point of view from which to judge it and a *savoir* for doing this. Smith's state is not frightening because it does not draw its strength from itself. It only assists in the accomplishment of an historical dynamic that owes nothing to it. The fact that the nature represented by the state takes the form of an historical dynamic rather than that of a static order has two consequences. On the one hand, the account which discovers it is exposed to refutation. This is not the case in Locke or Quesnay. On the other hand, one cannot claim that in the event of men proving to be defective agents of a rationality it would be appropriate for the state to impose this rationality on them. The possibility of this was foreseen by Locke, for example, in government by 'prerogative', that is to say, by the 'Power to act according to discretion, for the public good, without the prescription of the Law, and sometimes even against it' (Locke, 1963: 422). There are two guarantees here, if you like, given to the public by Smith's state.

Furthermore, the state is presented as having no autonomous force at its disposal: against what must be subjugated (ranks, monopolies . . .) it counterposes what exists in the 'natural movement' of men to which, as we have seen, history attests. It turns the force of the economy against capitalism.

In doing this Smith also provides a criterion and a *savoir* for judging the state. The criterion is its contribution to the material progress of society. Obviously the *savoir* is political economy, installed at the heart of the political set-up of modern societies: the language through which society can demand that the state account for itself. Smith, who affected to find no-one on whom his good state could lean, created a figure of the economist who is the solution to this problem. The economist is an individual who knows how to read the market. For both the state and the public he demonstrates the reality at work in things, that force in the name of which, ultimately, the state governs.

As discourse on reality on the one hand and on government on the other (insofar as it enables one to determine the opposition between good and bad forms of the state and the conditions of transition from one to the other) political economy is what L. Sfez calls a 'symbolic operation' (Sfez, 1978). Through it the real economy and state (cunning merchants, credulous landowners, prodigal state) are transmuted into this figure called upon to domesticate both of them: the orderly economy of the market and the state in the service of the nation's wealth.

Smith's system could have remained an appealing construction if an event had not occurred to confer upon it the verisimilitude necessary for its adoption as a discourse of government. In the perspective adopted here, the industrial revolution can be viewed as an event which came to verify Smith's account (in that industrial capitalism, in its forms and effects, is closer to Smith's economy than to merchant capitalism) at the same time as this account probably favoured its emergence. Hence it followed that the political management of societies strongly characterised by an industrial economy could support itself on the 'treaty' proposed by Smith. Rather than contradicting this treaty, *solidarisme* at the end of the nineteenth century (cf. Donzelot, 1984), Keynesianism, and the welfare state (*l'Etat Providence*) are its avatars.

Thus it is necessary to reply positively to the question of the pertinence of political economy's 'programme of truth' at the same time as it must be said that this pertinence is bound up with a particular form of capitalism, that is, let us say, that form which comes closest to the image that political economy gives of it so as to undertake the task of its domestication.

If, as Marx and most historians think, the Industrial Revolution is an outcome which gave capitalism its true face, there is no reason to think that political economy's pertinence is contradicted. On the other hand, if one thinks like Braudel (1985) that capitalism is 'eclectic' and that its industrial form is only one of its avators, then one must acknowledge that certain characteristics essential to the Smithian blueprint may disappear, calling its pertinence into question.

In particular, among the conditions for the pertinence of Smith's account two are likely to cease being fulfilled in the relatively short term:

- the insertion of capital in a national political space. The industrial revolution tied down a capital which has become once again extremely mobile. Nations are less the result of a 'natural' set of exchanges between their members, than the seat of particular economic strategies in a world economy which henceforth enter into competition with each other within a neo-mercantilist framework, discovering again the relation they maintained with capitalism before the nineteenth century;
- the social insertion of individuals through production. It is as a producer of wealth that Smith's individual is a citizen. In this respect, the unemployment which accompanied the 1929 crisis signalled a derailing of the machine whereas present-day unemployment – to the extent that it is not accompanied by an economic collapse – signals perhaps that the machine itself is in the process of changing its nature.

On this hypothesis, the current crisis is less economic than political.

A form of government almost 200 years old is struck with obsolescence manifested in the discredit into which the political class has fallen because it can neither truly manage the economy nor avoid promising that it will make it work.

We must therefore renew the treaty made with capitalism at the end of the eighteenth century. Failing this, it is less capitalism that will be threatened than the political regime which the old treaty inaugurated.

Ministry of National Education
Paris

Acknowledgements

Thanks are due to Graham Burchell, Jean Daniel Grousson, Fabio Petri, and Philippe Steiner for their criticisms and comments on an earlier version of this article. Obviously I am responsible for any remaining weakness in it.

Notes

1 The reader wanting to examine this approach in more detail is referred to the thesis in Political Sciences of which this article is a presentation: 'l'Economie Politique, comme discours de gouvernement', Paris IX, 1985.

2 In a more recent text Dumont abandons the Hayeckian tone of this passage from *Homo Aequalis* for the idea that 'the important thing is to subordinate necessary social disciplines to fundamental individual rights and freedoms' (Dumont, 1983: xv).

3 When Mun hopes that 'a very great multitude of the poor will be involved in the work of which consists the greatest strength and all the wealth of the Realm' one might see in this the sketch of a view of the internal economy. It is nothing of the sort since it is the work of the poor for export to which Mun appeals. In fact, in the same chapter he stresses that the poor who work for foreigners are more useful to the Republic than if they work for the wealth of their own country (Mun, 1650 Ch. 3).

4 This is a translation of the author's version of Montchrétien's text. The original text reads as follows: 'les vacations mécaniques sont opérations industrielles, qui concourrent à la publique, en laquelle elles sont arrêtées et confinées, et le tout sous la conduite du magistrat qui les améne à sa fin' (Montchrétien, 1889: 123).

5 Braudel himself notes the convergence between the distinction he makes and the one found in the texts of the eighteenth century: 'I found myself constantly faced with a regular contrast between a normal and often routine exchange economy (what the eighteenth century would have called the *natural* economy) and a superior, sophisticated economy (which would have been called *artificial*)' (1985: 22).

6 Mun combats 'prejudices' against commerce but, far from remonstrating against the limits imposed by the State on the export of money, he emphasises the

scrupulousness with which the East India Trade has respected them (Mun, 1621: 19).

7 In particular, it is a misinterpretation to assimilate his concept of intrinsic value to labour value and extrinsic value to the price. The first is only the effect of 'constant determinations' of the price, the second registering also those of 'fluctuating values'. Petty, like a merchant, wants to anticipate the real value and emphasises that for this one must take into account both types of determination. He doesn't have the economist's idea that the extrinsic gravitates around the intrinsic and that consequently only the latter matters. (Petty, 1905: 108).

8 'Whereas religious parties drew their strength from sources which were outside the jurisdiction of the Prince, the Prince could only succeed in imposing himself by breaking the primacy of religion' (Kosellek, 1973: 14 and 15).

9 Boisguilbert was not ignored but certainly underestimated in the eighteenth century (cf. Faccarello, 1987). Of the dozen authors cited by Appleby (1978) only three figure in Schumpeter's index (1955): Barbon, North and Coke. Schumpeter notes that Barbon's *Discourse of Trade* was quickly forgotten (p. 331).

10 Excepting the German school, no partisans of protectionism are found among Nineteenth century *economists*. By contrast, the mercantilist theory of the balance of trade is rediscovered unchanged in M. Decker's *Essai sur les causes du déclin du commerce du loin*, 1750 (Appleby, 1978: 158).

11 This conception of Smith's work is close to the view developed by Hont and Ignatieff (1983).

12 Schumpeter (1955: 186) thinks that in these last books Smith returns to the traditional form of economic discourses after freeing himself from it in the first two Books. Indisputably, Smith would consider that this would mean that he had failed completely.

13 This in a very concrete way. The aborted attempts to free prices under Turgot bear the mark of Quesney's approach: these attempts would have had to succeed immediately to testify in support of *l'Evidence*: failing which, it had to be renounced.

References

Appleby, J. O. (1978) *Economic Thought and Ideology in Seventeenth Century England*, Princeton.

Blaug, M. (1970) *Economic Theory in retrospect*, London.

Boisguilbert, P. de (1966) 'Dissertation sur la nature des Richesses, de l'Argent et des Tributs', in *P. de Boisguilbert ou la naissance de l'Economie Politique*, Paris.

Boulainvilliers, H. de (1727) *Mémoires au Duc d'Orleans*, The Hague and Amsterdam.

Braudel, F. (1985) *Civilization and Capitalism, 15th–18th Century, Volume Two, The Wheels of Commerce*, London.

Donzelot, J. (1984) *L'invention du social*, Paris.

Dumont, L. (1976) *Homo Aequalis*, Paris.

Dumont, L. (1983) 'Preface' to K. Polanyi, *la Grande Transformation*, Paris.

Faccarello, G. (1986) *Aux Origines de*

l'Economie Politique Liberale; Pierre de Boisguilbert, Paris.

Foucault, M. (1970) *The Order of Things*, London.

Hasbach, M. (1893) *Les fondements philosophiques de l'Economie Politique de Quesnay et de Smith, Revue d'Economie Politique*

Hirschman, A. O. (1977) *The Passions and the Interests*, Princeton.

Hont, I. and **Ignatieff, M.** (1983) *Wealth and Virtue*. Cambridge.

Kosselleck, R. (1973) *La règne de la critique*, Paris.

Lallement, J. (1984) 'Histoire de la pensée ou archéologie du savoir', in *Oeconomia*, cahiers de l'ISMEA, série PE, No. 2.

Lefort, C. (1986) *Essais Politiques*, Paris.

Lingren, J. R. (1975) *The social philosophy of Adam Smith*, The Hague.

Locke, J. (1963) *Two Treatises of Govern-*

ment, Cambridge.

Luftfalla, M. (1981) *Aux origins de la pensée économique*, Paris.

Montchrétien, A. de (1889) *Traité de l'Economie Politique*, Paris.

Montesquieu (1964) *L'Esprit des Lois*, Paris.

Mun, T. (1650) *England treasure by forraign trade*, London.

Mun, T. (1621) *A discourse of trade, from England to the East Indies . . .,,* London.

Petty, W. *A treatise of taxes and contributions* in (1905) *les oeuvres economiques de W. Petty*, Paris.

Plumb, J. H. (1981) *England in the Eighteenth Century*, Harmondsworth.

Pocock, J. G. (1975) *The Machiavellian Moment*, Princeton.

Schumpeter, J. A. (1955) *History of economic analysis*, London.

Sfez, L. (1978) *L'enfer et le paradis*, Paris.

Smith, A. (1976) *The Theory of Moral Sentiments*, Oxford.

Smith, A. (1976) *The Wealth of Nations*, Oxford.

Veyne, P. (1983) *Les grecs ont-ils cru à leur mythes?*, Paris.

5 Governing economic life

Peter Miller and Nikolas Rose

Abstract

This paper proposes some new ways of analysing the exercise of political power in advanced liberal democratic societies. These are developed from Michel Foucault's conception of 'governmentality' and addresses political power in terms of 'political rationalities' and 'technologies of government'. It draws attention to the diversity of regulatory mechanisms which seek to give effect to government, and to the particular importance of indirect mechanisms that link the conduct of individuals and organizations to political objectives through 'action at a distance'. The paper argues for the importance of an analysis of language in understanding the constitution of the objects of politics, not simply in terms of meaning or rhetoric, but as 'intellectual technologies' that render aspects of existence amenable to inscription and calculation. It suggests that governmentality has a characteristically 'programmatic' form, and that it is inextricably bound to the invention and evaluation of technologies that seek to give it effect. It draws attention to the complex processes of negotiation and persuasion involved in the assemblage of loose and mobile networks that can bring persons, organizations and objectives into alignment. The argument is exemplified through considering various aspects of the regulation of economic life: attempts at national economic planning in post-war France and England; the role ascribed to changing accounting practices in the UK in the 1960s; techniques of managing the internal world of the workplace that have come to lay special emphasis upon the psychological features of the producing subjects. The paper contends that 'governmentality' has come to depend in crucial respects upon the intellectual technologies, practical activities and social authority associated with expertise. It argues that the self-regulating capacities of subjects, shaped and normalized through expertise, are key resources for governing in a liberal-democratic way.

In advanced liberal democracies, political power has come to embrace many facets of economic, social and personal existence. Political power is exercised today through a multitude of agencies and techniques, some of which are only loosely associated with the executives and bureaucracies of the formal organs of state. In this paper we suggest that Michel Foucault's concept of 'government' provides a potentially fruitful way of analysing the shifting ambitions and concerns of all those social authorities that have sought to administer the lives of individuals and associations, focusing our attention on the diverse mechanisms through which the actions and judgements of persons

Published in *Economy and Society Volume 19 Number 1 February 1990*

and organizations have been linked to political objectives (e.g. Foucault 1979). We argue that an analysis of modern 'government' needs to pay particular attention to the role accorded to 'indirect' mechanisms for aligning economic, social and personal conduct with socio-political objectives. We draw upon some recent work in the sociology of science and technology in analysing these mechanisms, borrowing and adapting Bruno Latour's notion of 'action at a distance' (cf. Latour 1987b). We argue that such action at a distance mechanisms have come to rely in crucial respects upon 'expertise', the social authority ascribed to particular agents and forms of judgement on the basis of their claims to possess specialized truths and rare powers. And we contend that the self-regulating capacities of subjects, shaped and normalized in large part through the powers of expertise, have become key resources for modern forms of government and have established some crucial conditions for governing in a liberal democratic way.

We begin with a general discussion which sets out and seeks to develop the concept of 'governmentality'. In the remainder of the paper we seek to exemplify the mechanisms and processes discussed through a consideration of various aspects of the 'government' of economic life. We consider the 'government' of 'the economy', firstly through centralized systems of economic planning, and secondly through attempts to transform the calculative procedures of economic actors. We then turn to the 'government' of the internal world of the enterprise and examine this in relation to the changing techniques of management. We argue that management has come to depend upon expertise not only concerning the technical features of production, but also concerning the psychological features of the producing subjects. Finally, we look at the techniques by which the self-regulating capacities of subjects have become vital resources and allies for the 'government' of economic life, especially insofar as they have come to be understood and regulated in terms of the notions of autonomy and self-fulfilment. We link this to some remarks on contemporary transformations in 'governmentality'.

First, let us consider the notion of government. Michel Foucault argued that a certain *mentality*, that he termed 'governmentality', had become the common ground of all modern forms of political thought and action. Governmentality, he argued, was an 'ensemble formed by the institutions, procedures, analyses and reflections, the calculations and tactics, that allow the exercise of this very specific albeit complex form of power' (Foucault 1979: 20). And, he claimed, since the eighteenth century *population* had appeared as the terrain *par excellence* of government. Authorities have addressed themselves to the regulation of the processes proper to the population, the laws that modulate its wealth, health, longevity, its capacity to wage war and to engage in labour and so forth. Thus, he implies, societies like our own are characterized by a particular way of *thinking* about the kinds of problems that can and should be addressed by various authorities. They operate within a kind of political *a priori* that allows the tasks of such authorities to be seen in terms of the calculated supervision, administration and maximization of the forces of each and all.

This way of investigating the exercise of political rule has a number of advantages. Firstly, it refuses the reduction of political power to the actions of a State, the latter construed as a relatively coherent and calculating political subject. Instead of viewing rule in terms of a State that extends its sway throughout society by means of a ramifying apparatus of control, the notion of government draws attention to the diversity of forces and groups that have, in heterogeneous ways, sought to regulate the lives of individuals and the conditions within particular national territories in pursuit of various goals. Rather than 'the State' giving rise to government, the state becomes a particular form that government has taken, and one that does not exhaust the field of calculations and interventions that constitute it.

It is to the analysis of these aspirations and attempts that the notion of government directs us. This path may appear to lead, in a rather idiosyncratic way, to a familiar and well-trodden field – that of the historical and contemporary analysis of economic and social policy. However, the apparent familiarity of these concerns is likely to mislead. It is true that the earliest forms of governmentality in Europe went under the name of the science of 'police', and that 'police' and 'policy' share a common root. But the analysis of policy suggested by the concept of government implies that the very existence of a field of concerns termed 'policy' should itself be treated as something to be explained. It draws attention to the fundamental role that knowledges play in rendering aspects of existence thinkable and calculable, and amenable to deliberated and planful initiatives: a complex intellectual labour involving not only the invention of new forms of thought, but also the invention of novel procedures of documentation, computation and evaluation. It suggests that we need to consider under what ethical conditions it became possible for different authorities to consider it legitimate, feasible and even necessary to conduct such interventions. It suggests that the concerns that have occasioned and animated policy are not self-evident. The emergence of unemployment, crime, disease and poverty as 'problems' that can be identified and construed as in need of amelioration is itself something to be explained. It points to the diversity of the groupings that have problematized such aspects of existence in relation to social and political concerns, and that have developed and sought to implement policies. These are not just 'political' authorities, in the traditional sense, but also those whose basis is intellectual, spiritual, and so forth. It implies that there is no smooth path of development or evolution of policies, but that lasting inventions have often arisen in surprising and aleatory fashion and in relation to apparently marginal or obscure difficulties in social or economic existence, which for particular reasons have come to assume political salience for a brief period.

Hence the notion of government highlights the diversity of powers and knowledges entailed in rendering fields practicable and amenable to intervention. It suggests that the analysis of 'policy' cannot be confined to the study of different administrative agencies, their interests, funding, administrative organization and the like. A complex and heterogeneous assemblage of conditions thus makes it possible for objects of policy to be problematized, and rendered amenable to administration.

Of course, these dimensions can be studied, and have been studied, without drawing upon the notion of government. But the approach suggested by these writings of Michel Foucault has two further features that we consider important. Policy studies tend to be concerned with evaluating policies, uncovering the factors that led to their success in achieving their objectives or, more usually, deciphering the simplifications, misunderstandings, miscalculations and strategic errors that led to their failure (e.g. Williams *et al.* 1986). We, on the other hand, are not concerned with evaluations of this type, with making judgements as to whether and why this or that policy succeeded or failed, or with devising remedies for alleged deficiences (cf. Thompson 1987). Rather, we are struck by the fact that this very form of thinking is a characteristic of 'governmentality': policies always appear to be surrounded by more or less systematized attempts to adjudicate on their vices or virtues, and are confronted with other policies promising to achieve the same ends by improved means, or advocating something completely different. Evaluation, that is to say, is something internal to the phenomena we wish to investigate. For us, this imperative to evaluate needs to be viewed as itself a key component of the forms of political thought under discussion: how authorities and administrators make judgements, the conclusions that they draw from them, the rectifications they propose and the impetus that 'failure' provides for the propagation of new programmes of government.

'Evaluation' of policy, in a whole variety of forms, is thus integral to what we term the *programmatic* character of governmentality. Governmentality is programmatic not simply in that one can see the proliferation of more or less explicit programmes for reforming reality – government reports, white papers, green papers, papers from business, trade unions, financiers, political parties, charities and academics proposing this or that scheme for dealing with this or that problem. It is also programmatic in that it is characterized by an eternal optimism that a domain or a society could be administered better or more effectively, that reality is, in some way or other, programmable (cf. Gordon 1987; MacIntyre 1981; Miller and O'Leary 1989b; Rose and Miller 1988). Hence the 'failure' of one policy or set of policies is always linked to attempts to devise or propose programmes that would work better, that would deliver economic growth, productivity, low inflation, full employment or the like. Whilst the identification of failure is thus a central element in governmentality, an analysis of governmentality is not itself a tool for social programmers. To analyse what one might term 'the will to govern' is not to enthusiastically participate in it.

The discursive character of governmentality

Governmentality has a discursive character: to analyse the conceptualizations, explanations and calculations that inhabit the governmental field requires an attention to language. There is nothing novel in the suggestion that language and politics are interrelated, nor even in the suggestion that the relation between the two is neither one of simple homology or reflection, nor one of ideological mystification, but is mutually constitutive (e.g. Shapiro 1984; Connelly 1987; Taylor 1987). In relation to economic policy, a number of studies have directly addressed the discursive constitution of the domain and the component parts of the economy. They have demonstrated the conceptual conditions under which it came to be possible to conceive of a specifically economic domain composed of various economic entities with their own laws and processes that were amenable to rational knowledge and calculation, and hence to various forms of regulatory intervention (Birchell *et al.*, 1985; Hopwood 1987; Loft 1986; Tribe 1978; Thompson 1982; Tomlinson 1981a, 1981b, 1983). Jim Tomlinson has argued, in relation to the so-called Keynesian revolution in economic policy making, that whilst objects of economic policy are discursively constructed, such construction is dependent upon a complex and heterogeneous set of conditions that can neither be reduced to a recognition of eternal concerns or an expression of sectional interests, nor to a simple realization of a new economic theory (Tomlinson 1981a). Thus Keynesian policies for the political management of economic activity gained their power in relation to a pre-existing field of problems and depended upon the existence of a range of interlinked agencies, interests, calculations, theories and representations. The concern with 'full employment' in the post-war period depended upon a disparate set of conditions that included Keynesian economic theory, technocracy and total war, and was also made possible by diverse events such as the forced departure from the gold standard in 1931, the growth of government expenditure and a belief in the possibility of extending wartime planning to the post-war period (Tomlinson 1983).

Our approach has much in common with this. But we would like to place these concerns within a rather different framework. On the one hand, we suggest that policy should be located within a wider discursive field in which conceptions of the proper ends and means of government are articulated: an analysis of what Michel Foucault terms 'political rationalities'. On the other hand, we argue for a view of 'discourse' as a technology of thought, requiring attention to the particular technical devices of writing, listing, numbering and computing that render a realm into discourse as a knowable, calculable and administrable object. 'Knowing' an object in such a way that it can be governed is more than a purely speculative activity: it requires the invention of procedures of notation, ways of collecting and presenting statistics, the transportation of these to centres where calculations and judgements can be made and so forth. It is through such procedures of inscription that the diverse domains of 'governmentality' are made up, that 'objects' such as the economy, the enterprise, the social field and the family are rendered in a particular conceptual form and made amenable to intervention and regulation.

Political argument, no doubt, does not have the systematic and coherent character of theoretical discourse. Nonetheless, we suggest, it is possible to specify and differentiate political rationalities in terms of the relatively systematic discursive matrices within which government is articulated, the particular languages within which its objects and objectives are construed, the grammar of analyses and prescriptions, the vocabularies of programmes, the terms in which the legitimacy of government is established. It is out of such linguistic elements that rationalities of government such as welfarism or neo-liberalism – assemblages of philosophical doctrines, notions of social and human realities, theories of power, conceptions of policy and versions of justice – are elaborated and seek to specify appropriate bases for the organization and mobilization of social life.

All government depends on a particular mode of 'representation': the elaboration of a language for depicting the domain in question that claims both to grasp the nature of that reality represented, and literally to represent it in a form amenable to political deliberation, argument and scheming. This gives us a clue to a further way in which language is significant for government. For it is in language that *programmes of government* are elaborated, and through which a consonance is established between the broadly specified ethical, epistemological and ontological appeals of political discourse – to the nation, to virtue, to what is or is not possible or desirable – and the plans, schemes and objectives that seek to address specific problematizations within social, economic or personal existence. For example, in the early years of this century in Britain, the language of national efficiency served both to establish the proper role of government and the kinds of problems that it could and should address, to organize disputes between different political forces, and to articulate a range of different programmes that addressed themselves to managing specific aspects of the economic life and health of the population (Miller and O'Leary 1987; Rose 1985). Language here serves as a *translation mechanism* between the general and the particular, establishing a kind of identity or mutuality between political rationalities and regulatory aspirations.

The forms of political discourse characteristic of 'governmentality' open a particular space for theoretical arguments and the truth claims that they entail. The government of a population, a national economy, an enterprise, a family, a child, or even oneself becomes possible only through discursive mechanisms that represent the domain to be governed as an intelligible field with its limits, characteristics whose component parts are linked together in some more or less systematic manner (Burchell *et al.* 1985; Hopwood 1984, 1985, 1986; Miller 1989; Miller and O'Leary 1989a; Rose 1990). Before one can seek to manage a domain such as an economy it is first necessary to conceptualize a set of processes and relations as an economy which is amenable to management. The birth of a language of national economy as a domain with its own characteristics, laws and processes that could be spoken about and about which knowledge could be gained enabled it to become an element in programmes which could seek to evaluate and increase the power of nations by governing and managing 'the economy'. 'Government' that is to say, is always dependent on knowledge, and proponents of diverse programmes seek to ground themselves in a positive knowledge of that which is to be governed, ways of reasoning about it, analysing it and evaluating it, identifying its problems and devising solutions. Theories here do not merely legitimate existing power relations but actually constitute new sectors of reality and make new fields of existence practicable. Hence, as well as establishing the place of certain objects and problems within the legitimate obligations and powers of rulers, and enabling them to be formulated programmatically, it is through language that governmental fields are composed, rendered thinkable and manageable.

In drawing attention to the role of language in government in this way, we do not wish to suggest that the analysis of political power should become a sub-department of the history of ideas, nor that our concern should be with the problem of meaning. The features of language that we have described have a more active role than this, one perhaps best captured in the term *intellectual technology*. Language, that is to say, provides a mechanism for rendering reality amenable to certain kinds of action. And language, in this sense, is more than merely 'contemplative': describing a world such that it is amenable to having certain things done to it involves inscribing reality into the calculations of government through a range of material and rather mundane techniques (Rose 1988; cf. Latour 1987a). The events and phenomena to which government is to be applied must be rendered into information – written reports, drawings, pictures, numbers, charts, graphs, statistics. This information must be of a particular form – stable, mobile, combinable and comparable. This form enables the pertinent features of the domain – types of goods, investments, ages of persons, health, criminality, etc. – to literally be re-presented in the place where decisions are to be made about them (the manager's office, the war room, the case conference and so forth). From the eighteenth-century invention of statistics as the science of state, to the present attempts to evaluate the economic life of the nation by measuring the money supply or the efficiency of health services by turning their endeavours into cash equivalents, programmes of government have depended upon the construction of devices for the inscription of reality in a form where it can be debated and diagnosed. Information in this sense is not the outcome of a neutral recording function. It is itself a way of acting upon the real, a way of devising techniques for inscribing it (birth rates, accounts, tax returns, case notes) in such a way as to make the domain in question susceptible to evaluation, calculation and intervention.

The technologies of government

'Government', of course, is not only a matter of representation. It is also a matter of intervention. The specificity of governmentality, as it has taken shape in 'the West' over the last two centuries, lies in this complex interweaving of procedures for representing and intervening (cf. Hacking,

1983). We suggest that these attempts to instrumentalize government and make it operable also have a kind of 'technological' form (cf. Foucault 1986; 225–6). If political rationalities render reality into the domain of thought, these *technologies of government* seek to translate thought into the domain of reality, and to establish 'in the world of persons and things' spaces and devices for acting upon those entities of which they dream and scheme.

We use the term 'technologies' to suggest a particular approach to the analysis of the activity of ruling, one which pays great attention to the actual mechanisms through which authorities of various sorts have sought to shape, normalize and instrumentalize the conduct, thought, decisions and aspirations of others in order to achieve the objectives they consider desirable. To understand modern forms of rule, we suggest, requires an investigation not merely of grand political schema, or economic ambitions, nor even of general slogans such as 'state control', nationalization, the free market and the like, but of apparently humble and mundane mechanisms which appear to make it possible to govern: techniques of notation, computation and calculation; procedures of examination and assessment; the invention of devices such as surveys and presentational forms such as tables; the standardization of systems for training and the inculcation of habits; the inauguration of professional specialisms and vocabularies; building design and architectural forms – the list is heterogeneous and is, in principle, unlimited.

The classical terminology of political philosophy and political sociology – State v. Civil Society, public v. private, community v. market and so forth – is of little use here. Such language certainly needs to be investigated, to the extent that it functions in important ways within political rationalities and political programmes, providing them with an ethical basis and differentiating the legitimacy of varied types of governmental aspiration. But at the technical level, operationalizing government has entailed the putting into place, both intentionally and unintentionally, of a diversity of indirect relations of regulation and persuasion that do not differentiate according to such boundaries. In particular, the capacities that have been granted to expertise – that complex amalgam of professionals, truth claims and technical procedures – provide versatile mechanisms for shaping and normalizing the 'private' enterprise, the 'private' firm, the 'private' decisions of businessmen and parents and the self-regulating capacities of 'private' selves in ways that are simply not comprehended in these philosophies of politics. Yet it is precisely these indirect means of action and intervention that are central to modern 'mentalities of government' and crucial for the possibility of modern forms of rule (MacIntyre 1981; Miller and O'Leary 1989b; Rose 1986, 1989a). The analysis of such technologies of government requires a 'microphysics of power', an attention to the complex of relays and interdependencies which enable programmes of government to act upon and intervene upon those places, persons and populations which are their concern.

It is through technologies that political rationalities and the programmes of government they articulate become capable of deployment. But this should not be understood simply as a matter of the 'implementation' of ideal schemes in the real, still less as the extension of control from the seat of power into the minutiae of existence. By drawing attention to the technological dimension of government, we do not mean to summon up an image of a 'totally administered society'. It is true that, in certain European countries, the early versions of 'police' were inspired by the utopian dream that all regions of the social body could be penetrated, known and directed by political authorities. But, as Michel Foucault has pointed out, nineteenth-century liberalism marks the point from which this dream was abandoned in those nations that called themselves liberal democracies. The problem became, instead, one of governing a territory and a population that were independent realities with inherent processes and forces. With the emergence of such an idea of 'society', the question became 'How is government possible? That is, what is the principle of limitation that applies to governmental actions such that things will occur for the best, in conformity with the rationality of government, and without intervention' (Foucault 1986: 242).

It is for these reasons that we have suggested the need for the analysis of the 'indirect' mechanisms of rule that are of such importance in liberal democratic societies: those that have enabled, or have sought to enable *government at a distance*. In conceptualizing such indirect mechanisms by which rule is brought about, we adapt for our own ends Bruno Latour's notion of 'action at a distance' (Latour 1987b: 219 *et seq.*). He develops this notion in answering the question 'how is it possible to act on events, places and people that are unfamiliar and a long way away?' Eighteenth-century French navigators could only travel to unfamiliar regions of the East Pacific, colonize, domesticate and dominate the inhabitants from their European metropolitan bases because, in various technical ways, these distant places were 'mobilized', brought home to 'centres of calculation' in the form of maps, drawings, readings of the movements of the tides and the stars. Mobile traces that were stable enough to be moved back and forward without distortion, corruption or decay, and combinable so that they could be accumulated and calculated upon, enabled the ships to be sent out and to return, enabled a 'centre' to be formed that could 'dominate' a realm of persons and processes distant from it. This process, he suggests, is similar whether it is a question of dominating the sky, the earth or the economy: domination involves the exercise of a form of intellectual mastery made possible by those at a centre having information about persons and events distant from them.

Our notion of 'government at a distance' links this idea to a related approach developed in the work of Latour and that of Michel Callon (Callon and Latour 1981; Callon 1986; Latour 1986). In the context of analysing the establishment and generalization of scientific and technical innovations, Callon and Latour have examined the complex mechanisms through which it becomes possible to link calculations at one place with action at another, not through the direct imposition of a form of conduct by force, but through a delicate affiliation of a loose assemblage of agents and agencies into a functioning network. This involves alliances formed not only because one agent is dependent upon another for funds, legitimacy or some other resource which can be used for persuasion or compulsion, but also because one actor comes to convince another that their problems or goals are intrinsically linked, that their interests are consonant, that each can solve their difficulties or achieve their ends by joining forces or working along the same lines. This is not so much a process of appealing to mutual interests as of what Callon and Latour term '*interessement*' – the construction of allied interests through persuasion, intrigue, calculation or rhetoric. In the process occurs what Callon and Latour refer to as 'translation', in which one actor or force is able to require or count upon a particular way of thinking and acting from another, hence assembling them together into a network not because of legal or institutional ties or dependencies, but because they have come to construe their problems in allied ways and their fate as in some way bound up with one another. Hence persons, organizations, entities and locales which remain differentiated by space, time and formal boundaries can be brought into a loose and approximate, and always mobile and indeterminate alignment.

Language, again, plays a key role in establishing these loosely aligned networks, and in enabling rule to be brought about in an indirect manner. It is, in part, through adopting shared vocabularies, theories and explanations, that loose and flexible associations may be established between agents across time and space – Departments of State, pressure groups, academics, managers, teachers, employees, parents – whilst each remains, to a greater or lesser extent, constitutionally distinct and formally independent. Each of these diverse forces can be enrolled in a governmental network to the extent that it can translate the objectives and values of others into its own terms, to the extent that the arguments of another become consonant with and provide norms for its own ambitions and actions. The language of expertise plays a key role here, its norms and values seeming compelling because of their claim to a disinterested truth, and the promise they offer of achieving desired results. Hence expertise can appeal, in one direction, to the ambitions of politicians, administrators, educators and others seeking to achieve particular objectives in the most efficacious manner, and, on the other, to those who have come to feel the need for expert guidance for their conduct in the firm, the office, the airline, the hospital or the home.

Such networks are, of course, not the simple aggregate of rationally planned technologies for shaping decisions and conduct in calculated ways (Thompson 1982). 'Governmentality' is embodied in innumerable deliberate attempts to invent, promote, install and operate mechanisms of rule that will shape the investment decisions of managers or the child care decisions of parents in accordance with programmatic aspirations. But such attempts are rarely implanted unscathed, and are seldom adjudged to have achieved what they set out to do. Whilst 'governmentality' is eternally optimistic, 'government' is a congenitally failing operation. The world of programmes is heterogeneous and rivalrous, and the solutions for one programme tend to be the problems for another. 'Reality' always escapes the theories that inform programmes and the ambitions that underpin them; it is too unruly to be captured by any perfect knowledge. Technologies produce unexpected problems, are utilized for their own ends by those who are supposed to merely operate them, are hampered by underfunding, professional rivalries, and the impossibility of producing the technical conditions that would make them work – reliable statistics, efficient communication systems, clear lines of command, properly designed buildings, well framed regulations or whatever. Unplanned outcomes emerge from the intersection of one technology with another, or from the unexpected consequences of putting a technique to work. Contrariwise, techniques invented for one purpose may find their governmental role for another, and the unplanned conjunction of techniques and conditions arising from very different aspirations may allow something to work without or despite its explicit rationale. The 'will to govern' needs to be understood less in terms of its success than in terms of the difficulties of operationalizing it.

Governing the national economy

In the remainder of this paper, we wish to illustrate some of the mechanisms to which we have drawn attention by means of a number of examples. None of these is intended as an exhaustive historical account of policy development and implementation, let alone an evaluation of policies or the politics behind them. Our concern is with 'governmentality' in the sense in which we have discussed it above, with the mentalities that have constituted the changing attempts to modulate economic activity, the varying vocabularies through which economic activity has been rendered thinkable, the different problems that have concerned them, the role of intellectual technologies of theorization and inscription within them, the diversity of regulatory technologies that have been invented together with the difficulties of implanting them and the key role that has been taken by expertise. It is in the assemblage formed by this heterogeneity, and in particular in the part accorded to the self-regulating activities of 'private' social actors under the guidance of expertise, that the possibility has emerged for governing the economic life of the nation in ways consonant with liberal democratic ideals.

We begin with an investigation of one attempt to 'govern' the economy through a centralized system of economic planning. Even in consideration of such 'centralized' mechanisms, it is necessary to recognize that programmes for the government of economic life do not emanate from a central point – the State. The notion of government directs attention instead to the diversity of the elements out of which particular rationalities are formed, and to the mechanisms and techniques through which they are rendered operable. Whilst the rationalities and technologies do not stand in a one-to-one relationship, the relays and linkages between them are decisive conditions for the elaboration of each. The emergence of a particular political vocabulary requires as one of its conditions of possibility the implanting of a number of mechanisms of inscription, recording and calculation. Political rationalities, even those which profess to limit the scope of government and promote autonomy and freedom of choice, require for their functioning a complex array of technologies if they are to operate.

We can illustrate the complexity of these relays and linkages between a particular political vocabulary and a range of devices for producing, tabulating and calculating information through a discussion of the development of national accounting and planning in post-war France (Fourquet 1980; Miller 1986a). National accounting is not a simple matter of mirroring the dispersed activities of individual enterprises and producers at the macro-level of the nation. Rather it is the opening up of a new domain of knowledge, involving not merely the installation of a new set of concepts by which to think of 'the economy' as an economy, but also the construction of a vast statistical apparatus through which this domain can be inscribed, tabulated, calculated and acted upon. It entails the formation of a novel relationship between government and society which makes possible distinctive forms of calculation and management of economic and social life. The process by which the national economy becomes an object of possible knowledge, calculation and possible intervention is not an unproblematic linear unfolding. The language through which the economy comes to be understood does not emerge effortlessly in the realm of an autonomous theoretical debate. And once formulated it is not a simple matter of its 'application'.

At stake in the complex process of articulating the national economy as an object to be known, recorded, calculated and operated upon is a decisive shift in the principles of government. The shift is from a notion that the ruler need do no more than extract from his or her subjects whatever wealth they may produce, to a notion that a ruler should seek to renew and even augment such wealth. This shift places the calculation of national economic resources at the heart of the objectives of government. It entails the integration of the different activities of production, consumption and investment into a table, the calculation of the proportion and movement of each of these elements, and an indication of the activities to be encouraged, the fiscal system deemed appropriate, and the correct allocation of public expenditure.

In the case of France the development of national accounting is inseparable from the project of national planning as developed under Jean Monnet. National accounting is implicated in the attempt to undertake post-war economic reconstruction, itself part of a project of political modernization designed to eliminate elements of 'backwardness' from French society. The political vocabulary through which the project to modernize French society was formulated had as its central terms the notions of 'growth', 'progress' and 'solidarity'. It was through this political language that a variety of concrete and micro-level issues were to be thought about and acted upon. And it was by reference to this language that the categories of national accounting were articulated.

The category of production was central to this process of translating a political vocabulary into a set of techniques of recording and calculation. By means of the category of production it was possible to introduce a fundamental distinction between activities regarded as productive and those regarded as unproductive. What is production? Who is productive? Both questions lead us to the citizens for it is through them that wealth is created and it is to them that government must look if it is to enhance its resources. Whilst one can trace certain elements of such a tradition to the late seventeenth century through the writings of Petty, King and Davenant, it is in the early post-war years that such an objective was provided with a language in terms of which it could be thought, an institutional apparatus through which it could be enacted, and a set of statistical and economic-calculative techniques through which it could be rendered operable.

It was during World War II that the process of elaborating a conceptual architecture for national accounting and establishing its statistical basis commenced in France. The role of the Vichy regime in installing a statistical infrastructure which would provide an 'avalanche of numbers' was crucial in this process. After the war these developments provided a basis for the 'programming of hope' that was national planning, the attempt to deploy the language of growth and modernization in turning France 'into a truly developed country'.

To construct a set of national accounts which would enable the requirements of planning, modernization and growth to be achieved is not a simple matter of implementing a given political vocabulary. In trying to render activities and processes in a certain manner, technologies encounter various difficulties. One important component of a system of national accounts is the input-output table. Between 1952 and 1960 the French attempted to construct a table divided according to sectors (a group of enterprises defined by their principal activity; a sector can produce various products) rather than branches (the ensemble of divisions of enterprises producing one product only) of industry. It was thought that a table organized according to sectors could be immediately integrated into the accounting system since it was based on the actual loci of decisions. But despite the massive commitment of personnel and resources, and the conceptual acrobatics of those who tried to translate accounts of enterprises organized according to sectors into accounts organized according to branches, the attempt to devise a table organized around sectors ended in failure. Statistically, the notion of a table organized according to sectors made good sense. But to work with the planning commission, a table organized around branches was required (Fourquet 1980; Miller 1986a).

A degree of congruence or translatability is thus necessary between calculative technologies and the programmes they are designed to instrumentalize. Different modes of aggregating the economic activities of the nation bring different results. One can, for instance, utilize an 'institutional' basis for aggregation (in which economic agents are grouped according to their socio-juridical characteristics – individuals, private enterprises) or a 'functional' basis (a system based on the principal activity – production, consumption, savings). The adoption of the former in the French system can be understood by reference to its utility for a system of economic forecasting. The French argued that, if the economic activities of the nation take place through agents who are physically and institutionally distinct, it made sense to construct one's accounts around these real economic agents rather than an abstract entity composed of different forces.

Programmes of government are idealized schema for the ordering of social and economic life. As such they are not simply 'applied' through techniques such as national planning and accounting. Programmes constitute a space within which the objectives of government are elaborated, and where plans to implement them are dreamed up. But the technologies which seek to operate on activities and processes produce their own difficulties, fail to function as intended, and sometimes intersect poorly with the rationalities in terms of which their role is conceived. The example of attempts at economic planning in post-war France not only illustrates the importance of the 'technological' side of intellectual labour in rendering a domain amenable to government – in particular the key role of inscription of technologies – but also shows that governing is not the 'realization' of a programmer's dream. 'The real' always insists in the form of resistance to programming; and the programmer's world is one of constant experiment, invention, failure, critique and adjustment.

In the theoretico-practical matrix of government, political programmes are inescapably associated with operational devices and critical judgements. Whilst a particular political programme sets out specific objectives for government, and proposes mechanisms to realize them, the operationalization of a programme is achieved through a complex and difficult process: formulating the categories and techniques to make it realizable; assembling and sometimes devising technologies to give effect to its objectives in the lives of individuals, enterprises and organizations; and evaluating, debating and contesting the consequences of such programmes and the conditions of their failure and success.

Governing the economy at a distance

We have argued that contemporary 'governmentality' accords a crucial role to 'action at a distance', that is to say, to mechanisms which promise to shape the economic or social conduct of diverse and institutionally distinct persons and agencies without shattering their formally distinct or 'autonomous' character. And we have suggested that vocabularies and expertise have played a very significant part in inventing and seeking to operationalize such mechanisms of government, both in the sense that they have been involved in calculated attempts to implant such technologies, and in the sense that the existence of experts has made it possible for self-regulation to operate in a way that minimizes the need for direct political intervention. In the government of the economy, one important mechanism has operated through the transformation of the calculative procedures of economic actors. We can illustrate this through a discussion of economic regulation in the UK in the 1960s.

Conventionally, the politics of the UK from about 1962 to 1975 is seen as the high point of the interventionist State. Political arguments, from both the Conservative and Labour parties, diagnosed a failure in 'hands off' techniques of economic regulation, in which government did not intervene directly in economic decisions, and in which the Treasury pulled various levers in order to set the overall framework within which the various economic actors would make their calculations and decisions. This registration of failure was itself dependent in part upon the political vocabularies and techniques of inscription that we have discussed in the previous section. At the level of what we have termed 'political rationalities', 'growth' had emerged as a key indicator of the economic health of the nation, and one by which the success or failure of economic policy was to be judged (cf. Leruez 1975). There were many differences in understanding what growth was and how it was to be achieved. For example, for the Federation of British Industry and similar organizations, the imperative was for Britain to compete with other nations in the international economic order. For Labour, on the other hand, growth was to be the motor of a social dynamic for eliminating poverty and building a fair and just society. But these differences operated upon a common ground: politicians, businessmen and academics across a large swathe operated upon the *a priori* that 'growth' was a national goal and that new policies needed to be set in place to achieve it.

There were very specific intellectual preconditions for the emergence of a discourse of growth, and of Britain's low 'rate of growth', in this particular form: growth as a calculable entity rather than a vague attribution. Systems of national accounting such as those discussed earlier had rendered national economic activity into thought as a calculable and comparable entity. International bodies such as the OECD produced tabular comparisons of the 'rates of growth' of the industrial nations, which could then be utilized in political arguments. Only thus could it be established that Britain's rate of growth was low in relation to her international competitors. And only thus could the general argument that 'something should be done' be translated into specific programmes for realizing growth and particular technologies for operationalizing them.

The policy changes of the sixties are usually seen as a strengthening of the State's powers of planning and regulation of economic life. Certainly, many argued that the way in which economic agents made their decisions had to be transformed if 'growth' was to occur. But applying the notion of government to such a period suggests it is misleading to counterpose an interventionist to a non-interventionist state. One needs to conceptualize the relations differently, to attend to the diversity of mechanisms, both direct and indirect, through which political authorities have sought to act upon the entities and processes that make up a population in order to secure economic objectives, and the loose tie-ups between political ambitions, expert knowledge and the economic aspirations of individual firms.

Within the political vocabulary of the 1960s in the UK, the objective of economic growth was to be achieved through a number of mechanisms. Central to these were increased industrial output, improved efficiency within the enterprise, and better investment decisions. There were many initiatives through which it was hoped that this objective might be achieved, including the *National Plan*, the National Economic Development Council, the Industrial Reorganization Corporation, Regional Employment Premiums, and the legal regulation of industry through the 1965 Monopolies and Mergers Act. But whilst all these projects are indicative of an interventionist political aspiration, they are all equally constrained when it comes to intervening directly within the 'private' enterprise and at the micro-level of individual decisions. This is particularly so for interventions that would bear directly on the question of economic growth: investment decisions. It is here that a new relationship between thinking and doing was called for as a way of operationalizing the vocabulary of economic growth. It is here that a way of conceptualizing investment decisions and calculating them within the enterprise was called for to actually deliver the objective of growth through individual investment decisions. Whilst politicians and their economic advisers could not themselves control the decisions of individual enterprises, whether private or nationalized, persuading managers of the advantages of the technique of Discounted Cash Flow Analysis (DCF) held out the promise of delivering economic growth (Miller 1989).

DCF techniques were not invented in the 1960s. But it was during this period that they were actively promoted through government bodies such as the NEDC and strongly recommended by the Treasury for the Nationalized Industries (HC 440/VIII 1967; NEDC 1965). In the context of a government policy committed to some form of intervention and planning, the regulation of individual investment decisions by means of the calculus of DCF techniques made it possible to weaken the distinction between a centre which would direct the economy, and individual enterprises which would act according to instructions and inducements. DCF techniques offered the prospect that individual firms and individual managers within them would willingly transform the manner in which they thought about and calculated investment opportunities. Intuition and rule of thumb would be replaced by a new knowledge which allowed management to increase the 'productivity of capital', in particular through the concept of the time value of money. Personal judgement was to be replaced by the objectivity of economic-financial calculation which allowed management to rank investment opportunities, compare alternatives, and consider the net economic worth of particular options to the company. The widespread failure of management to objectively calculate the investment value of individual proposals would be counteracted by economic theory, financial mathematics, economic forecasting, projection and control techniques. New teams of specialists would be needed within firms to provide this expertise. Once installed, the 'directional beam of capital productivity' would allow management to calculate and evaluate not just investment in plant and machinery, but welfare and prestige investments such as gymnasiums, country clubs and palatial office buildings. Departures from this beam were not necessarily wrong, but top management would not be able to record, calculate and evaluate the *costs* of such projects, conceptualizing them in terms of the amount of earnings foregone, thereby putting them on the same plane as other capital expenditures. The language of the productivity of capital, and the technique of DCF analysis as a way of translating this into individual investment decisions, would enable a fundamental transformation in the nature and quality of investment decisions.

It was not just for the private sector that DCF techniques were promoted as a way of delivering economic growth. DCF techniques were identified as a central mechanism for specifying more precisely the economic and financial obligations of the Nationalized Industries. With an annual investment equivalent to that of the whole of manufacturing industry, and contributing about 10 per cent of the gross domestic product, it is not surprising that the efficiency of so large a sector should be singled out for its impact on the growth of the whole economy (HC 440/VIII 1967). The 1967 White Paper stated clearly and explicitly the government's commitment to economic growth, the need for investment to secure such an objective, and the role that DCF techniques should play in ensuring that the latter was congruent with the former (Cmnd 3437 1967).

The regulatory role of DCF techniques in the context of the Nationalized Industries was of course a specific one. Free from day to day government control, yet obliged to operate 'efficiently', the criteria by which individual investment decisions were to be made within the Nationalized Industries were only specified in broad terms prior to 1967 (Cmnd 1337 1961). In such a context DCF techniques offered the possibility of installing a most appropriate regulatory mechanism. Investment decisions were henceforth to be made by the application of DCF techniques, and these were to be guided by a specified discount rate. A calculus was thus installed as the basis on which individual decisions by management should be made. In exceptional circumstances it might be legitimate to depart from this calculus. But such possible departures would be made visible by the application of DCF techniques. And in principle the investment review procedure overall was to be one of partnership between the industry, the responsible department, and the central economic department.

DCF techniques thus helped to retain the notion that individual investment decisions within the Nationalized Industries should be kept at arms length from the government. Yet at the same time a calculative norm would serve as a regulatory mechanism. Departures from the 'directional beam of capital productivity' could in this way be clearly identified as exceptions, and the loci of these decisions shifted toward the centre. The language of 'growth' could thus be instrumentalized by a specific calculative regime within this crucial area of economic life.

Thus, whilst the language of growth was one of the central features of the political rationality of the mid-1960s, to realize such an objective at the level of individual enterprises and in the public sector was far from easy. Even a government disposed towards the regulation and supervision of industry could not take over day-to-day investment decisions within private firms or even the Nationalized Industries. The technique of DCF analysis provided an ideal mechanism for such a situation. DCF techniques made possible a range of renewed attempts to govern economic life 'at a distance'. If government could not intervene directly, it could certainly seek to act upon that group whose responsibility investment decisions were by translating their decisions and judgements into a particular form of calculative expertise. By promoting DCF techniques for private industry, by insisting on their use in the National-ized Industries, and by recommending that they be taught to management within the new business schools, the ideal of economic growth was rendered congruent with democratic freedom, social justice and a fair standard of living. Social and private net returns on investment could be reconciled, so it was held, by transforming ways of thinking about and calculating investments. The political rationality of growth and its orientation toward the future could be rendered operable within the enterprise by a technology which made the future actually calculable. The processes of calculation would take place at the micro-level of the enterprise, but they would henceforth be congruent with national economic growth. 'Growth' as an ideal to be sought, an objective to be realized and a rationality by which to evaluate society was to be delivered in the final analysis not by politicians and planners but by a multitude of local centres of calculation. A political programme, it was hoped, could be rendered oper-able by installing a technology of incessant calculation.

Governing the psychological world of the enterprise

Governing involves not just the ordering of activities and processes. Governing operates through subjects. The individual manager who comes to think of investments in terms of the discounting of future cash flows is a resource for a strategy of government oriented toward economic growth. Government to that extent is a 'personal' matter, and many programmes have sought the key to their effectiveness in enrolling individuals as allies in the pursuit of political, economic and social objectives. To the extent that authoritative norms, calculative technologies and forms of evaluation can be translated into the values, decisions and judgements of citizens in their professional and personal capacities, they can function as part of the 'self-steering' mechanisms of individuals. Hence 'free' individuals and 'private' spaces can be 'ruled' without breaching their formal autonomy. To this end, many and varied programmes have placed a high value upon the capacities of subjects, and a range of technologies have sought to act on the personal capacities of subjects – as producers, consumers, parents and citizens, organizing and orienting them in the decisions and actions that seem most 'personal', and that confront them in the multitude of everyday tasks entailed in managing their own existence.

Experts have played a key role here. They have elaborated the arguments that the personal capacities of individuals can be managed in order to achieve socially desirable goals – health, adjustment, profitability and the like. They have latched on to existing political concerns, suggesting that they have the capacity to ameliorate problems and achieve benefits. They have allied themselves with other powerful social authorities, in particular businessmen, translating their 'lay' problems into expert languages and suggesting that rational knowledges and planned techniques hold the key to success. They have problematized new aspects of existence and, in the very same moment, suggested that they can help overcome the problems that they have discovered. And they have acted as powerful translation devices between 'authorities' and 'individuals', shaping conduct not through compulsion but through the power of truth, the potency of rationality and the alluring promises of effectivity.

Again, we will take our examples from economic life, focusing here upon the internal world of the enterprise and the management of the productive subject. The government of economic life across the twentieth century has entailed a range of attempts to shape and modulate the relations that individuals have with society's productive apparatus (Miller 1986b; Rose 1990). In the process, the activities of individuals as producers have become the object of knowledge and the target of expertise, and a complex web of relays has been formed through which the economic endeavours of politicians and businessmen have been translated into the personal capacities and aspirations of subjects.

The programmes of 'scientific management' that were devised in the first two decades of this century – called Taylorism after their leading proponent – are often taken as the paradigm of all 'scientific' attempts to make the worker an object of knowledge and an asset for management. Within Taylorism and associated techniques such as standard costing (Miller and O'Leary 1987) the worker was depicted as a brute, the motivations of the person were viewed as purely economic, and the only tactic available to management was to issue commands derived from the imperatives of the productive process. But Taylorism was not merely a cynical attempt to increase control over the workplace and maximize the rate of exploitation of the worker. Rather, it was one of a set of programmes articulated in the language of 'efficiency', entailing an alliance between macro-political aspirations and the powers of expertise. These programmes sought to increase the national wealth and international competitiveness of states through employing scientific knowledge and rational techniques to make the most productive use of natural, mechanical and human resources. The labouring subject came into view as an object of knowledge and a target of intervention, as an individual to be assessed, evaluated and differentiated from others, to be governed in terms of individual differences.

The productive subject, for Taylorist programmes and the technologies that sought to implement them, was essentially a passive entity to be managed externally through a complex technology of the workplace. This entailed assembling and creating a range of practical and intellectual instruments to produce what Taylor termed the 'mechanism' of scientific management: standard tools, adjustable scaffolds; methods and implements of time study, books and records, desks for planners to work at, experiments leading to the establishment of formulae to replace the individual judgement of workmen, a differentiation of work into standard tasks, written instructions and instruction cards, bonus and premium payments, the scientific selection of the working man and many more (Thevenot 1984). This list may be heterogeneous, but as Thevenot points out, for Taylor its elements were parts of a single mechanism. Taylor here provides a perfect example of what we have termed a technology of government, an attempt to produce a stable, standard and reproducible form of relations amongst persons and things that purports to enable production to be predictably undertaken in the most efficient manner.

But Taylorism does not provide a diagram for all technical interventions to govern the productive subject through expertise. In Britain in the inter-war years, a new vocabulary and technology for programming the employment relationship was born, associated in particular with the writings of Charles Myers and the work of the National Institute of Industrial Psychology (cf. Myers 1927). This new way of construing the productive subject had its own intellectual conditions of possibility, in the 'new psychology' of instincts and adjustment that had been formulated in the years following the First World War, and in the mental hygiene movement that sought the roots of a plethora of social troubles in the minor and untreated problems of mental life that prevented efficient functioning (Rose 1985). When this new intellectual technology was applied to industry, it had three distinctive features. First, it addressed the relationship individuals have with their selves in their work. The worker came to be viewed as having a personal life that continues into his or her productive work, and that influenced the ways in which it was carried out. The worker was to be understood as an individual with a mind, with fears and anxieties. Not just monotony, fatigue, and attentiveness, but motivation and morale became a concern for various expertises of the psyche. This way of construing the psychology of the working individual was linked to a range of attempts to produce a congruence between the needs of production and the motives, fears and wants of the worker. Second, this new vocabulary brought into view the relationships that individuals have with other workers – colleagues, superiors and subordinates. The informal life of the enterprise emerged as a new terrain to be known through expert investigations and administered by expertise. Third, this language established an interdependence between the worker as a productive machine and the worker as a person with a family and home life. Departures from specified norms in a worker's home and personal life could henceforth be seen to have possibly disruptive effects on his or her work performance. From now on, the mental hygiene of the worker would be a key concern for experts, for managers, for bosses and for politicians (Miller and Rose 1988).

At issue in this new attentiveness to the personal dimension of the productive process is more than simply a concern to increase productivity. Doubtless this is an objective that animates the history of the capitalist enterprise. Doubtless too the new promoters of mental hygiene sought to convince the bosses that their expertise would contribute to such an end. But the novel ways of understanding the relationship of the worker to the productive apparatus in the inter-war years contributed more than this. They opened up a new domain of knowledge and possible intervention. A new conception and practice of the worker emerged. This had as its objective to ensure that the bond linking the individual to the enterprise, and also the individual to society, would henceforth not be solely economic. The wage relation and the power of the boss would be supplemented by a personal bond that would attach individuals to the lives they lived in the world of work, to their co-workers and bosses, and to society as a whole (Miller 1986b). It would be possible to conceive of administering the working environment in such a way as to ensure simultaneously the contentment and health of the worker and the profitability and efficiency of the enterprise. Macro-political programmes, the quest for profit of entrepreneurs and the personal well-being of employees could be brought into alignment through a psychological expertise that was allied with none of these parties but only with the values of truth and rationality.

Within this new set of programmes and technologies of the productive subject, the subjectivity of the worker still tended to be viewed in terms of individual capacities, and judged in the negative sense of departures from norms. The worker was still to be administered externally, by a wise and prescient management informed by a rational knowledge and a neutral expertise. Following World War II a further transformation occurred in conceptions of the worker which entailed the formulation of a concern with *positive* mental health in the workplace. 'Defective' individuals still had to be identified, but a more important terrain was to be opened up – one which would seek to optimize the mental health of all individuals in their relation to their work. New alliances had been forged between industrialists, psychologists, managers and politicians in the course of managing the human problems of the war: it appeared that the enlightened administration of human relationships in work and elsewhere could maximize contentment at the same time as it maximized productivity, as well as corresponding to the values of democracy with its respect for the citizen. (e.g. Taylor 1950; Brown 1954). The responsibility for promoting the health of a society did not reside just in its medical services, but in its social practitioners – managers, politicians, teachers and others in positions of leadership. These new concerns were articulated in terms of the expert management of human relations in groups. In the new vocabulary of group relations, the intersubjective life of the enterprise could be construed as a vital mechanism upon which government should operate, not only binding the individual psychologically into the production process, but also, through work, linking the worker into the social order as a democratic citizen with rights and responsibilities.

The new technologies of the enterprise promoted by government reports, management organizations and industrial psychologists, sought to instrumentalize its relational life for economic ends (Miller and Rose 1988). It appeared that the subjective capacities and intersubjective dynamics of employees could be shaped and utilized in such a way that would simultaneously recognize the stake of the employee in the firm and the stake of the firm in the employee. Leadership could be utilized as a resource for management, not only the leadership capacities of the top employees, but also those of crucial intermediaries such as foremen. The key to this technology was that leadership could be re-conceptualized, not as an individual quality to be obtained by careful selection procedures, but as the effectiveness of an individual in a specific role within a specific group united for a particular purpose. Hence leadership could be produced and promoted by a relational technology of the workplace, a calculated reorganization of the relations of persons and tasks.

Similarly it was argued by industrial psychologists that industrial accidents should not be understood as the result of personal attributes. 'Accident-proneness' rather should be understood as a phenomenon of the group. Accidents were to become social as well as personal events, caused by virtue of the fact that the people concerned are members of some kind of work organization. In this and other ways, the vocabulary of the group provided here a new route for understanding and operating on the personal dimension of productive activity. Productivity and efficiency were now to be understood in terms of the attitudes of workers to their work, their feelings of control over their place of work and environment, their sense of cohesion within their small working group, and their beliefs about the concern and understanding that the bosses had for their individual worth and their personal problems.

The point here is not just that a new vocabulary emerges for speaking about the tasks of management. It is that a new importance is accorded to regulating the internal psychological world of the worker through a calculated administration of the human relations of the workplace, in order to turn the personal wishes of the employee from an obstacle into an ally of economic efficiency. This would profess to overcome the centuries old opposition between work as a sphere of dull compulsion within which selfhood is denied or suppressed, and the home, family and leisure as spheres for the satisfaction of personal wants and the realization of the self. From this time forth, management would seek to recruit the self-regulating capacities of the worker, and the desires of the worker for personal goals, for its own ends. A neutral, rational and humane expertise was to assume the task of aligning the ethics of the worker as a psychological individual whose needs were worthy of consideration with the bosses' quest for profitability.

A range of new tasks emerged to be grasped by knowledge and managed in the factory. Rendering the intersubjective world of the factory into thought as a calculable entity required more than a new theory, it entailed the invention of new devices to chart and evaluate it. Social psychologists were to enter the workplace, using such instruments as non-directed interviews to get at the thoughts, attitudes and sentiments amongst workers, foremen, supervisors and so forth which gave rise to problems, dissatisfactions and conflict (Rose 1989a; 1990). Techniques of measurement and scaling could be developed and deployed in order to render intersubjectivity into tables and charts which could give management material upon which to calculate, to diagnose the problems of the factory, to evaluate the consequences of this or that initiative. And the technology of the interview was a regulatory mechanism in its own right, for in speaking and being heard, worker's subjective states were to be transformed: frustrations dispelled, anxieties reduced, contentment increased and solidarity and commitment enhanced.

In the 1950s and 1960s, the social psychological experts of industry, and the management theorists with whom they allied, did not confine their programmatic aspirations within the factory walls. The new vocabulary of the group and its attendant technologies established a series of relays that enabled connections to be made between interventions on the interior life of the enterprise and calculations concerning the economic well-being of the nation. The notion of the proper sphere of politics and appropriate modes of intervention by the State could be transformed. A variety of programmes argued for little less than a complete reorganization of industry and the economy along social-psychological lines (e.g. Taylor 1950; Trist *et al.*, 1963; Brown and Jaques 1965; Emery and Thorsrud 1969). These programmes may have remained little more than a dream in the United Kingdom, though not in Denmark, Norway, Sweden and elsewhere. The point we wish to make concerns not their implementation, or lack of it, but rather the new relations that they make possible: expertise could secure its position by finding a way of linking the values of economic productivity, political democracy and personal contentment into a single theoretico-practical matrix.

Governing the autonomous self

The forms of political rationality that took shape in the first half of this century constituted the citizen as a social being whose powers and obligations were articulated in the language of social responsibilities and collective solidarities. The individual was to be integrated into society in the form of a citizen with social needs, in a contract in which individual and society had mutual claims and obligations. A diversity of programmes for social security, child welfare, physical and mental hygiene, universal education and even for the form and content of popular entertainment operated within this rationale and numerous technologies were invented – from social insurance to the child guidance clinic – that sought to give effect to it.

Whilst the decade or so after the Second World War may be seen as the culmination of this period, marked by attempts to weld these diverse programmes and technologies into a coherent and centrally directed system, the past decade has seen an apparently decisive displacement of these political rationalities. Not only within the revived vocabulary of neo-liberalism, but also in many of the political programmes articulated from the centre and the left of the political field as well as from radical critics of the present, the language of freedom and autonomy has come to regulate arguments over the legitimate means and ends of political power.

No longer is citizenship construed in terms of solidarity, contentment, welfare and a sense of security established through the bonds of organizational and social life. Citizenship is to be active and individualistic rather than passive and dependent. The political subject is henceforth to be an individual whose citizenship is manifested through the free exercise of personal choice amongst a variety of options (cf. Meyer 1986). Programmes of government are to be evaluated in terms of the extent to which they enhance that choice. And the language of individual freedom, personal choice and self-fulfilment has come to underpin programmes of government articulated from across the political spectrum, from politicians and professionals, pressure groups and civil libertarians alike.

This new political language may be seen as an ephemeral phenomenon, as ideology, or as merely a reprise on the atomistic individualism characteristic of capitalism. However the perspective we have sketched out in this paper would suggest a different approach, one that emphasized the manner in which this new language served not only to articulate and legitimate a diversity of programmes for rectifying problematic areas of economic and social life, but also enabled these programmes to be translated into a range of technologies to administer individuals, groups and sectors in a way that was consonant with prevailing ethical systems and political mentalities (Rose 1989b). We can illustrate this by focusing upon one particular notion that has been so central to the doctrines of the new right in Britain, Europe and America – that of 'enterprise'.

The language of enterprise has become so significant, we suggest, because it enables a translatability between the most general *a priori* of political thought and a range of specific programmes for administering the national economy, the internal world of the firm and a whole host of other organizations from the school to the hospital. But further, it enables such programmes to accord a new priority to the self-regulating capacities of individuals (cf. Gordon 1987). At the level of the macro-economy, the argument that an economy structured in the form of relations of exchange between discrete economic units pursuing their undertakings with confidence and energy will produce the most social goods and distribute them in the manner most advantageous to each and to all has not spelt an end to programmes for the 'government' of economic life. Rather it has given rise to all manner of programmes for reforming economic activity in order to construct such a virtuous system, and to a plethora of new regulatory technologies that have sought to give effect to them (see Thompson 1990; Rose and Miller 1989).

Within these rationalities, new relations can be formed between the economic health of the nation and the 'private' choices of individuals. The citizen is now assigned a vital economic role in his or her activity as a consumer. To maintain the economic health of the societies of the west, construed both in terms of budgetary discipline and high levels of employment, a constant expansion in consumption is required. Economies are successful to the extent that they can promote this, at one and the same time proliferating and differentiating needs, producing products aligned to them and ensuring the purchasing capacity to enable acts of consumption to occur. However, whilst the language of the consumer, and consumer responsiveness structures political argument, providing the rationale for programmes of reform in domains as diverse as the organization of the car industry, delivery of health care and the organization of water and sewage systems, consumption is itself shaped by a differentiated range of practices and techniques whose mentalities are not those of government but of profit. This reveals the extent to which certain conditions of existence are necessary for particular political rationalities to be made operable. In this case, the rationalities of autonomy have become operable, in part, because of the emergence of a plethora of discourses and practices for shaping and regulating the conduct, choices and desires of individuals: popular television and entertainment, and particularly the transformation of the world of goods through expert techniques of product differentiation, targeting and marketing.

Thus whilst the aim of maximizing consumption may be a matter of state, the executive power operates in an indirect manner upon it, by policies on advertising, interest rates, credit and the like. The language of enterprise again forms a kind of matrix for thought here, consumers being considered as, in a sense, entrepreneurs of themselves, seeking to maximize their 'quality of life' through the artful assembly of a 'life-style' put together through the world of goods. Within this politico-ethical environment, the expertise of market research, of promotion and communication, provides the relays through which the aspirations of ministers, the ambitions of business and the dreams of consumers achieve mutual translatability. Design, marketing and image construction play a vital role in the transfiguring of goods into desires and vice versa, imbuing each commodity with a 'personal' meaning, a glow cast back upon those who purchase it, illuminating the kind of person they are, or want to become. Product innovation and consumer demand are connected through the webs of meaning through which they are related, the phantasies of efficacy and the dreams of pleasure which guide both. Through this loose assemblage of agents, calculations, techniques, images and commodities, consumer choice can be made an ally of economic growth: economic life can be governed through the choices consumers make in their search for personally fulfilling forms of existence.

The rationalities of personal autonomy and self-fulfilment are also linked to a transformation in programmes and technologies for regulating the internal world of the enterprise (e.g. Peters and Waterman 1982; see Rose 1990). Once again, expertise plays a vital translating role, promising to align general politico-ethical principles, the goals of industry and the self-regulatory activities of individuals. The vocabulary of enterprise provides versatile tools for thought: the worker is no longer construed as a social creature seeking satisfaction of his or her need for security, solidarity and welfare, but as an individual actively seeking to shape and manage his or her own life in order to maximize its returns in terms of success and achievement. Thus the vocabulary of entrepreneurship does not merely seek to shape the way bosses calculate and activate business strategies in the external world of the market, but also can be formulated by the experts of management into a new set of techniques for ensuring business success. In these programmes, the world of the enterprise is reconceptualized as one in which productivity is to be enhanced, quality assured and innovation fostered through the active engagement of the self-fulfilling impulses of the employee from lowliest worker to highest manager, aligning personal desires with the objectives of the firm. Organizations are to get the most out of their employees, not by managing group relations to maximize contentment, or by rationalizing management to ensure efficiency, but by releasing the psychological strivings of individuals for autonomy and creativity and channelling them into the search of the firm for excellence and success. Psychological consultants to the organization provide the techniques for charting the cultural world of the enterprise in terms of its success in capitalizing upon the motivations and aspirations of its inhabitants. And these experts have invented a whole range of new technologies in order to give effect to these programmes, techniques for promoting motivation through constructing a regime of values within the firm, for reducing dependency by reorganizing management structures, for encouraging internal competitiveness by small group working, for stimulating individual entrepreneurship by new forms of staff evaluation and reward.

The 'autonomous' subjectivity of the productive individual has become a central economic resource; such programmes promise to turn autonomy into an ally of economic success and not an obstacle to be controlled and disciplined. The self-regulating capacities of individuals are to be aligned with economic objectives through the kinds of loose and indirect mechanisms that we have described earlier: the capacities of language to translate between rationalities, programmes, technologies and self-regulatory techniques, and the particular persuasive role of expertise. Significantly, these programmes do not merely seek to instrumentalize the aspirations of workers, but also seek to act upon the selves of managers. There is no opposition between the modes of self-presentation required of the manager and the ethics of the personal self, indeed becoming a better manager is to become a better self, and innumerable training courses and seminars operate in these terms. The values of self-realization, the skills of self-presentation, self-direction and self-management are both personally seductive and economically desirable. Again, expertise plays the role of relay, teaching managers the arts of self realization that will fulfil them as individuals as well as employees. Economic success, career progress and personal development intersect in this new expertise of autonomous subjectivity.

No doubt there is a considerable discrepancy between the images portrayed in the proliferating texts written along these lines, and the reality of the practices of management. And, no doubt, the promises of this new generation of programmers of the enterprise will soon be deemed to have failed: increased productivity, improved flexibility and enhanced competitiveness will still prove elusive goals. But it is more than ideology that can be observed here. As with the previous illustrations, what is at issue here is the establishing of connections and symmetries, at both the conceptual and practical level, between political concerns about the government of the productive life of the nation, the concerns of owners of capital to maximize the economic advantages of their companies, and techniques for the governing of the subject. Expertises of the enterprise play a crucial role in linking up these distinct concerns into a functioning network. Their languages and techniques provide both the necessary distance between political authorities and organizational life, and the translatability to establish an alliance between national economic health, increased organizational effectiveness, and progressive and humanistic values.

The rapprochement of the self-actualization of the worker with the competitive advancement of the company enables an alignment between the technologies of work and technologies of subjectivity. For the entrepreneurial self, work is no longer necessarily a constraint upon the freedom of the individual to fulfil his or her potential through strivings for autonomy, creativity and responsibility. Work is an essential element in the path to self-realization. There is no longer any barrier between the economic, the psychological and the social. The government of work now passes through the psychological strivings of each and every individual for fulfilment.

Conclusion

In this paper we have suggested that Michel Foucault's concept of 'governmentality' can be usefully developed to analyse the complex and heterogeneous ways in which contemporary social authorities have sought to shape and regulate economic, social and personal activities. We have proposed an analysis of political rationalities that pays particular attention to the role of language, and the language of social science in particular. Vocabularies and theories are important not so much because of the meanings that they produce, but as intellectual technologies, ways of rendering existence thinkable and practicable, amenable to the distinctive influence of various techniques of inscription, notation and calculation.

We have sought to draw attention in particular to the programmatic character of government, and to suggest that an analysis of this programmatic field of government should not be restricted to a judgement of success or failure. We have highlighted the ways in which expert knowledges, and experts as accredited and skilled persons professing neutrality and efficacy, have mobilized, and have been mobilized within such programmes. We have argued that an analysis of modern 'governmentality' needs to free itself from a focus upon 'the state' and from a restricted conception of the kinds of mechanism through which authorities seek to regulate the activities of a differentiated assembly of social agencies and forces. Further, we have proposed that the analysis of 'governmentality' needs to be accompanied by an investigation of the 'technologies' which seek or claim to give effect to the aspirations of programmers. Our argument has been that in advanced liberal democracies such as our own, these technologies increasingly seek to act upon and instrumentalize the self-regulating propensities of individuals in order to ally them with socio-political objectives.

A range of 'new technologies' has been devised which provide citizens as economic and social actors with numerous techniques through which they can instrumentalize the diverse spheres of social life themselves in order to avoid what they have come to consider unwelcome and achieve what they have come to believe they want. In this context, the rise to prominence in the last decade of political rationalities placing emphasis upon the self-government of individuals, and seeking to limit the incidence of 'the state' upon the lives and decisions of individuals, can be seen as one articulation, at the level of a political rationality, of the new possibilities for political rule which these technologies have established. Political authorities no longer seek to govern by instructing individuals in all spheres of their existence, from the most intimate to the most public. Individuals themselves, as workers, managers and members of families can be mobilized in alliance with political objectives, in order to deliver economic growth, successful enterprise and optimum personal happiness. Programmes of government can utilize and rely upon a complex net of technologies – in management, in marketing, in advertising, in instructional talks on the mass media of communication – for educating citizens in techniques for governing themselves. Modern political power does not take the form of the domination of subjectivity (Miller 1987). Rather, political power has come to depend upon a web of technologies for fabricating and maintaining self-government.

P.M.
Dept. of Accounting and Finance,
London School of Economics and Political Science,
Houghton St., London WC2A 2AE
N.R.
Dept. of Sociology
Goldsmiths' College, University of London

Note

This is an extensively revised version of a paper first presented at a Colloquium on Language and Politics, University of Helsinki, December 1988 and published in Finnish in Politiikka, 1989 and in English in S. Hanninen and K. Palonen (eds), *Texts, Contexts, Concepts*, Helsinki: Finnish Political Science Association, 1989. Thanks to Grahame Thompson and anonymous reviewers of this Journal for critical comments that have helped us to clarify our argument.

References

Brown, J. A. C. (1954) *Social Psychology of Industry*, Harmondsworth: Penguin.

Brown, W. and Jaques, E. (1965) *Glacier Project Papers*, London: Heinemann Educational Books.

Burchell, S., Clubb, C. and Hopwood, A. G. (1985) 'Accounting in Its Social Context: Towards a History of Value Added in the United Kingdom', *Accounting, Organizations and Society*: 381–413.

Callon, M. (1986) 'Some elements of a sociology of translation', in J. Law (ed.), *Power, Action and Belief*, London: Routledge & Kegan Paul.

Callon, M. and Latour, B. (1981) 'Unscrewing the Big Leviathan: how actors macro-structure reality and how sociologists help them to do so,' in A. Cicourel and K. Knorr-Cecina (eds) *Advances in Social Theory* (London).

Cmnd 1337 (1961) *The Financial and Economic Obligations of the Nationalised Industries*, White Paper.

Cmnd 3437 (1967) *Nationalised Industries: A Review of Economic and Financial Objectives*, White Paper.

Connelly, W. (1987) 'Appearance and Reality in Politics', in M. T. Gibbons (ed.), *Interpreting Politics*, Oxford: Basil Blackwell.

Emery, F. and Thorsrud, E. (1969) *Form and Content in Industrial Democracy*, London: Tavistock.

Foucault, M. (1979) 'On governmentality', *I & C*, 6: 5–22.

Foucault, M. (1986) 'Space, Knowledge and Power', in P. Rabinow (ed.), *The Foucault Reader*, Harmondsworth: Penguin.

Fourquet, F. (1980) *Les comptes de la puissance*, Paris: Encres.

Gordon, C. (1987) 'The Soul of the Citizen: Max Weber and Michel Foucault on Rationality and Government', in S. Lash and S. Whimster, *Max Weber, Rationality and Modernity*, London: Allen & Unwin.

Hacking, I. (1983) *Representing and Intervening*, London: Cambridge University Press.

H.C. 440/VIII (1967) *Select Committee on Nationalised Industries; Sub-Committee A*, Minutes of Evidence, Memorandum submitted by HM Treasury, including Appendix A.

Hopwood, A. G. (1984) 'Accounting and the Pursuit of Efficiency', in A. G. Hopwood and C. Tomkins, *Issues in Public Sector Accounting*, Oxford: Philip Allan.

Hopwood, A. G. (1985b) 'Accounting and the domain of the public: some observations on current developments', The Price Waterhouse Public Lecture on Accounting, University of Leeds. Reprinted in A. G. Hopwood (1988), *Accounting from the Outside: The Collected Papers of Anthony G. Hopwood*, New York and London: Garland.

Hopwood, A. G. (1986) 'Management accounting and organizational action: an introduction', in M. Bromwich and A. G. Hopwood (eds), *Research and Current Issues in Management Accounting*, London: Pitman.

Hopwood, A. G. (1987) 'The archaeology of accounting systems', *Accounting, Organizations and Society*: 207–34.

Latour, B. (1986) 'The powers of association' in J. Law (ed.) *Power, Action and Belief*, London, Routledge and Kegan Paul.

Latour, B. (1987a) 'Visualization and cognition: thinking with eyes and hands', *Knowledge and Society: Studies in the Sociology of Culture, Past and Present*, 6: 1–40.

Latour, B. (1987b) *Science in Action*, Milton Keynes: Open University Press.

Law, J. (ed.) (1986) *Power, Action and Belief*, London: Routledge & Kegan Paul, 1986.

Leruez, J. (1975) *Economic Planning and Politics in Britain*, tr. M. Harrison, London: Martin Robertson.

Loft, A. (1986) 'Towards a critical understanding of accounting: the case of cost accounting in the U.K.', *Accounting, Organizations and Society*: 137–69.

MacIntyre, A. (1981) *After Virtue: A Study in Moral Theory*, London: Duckworth.

Meyer, J. (1986) 'The Self and the Life Course: Institutionalization and its Effects', in A. Sorensen, F. Weinert and L. Sherrod (eds), *Human Development and the Life Course*, Hillsdale, NJ: L. Erlbaum.

Miller, P. (1986a) 'Accounting for Progress – National Accounting and Planning in France', *Accounting, Organizations and Society*: 83–104.

Miller, P. (1986b) 'Psychotherapy of Work and Unemployment' in P. Miller and N. Rose (eds), *The Power of Psychiatry*, Cambridge: Polity Press.

Miller, P. (1987) *Domination and Power*, London: Routledge & Kegan Paul.

Miller, P. (1989) 'Managing Economic Growth Through Knowledge: The Promotion of Discounted Cash Flow Techniques', Working Paper.

Miller, P. and **O'Leary, T.** (1987) 'Accounting and the Construction of the Governable Person', *Accounting, Organizations and Society*: 235–65.

Miller, P. and **O'Leary, T.** (1989a) 'Hierarchies and American Ideals, 1900–1940', *Academy of Management Review*: 250–65.

Miller, P. and **O'Leary, T.** (1989b) 'Accounting expertise and the entrepreneurial society: new rationalities of calculation, paper presented at Conference on Accounting and the Humanities, University of Iowa, September 1989.

Miller, P. and **Rose, N.** (1988) 'The Tavistock Programme: The Government of Subjectivity and Social Life', *Sociology*, 22 (2): 171–92.

Myers, C. S. (1927) *Industrial Psychology in Great Britain*, London: Cape.

NEDG (1965) *Investment Appraisal*, London, HMSO.

Peters, T. J. and **Waterman, R. H.** (1982) *In Search of Excellence*, New York: Harper & Row.

Rose, N. (1985) *The Psychological Complex: Psychology, Politics and Society in England 1869–1939*, London: Routledge & Kegan Paul.

Rose, N. (1986) 'Beyond the public/private division', in P. Fitzpatrick and A. Hunt, *Critical Legal Studies*, Oxford: Blackwell.

Rose, N. (1988) 'Calculable Minds and Manageable Individuals', *History of the Human Sciences*, 1: 179–200.

Rose, N. (1989a) 'Social psychology as a science of democracy', paper presented at Cheiron-Europe Conference on the History of the Human Sciences, Goteborg, August 1989.

Rose, N. (1989b) 'Governing the enterprising self', paper presented at Conference on the Values of the Enterprise Culture, University of Lancaster, September 1989.

Rose, N. (1990) *Governing the Soul: The Shaping of the Private Self*, London: Routledge.

Rose, N. and **Miller, P.** (1989) 'Rethinking the state: governing economic social and personal life', Working Paper (available from the authors on request).

Sofer, C. (1972) *Organizations in Theory and Practice*, London: Heinemann.

Shapiro, M. (ed.) (1984) *Language and Politics*, Oxford: Blackwell.

Taylor, C. (1987) 'Language and Human Nature', in M. T. Gibbons (ed.), *Interpreting Politics*, Oxford: Basil Blackwell.

Taylor, G. R. (1950) *Are Workers*

Human, London: Falcon Press.
Thevenot, L. (1984) Rules and
implements: investment in forms, *Social
Science Information*, 23 (1): 1–45.
Thompson, G. (1982) 'The firm as a
"dispersed" social agency', *Economy and
Society*, 11: 233–50.
Thompson, G. (1987) 'The American
industrial policy debate: any lessons for
the U.K.?', *Economy and Society*, 16:
1–74.
Thompson, G. (1990) *The Political
Economy of the New Right*.
Tomlinson, J. (1981a) 'Why was there
never a "Keynesian Revolution" in
economic policy', *Economy and Society*,
10: 73–87.

Tomlinson, J. (1981b) *Problems of
British Economic Policy 1870–1945*,
London: Methuen.
Tomlinson, J. (1983) 'Where do
economic policy objectives come from?
The case of full employment', *Economy
and Society*, 12: 48–65.
Tribe, K. (1978) *Land, Labour and
Economic Discourse*, London: Routledge
& Kegan Paul.
Trist, E. L., Higgins, G. W., Murray,
H. and Pollock, A. B. (1963)
Organizational Choice, London:
Tavistock.
Williams, K. *et al.* (1986) 'Accounting
for failure in the nationalised
enterprises: coal, steel and cars since
1970', *Economy and Society*, 15: 167–219.

6 The promotion of the social*

Jacques Donzelot
Translated by Graham Burchell

With the invention of the notion of solidarity, the Third Republic found a way to resolve the antinomies inherent in its *political foundation* on the equal sovereignty of all. Solidarity is the principle of government that makes it possible to convert the conflicting demands and fears generated by the proclamation of the Republic into a common faith in progress. At least, that is what is claimed by those who direct this new orientation in these closing years of the nineteenth century which are often represented as our Golden Age, when the Republic seems well on its way to a definitive triumph over its demons, wrenching itself free from the troubles of this closing century, and completing its self-realisation by creating the figure of the *State as guarantor of society's progress*.

But, as men like Georges Sorel point out at the time, this process has its reverse side. Since it consists in removing political contradictions in the name of a general progress of society made possible by solidarity, it ensures that for citizens the Republic's validity will be linked to the value of that progress. The Republic is only credible to the extent that progress provides proof that it is not an empty slogan and that solidarity is not a simple phrase which is clever but vague and of dubious content.

What means, then, does the republican State have at its disposal for securing the progress of civil society? The Republic not only suffered from the aporia of its political foundation – the question of sovereignty – but equally from the failure of its privileged instrument – the *language of right*. It might have been hoped that the proclamation of rights would by itself restore harmony to society, but this discourse split into two interpretations with contradictory implications concerning the role to be given to the State, thereby condemning the latter to a role of inertly waiting on events which had already once proved fatal for the Republic in 1848.

*This paper is a chapter from Jacques Donzelot, *L'invention du sociale*, Paris, 1984.
Published in *Economy and Society Volume 17 Number 3 August 1988*

It's your responsibility, some told the government of 1848, to raise the civil condition of individuals to the level of their new political dignity, to abolish the shameful opposition between owners of capital and those who, living only by their labour, remain enslaved to them at the same time as they are proclaimed politically sovereign. On the other hand, others held that if the republican government complied with this demand it risked suppressing any notion of responsibility and abolishing the autonomy of civil society and individual freedom. Only the security of property and personal freedom can guarantee respect for contracts, can safeguard the capacity of some for enterprise and the fulfilment by others of their obligations. Caught in this way between its new *political responsibility*, based on a requirement of justice, and its *civil responsibility*, based on respect for freedom, the republican state had found itself already paralysed in 1848. Abandoning society to the confrontation between capital and labour, it fell prey to a political adventurer, paying the price of the neutrality it sought to maintain in this decisive conflict.

Solidarity was the remedy found for the difficulties inherent in the Republic's political foundation. But what is the practical worth of this notion when it comes to determining concretely the State's action on civil society? Solidarity is a fine theory, but does it have a practical value as well?

At the end of the nineteenth century, a whole current of legislation developed under the sign of solidarity which laid the foundations of what may best be termed *social right*. This comprised laws dealing with work conditions and the protection of workers in the various circumstances in which they lose the use of their labour power: accidents, illness, old age, unemployment. Laws protecting women and children in the family are also usually included under this rubric, as well as the many measures aimed at securing conditions for the health, education and morality of all members of society.

In the name of social right the public power increasingly intervenes in the sphere of civil and private relations. It is deployed wherever the sense of responsibility of the head of the family or of a business seems inadequate for meeting these requirements or, conversely, when this avowed responsibility serves as an alibi for maintaining personal dependency and for individual shortcomings as harmful to individual happiness as to the smooth running of society.

Social right presents itself, therefore, as the practical application of the theory of solidarity. But how, up to what point and at what price, can this instrument be expected to resolve the contradiction within classical right brought to light in 1848?

Social right is intended to promote the popular classes and the more fragile social categories generally. But *how* can the demand be met that the public power improve popular conditions while at the same time removing liberal distrust of an increase in the State's role and of the risk of it being used in a partisan way when intervening to relieve the problems of a particular class? How can rights be given to the popular classes without giving them a right over the State, a subversive hold over it, as was the case with the right to work of the Second Republic?

In conformity with the doctrine of solidarity, social right seeks only to make up for the shortcomings of society, to compensate for the effects of poverty and reduce the effects of oppression. It aims to mitigate society, not reorganise it. But *how far* can it lessen the fundamental anatagonism between labour and capital around which the social question turns? *How far* can it reduce the latter's economic subjugation of the former which makes the equal political sovereignty of all in the Republic seem a sham?

The interest of republicans in the idea of solidarity stems from the fact that it allowed a positive role for the State to be defined while maintaining its neutrality vis-à-vis the forces dividing society. Now, the State's intervention through social right, by operating towards the extinction of these forces, necessarily tends to transfer back to itself responsibility for the general movement of society. Henceforth, *what will be the cost* of protecting its republican neutrality vis-à-vis the forces making up society, while at the same time guaranteeing society's progress? Can it '*faire du social*' without securing the economic progress which is the condition of this, and how can it successfully accomplish this task without opting for one or other of the ideologies which claim exclusive rights over the direction of social progress?

Through these questions we want to undertake a genealogy of the Welfare State (*l'État-providence*) which will consist in showing how the reduction of sovereignty in politics calls for an equal reduction of responsibility on the civil level.

I Social right

At the start of the nineteenth century, we see coming together under the term *social economy*, attempts to find practical solutions to the social problems that seemed to result from the pure and harsh application of the laws of classical political economy. This 'social economy' constituted a relatively weak discipline. Notwithstanding various attempts, and particularly Sismondi's, it was never more than the lumping together under a single label of a whole range of concrete solutions to different aspects of social problems. It never succeeded in designating its object, concepts and methods with any rigour. Private charity, philanthropy, agricultural colonies, mutual aid societies, saving, and cooperatives are so many 'solutions' which in different ways remain tied to the main ideological currents of the nineteenth century. Liberals are keen on private charity and saving. Conservatives go for mutual aid societies under the tutelage of *notables*, and for agricultural colonies and the more or less forced repopulation of country areas. Socialists are for cooperatives and the Statist organisation of the economy.

At the end of the eighties, a 'new school', to use Charles Gide's term, emerges in this overcrowded and underorganised domain, confident of finally providing it with scientific credentials. Organised around the idea of solidarity, it claims to provide both a theory of society and a technique for solving social problems which harmonise perfectly with each other.[1]

On the theoretical level, the 'new school' results from a synthesis of various currents of thought that had recently tried to depart from the beaten tracks of liberalism and traditionalism, as well as from those of socialism in its many variants. In the first place, historical inquiries, like those of Émile de Laveleye on 'the primitive forms of property', showed that the institutions of property and wage-labour are by no means immutable, but rather historical and evolutionary.[2] Thus it is possible to change them, but only in a gradual manner, taking into account the special laws which appear to govern their evolution and direction. Works like these confirmed those of Durkheim and, in a way, provided him with an historical verification, since he taught the irreducibility of social phenomena either to the psychological motives of the individual, or to the dreams of pure political will. To understand and act on social phenomena it is necessary to start – always and exclusively – from social fact. In other words, it is by acting on the social milieu that one makes changes, not by declaiming moral and political maxims. Finally, the German school conveyed the idea of a specific mission of the State within the framework of social solidarity. Bismarck's social politics, known in France through the work of Lujo Brentano and Schäffle, showed that subversion can be combatted only by freeing the State from the so-called liberal definition which limits its role to guaranteeing the established order – an easy target for revolutionaries[3] – and by realising its true vocation as society's cement.

Thus there is a total of three components in this approach which appear in this order, moreover, in Charles Gide's presentation of the 'new school' as 'the exercise of a method which studies societies in their historical development and aims by its practical action to modify man by firstly modifying his environment through action by the State understood as the visible expression of the invisible bond uniting living men in the same society'.[4]

On the practical level, what technique can realise this solidarity, modify the relations between capital and wage-earners without distorting the historical logic on which they rest, ensure a better moralisation of the individual by transforming the social milieu and, especially, concretise the invisible bond between men of which the State is the visible expression? According to the members of the new school there is one answer: the *insurance technique*. Bismarck had successfully employed this technique in Germany, making it the Mecca for the 'new social economists' and a place of pilgrimage for anyone concerned with social problems. For thirty years, up until the First World War, the insurance technique is central to debates on the social question. Discussion is international in scope and organised in numerous colloquia where the new school makes a speciality of showing how the insurance technique is most in conformity with the contemporary idea of solidarity and with the need making itself felt everywhere. Thanks to this technique, the new school succeeds in making the discourse of solidarity prevail over rival schools – liberal, traditionalist or socialist.[5]

To start with, it is against the classical liberal school and the juridical individualism that it claims must exclusively govern relations at work that the excellence of the method of insurance succeeds in imposing itself. According to the liberal school everything boils down to a question of contracts between individuals, and problems arising in the framework of these relations call only for a procedure for assigning fault to one or other of the parties concerned, worker or boss. Now, if this is truly the way things go in society, then precisely they go badly. Proponents of the new school point to the sensitive question of accidents at work. If there is a domain which inordinately nourishes social antagonisms, that is surely it. With accidents and physical exhaustion, mutilation and death enter into relations between workers and bosses. The presence or threat of such a cortege of sufferings, always inflicted on the same class, can only encourage this class in the idea of a merciless struggle against those who control production. And what has one had at one's disposal to deal with this question until now? A judicial investigation into responsibility for the fault committed at the origin of the accident. To obtain legal compensation, the worker injured by an accident must prove that it is the employer's fault, that he has not kept to his agreements concerning the condition of machinery or hours of ·work – matters which, moreover, refer to factory regulations which the employer decrees as he likes. This, in addition to the worker's state of economic dependence, is enough to explain why two thirds of this kind of case are without juridical result. And if by chance the worker obtains justice, liberal logic, besides its practical immorality, also reveals its economic dangerousness. In the case of a death, the amount of compensation payable by a boss whose responsibility has been demonstrated can very quickly bankrupt his business. In terms of how the question is formulated around 1880, this amounts to saying that the juridical search for responsibility is no solution. It cannot give a penalty in most accident cases, and when it does it threatens to give rise to other problems on the economic level. In either case, the judicial pursuit of individual responsibility succeeds only in poisoning the already difficult climate of relations of production.

The insurance technique clearly demonstrates the superiority of the notion of collective solidarity over that of individual responsibility precisely on this question of accidents at work. With so many cases remaining unresolved due to the characteristic difficulty of ascribing fault to anyone, wouldn't it be better to regard accidents as effects of an unwilled *collective reality*, not of an individual will but effects arising from the general division of labour which, by making all actors interdependent, results in none of them having complete control over their work or, consequently being in a position to assume full responsibility. We can say that an accident is usually the occasional, *aleatory* result of all the combined processes of work and that everyone involved in these processes is thereby implicated in its occurrence and, consequently, in compensating the harm caused. There are no culpable individuals to be found then, save in exceptional and blatant cases of malice or specified negligence.[6]

The method of calculating insurance is applicable to every problem of accidents in the work situation. The substitution of the notion of occupational risk for that of fault opens the way for a systematic settlement in advance as it were. Insurance had already provided the example and effective proof of this in other domains (notably vis-à-vis possible risks to goods arising in the framework of commercial transactions). So, each party makes a kind of prior sacrifice in exchange for security against difficulties that might result from an unforeseen eventuality, the accident. Thanks to this *socialisation of risk*, the injured worker, while admittedly not receiving complete amends for the injury suffered, is always indemnified without having to institute proceedings, and so without risking coming up against a legal rejection. The employer, while no longer protected by the worker having to prove fault, as previously was the case, escapes the risks of total reparation, and notably the risk of bankruptcy threatened by jurisprudence when it tried to be humanitarian.

Through the notion of occupational risk, applications of the insurance technique can be extended to other problems than accidents at work. Is not illness resulting from an unhealthy occupation also an occupational risk? Is not old age, with the physical inability to work that comes with it, a disability that can also be foreseen and indemnified according to the same procedure? And what after all is unemployment, other than a kind of economic disability calling for the same kind of compensation as physical disabilities?

From the moment that social problems are viewed from the angle of interdependence between people, rather than in terms of the argument about individuals' respective duties and faults, the insurance technique offers a considerably *more effective* and *more moral* kind of solution. It makes it possible to take into account the social division of labour and the organic solidarity that, as Durkheim explained, derives from it, rather than, as liberal ideology would like, being confined solely to the register of individual contracts which is only secondary and derivative in relation to that primary solidarity. The same analysis applies against the theses and recipes of the traditionalist school when they claim that to solve the social question it is enough to restore *Ancien Régime* forms of social dependence, in the name of the employer's responsibility.

Under the second Empire and at the beginning of the Third Republic, the traditional school set up by Frédéric Le Play represented an important movement and gathered around it the best minds concerned with finding concrete, non-revolutionary, solutions to social problems. Frédéric Le Play gave them a famous method: the comparative study of monographs of popular families; together with an historical analysis which postulated as the source of all social evils the splitting up of property by the equal division of an inheritance between successors. This shows how much the solutions put forward by this school turned entirely on the restoration of the family's role. In the case of returning to the right of primogeniture and the moralising practice of saving, it was a question of restoring strength to the family and giving it a capacity to keep hold of its members, and so of developing its social role. With the promotion of well-regulated agricultural colonies for decanting the overflowing masses of the towns back into the country, with properly conceived mutual aid societies, that is to say administered under the auspices of philanthropic *notables*, the overarching concern is with recovering a familial role for society.

From the beginning of the eighties it is easy to see why this doctrine becomes difficult to sustain. An ideology hardly appropriate except for rural society and an archaic kind of family was made obsolete by economic development as well as by the development of mores. We also find members of the traditional school splitting in opposite directions. Some join the new school, recognising in the insurance technique the modern principle for bringing workers and bosses together that previously they had tried to achieve by methods that now look outdated. This is the case, for example, for men like Eugène Rostand and Émile Cheysson, who are among the major propagandists of 'the new school'.[7] Others, allergic to 'this calamitous principle of universal insurance of every risk by the State', join with Claudio Jannet and proponents of the English school in regarding the Anglo-Saxon model of mutual aid societies more respectful of the spirit of moral rearmament advocated by their master Le Play.[8]

But the English mutual aid societies have their own weaknesses which the solidarity school proceeds to point out. In the first place, the level of cover which they offer their members varies widely and may be either insufficient or excessive. Contributions are easy to collect in occupations where there is security of employment and wages are already high, but they become derisory where employment and income are uncertain. From the sometimes excessive, sometimes inadequate character of the cover provided for the working class by mutual aid societies stems a whole series of obvious drawbacks. In fact, in industries where the societies have abundant resources, these can easily serve as war funds for directing strikes as lengthy as they are economically unrealistic for a business, thus contributing to the restoration of a disguised form of corporatism. While in low-paid sectors, the manifest insufficiency of these societies' resources obliges the State to provide means of survival directly to this section of the population.

In relation to the mutual aid societies advocated by the Anglo-Saxon school, the insurance method thus offers the considerable advantage of an equal solidarity for all social categories, making up for differences between contributions thanks to the size of the population involved. Furthermore, through its abstract and automatic form of allocating payments, the method seems resistant to perversions of the meaning of solidarity: there is no question of using it to finance strikes with money intended for pensions. The insurance technique also wins out over the call for individual saving since it can be applied even when precarious income prevents the accumulation of savings. And then it has the advantage over the latter of being more moral: after all, saving rests on a selfish philosophy, whereas with insurance the money put aside is intended for a use that no-one hopes to benefit from, while everyone gains in feeling solidarity from the fact of a levy imposed on all and intended for whoever will need it.

The new school thus sees the error of the traditional school as wanting to resolve the social problem by acting on the individual's motivation, as seeking once again to moralise him directly by restoring 'dignity' to the poor and concern in the rich. That this is to look at the problem the wrong way round is clearly shown by the negative effects this attitude generates, by its global inneffectiveness and by the immorality that paradoxically it maintains in the spirit of dependence and vengeance that animates the working classes wherever the traditionalist perspective still seeks to install the reign of social peace. It is necessary, on the contrary, to act on the environment in order to modify behaviour, to weave effective bonds of collective solidarity between members of society if one wants to see the violence of conflict softened. But isn't acting on the social environment instead of moralising individuals what socialists aim to do? Is it not for this reason that they advocate the right to work and State intervention in the domain of production? By making insurance obligatory, by organising insurance through the State, aren't we slowly installing socialism from above, aren't we preparing the way for the reign of State socialism?

Supporters of the new school have to apply themselves to removing any suspicion of latent socialism from the insurance system so as to demonstrate that its technical and moral superiority is not paid for at an exorbitant political price. By putting the debt of all before the right of any class, the method of insurance, they reiterate, corresponds well with the requirements of solidarity and not at all with socialist dreams of the reorganisation of society. The principle of a pre-existing debt provides it with the means for dealing with social problems as eventualities calling for compensation rather than as the fruit of original injustices calling for the global reconstruction of society. Thus the rights introduced by insurance cannot give rise to subversion. They are secondary in relation to the debt of each towards all. Modelled on this debt, they are established on an inclusive basis as a function of the extent of material harm suffered and in accordance with a tariff fixed in advance. Consequently, the role this method gives to the State is by no means that of being the agent of a deliberate transformation of the structure of society, but of maximising effective bonds of solidarity within the existing structure. In so doing the State can at last become that 'visible expression of the invisible bond' that, according to Gide, unites members of society. By the method of insurance it establishes between individuals and social classes the federating bond which makes everyone's interdependence tangible, even where the structures of production tend to make social classes think that they are irreducibly opposed to each other. Insurance is not then the anti-chamber of socialism, but its antidote. It is indeed, according to Émile Cheysson's oft-repeated formula, 'the only science to have mathematics as its basis and morality for its crown'.

Since 1848 a way had been sought for giving rights to the poor classes without this resulting in them obtaining a right over the State. Proponents of solidarity provided a rigorous solution to this problem by actualising the insurance technique. Giving precedence to a debt over rights does not authorise the State being highjacked for partisan ends. The State manages everyone's contribution with a view to improving the whole of society. Moreover, the rights involved do not call for a reorganisation of society but for the compensation of injuries caused by the hazards of the social division of labour – and not in the name of an original injustice.

The injured, sick or unemployed worker no longer demands justice before the courts or by taking to the streets. He presents his entitlement to administrative authorities who, after examining the justified grounds of his claim, dispense predetermined indemnities. It is not by proclaiming the injustice of his condition that the worker benefits from social right, but as a member of society insofar as society guarantees the solidarity of everyone with those who find themselves in a particular situation of need as a result of the hazards of its development. All the guarantees from which he benefits thanks to this method give him a right to possible compensations, and therefore to a protection of his wage or capacity. But this does not give him any power of direction over the business or the State. The set of these social rights form what can best be termed his status. Like the shadow of the State cast over the individual, status, in the etymological sense of the word, places its beneficiary in the situation of being society's ward in proportion to the injuries inflicted on him by the social division of labour. Status is a protection due to the individual, but which can only be extended on demonstration of the claimant's extremely weak situation. The introduction of social rights at the end of the nineteenth century thus makes it possible to exchange a general demand for social justice for the collectivity's local protection of those of its members who incur a particular risk.

Social right is thus established on the basis of the socialisation of risk and not on the extension of classical right. In its principles the latter is absolute but, through the manifest opposition between the right to work and the rights of property, it showed itself to be contradictory in its effects. Through the socialisation of risk, social right can establish itself on the *relative and homogeneous language of statistics* and thereby dissolve the contradictions of classical right. To rights which are in principle absolute, this language counterposes the relative and aleatory character of events, situations, and injuries. To the contradiction between different interpretations of the law it counterposes the homogeneous form of a levy on all individuals and classes. Supporting itself on this new language of statistics, social right can claim to substitute the mechanism of a *promotion of the social*, that is to say a *reduction of the risks of all* and the *simultaneous augmentation of the chances of each*, for the original opposition between the right to work and the rights to property. The right to work is rigorously indefensible for it opens the door to all kinds of plunder and the suppression of freedoms. Contrariwise, it can be acknowledged that some incur *more risks* than others, and, by this very relativity, a consequent levy on wealth in order to *compensate* for the harms associated with them can be justified. The rights of property are in principle unassailable, but debatable – and debated – in respect of their actual distribution. It may, accordingly, make sense here to pose this issue rather in terms of the greater or lesser *chances* open to each to achieve the situation they desire: in this way a justification is found at once for property and for imposing a levy on it insofar as this is for the purpose of improving the chances for everyone to acquire it.

II The separation of the social and the economic

The insurance technique, by eliminating the question of individual responsibility from social dramas, effectively makes possible the introduction of a mechanism for their resolution in conformity with the solidarist definition of the State which requires it to act on the forms of the social bond and not on the structures of society. For the moral demand of justice it substitutes the principle of a social compensation for essentially aleatory harms. To pressure exercised on the State for a reorganisation of society it counterposes the principle of a promotion of the social, of an increase of the chances of each through the reduction of the risks of all. But is acting only on the form of the social bond any more than a surface solution which leaves intact the fundamental causes of the social question, that is, the natural antagonism between workers and capitalists and the oft-denounced subjection of the former to the latter? *To what extent* then was social right genuinely able to act on the oppressive situation that the working class had complained about since the beginning of the nineteenth century?

The hypocritical nature of the contractual form – the one-sided terms of exchange it offers between an individual with capital and another who lives only by his labour-power – is usually held responsible for the situation of the subjection of the working class. And it is the famous Le Chapelier law of 1792 that is held responsible for installing this pitiless regime of the contract. It is seen as the very expression of bourgeois hypocrisy, advancing modern mechanisms of exploitation under the cover of grand speeches on the Rights of Man.

At the very least there is an historical error here concerning the conditions under which this law was conceived. The Le Chapelier Law was not passed surrepticiously, hiding behind grand humanitarian declarations of the Revolution, but immediately in the wake of the abolition of privileges on the night of August 4th. From that moment the order of masters, and so the power of corporations to authorise or prohibit work, is disrupted. Inventors then claimed the right to set up in production on the basis of their industrial discovery, while unqualified workers, the very ones rejected by the corporations, claim the right to work. It is true that in response to employers' demands the law was directed at worker combinations, but it was equally directed at corporative powers in response to the demands of workers, of those much-discussed 'workers *sans qualité*', in the expression of the period, who wanted to open a stall and to work freely. Workers' combinations and corporatist monopolies go together therefore like two dangers which entail and nourish each other. In the proliferating arguments and confrontations between workers and bosses the State is appealed to and the Le Chapelier Law seeks first of all to respond to these incessant entreaties. It does so by referring the problem of work to a forced *tête-à-tête* between bosses and employees. This was not at all unrealistic, nor particularly hypocritical, at a time when production was still overwhelmingly organised on the model of an artisan employer and some journeymen.[9]

But difficulties arise precisely from the artisanal context in which the law governing relations between bosses and workers originates. More precisely, they arise from the fact that the type of contract that serves as reference is the one then in use for relations between an artisan and the person employing him, as still a relation between servant and master – *the contract for the hire of service*. This refers to a commitment to global availability for carrying out a job. It is more a contract for the hiring of persons than the establishment of respective relations between worker and employer in a given work situation. However, to say that this form of contract was made to suit the employers is certainly excessive. They are the first to complain about it and from these complaints came the three major instruments of nineteenth century paternalism: industrial tribunals (*conseils de prud'hommes*), the workers' passbook (*livret ouvrier*), and the system of factory regulations.

Under the Consulate, the bosses – and in particular those from Lyon – call on Chaptal, the Minister for the Interior, to restore structures of authority in the enterprise. Their argument consists in a lengthy enumeration of their disappointing experiences of free contractual relations between bosses and workers. Aren't they essentially the victims of this so-called contractual equality, they ask? When conflicts arise over an accident or stoppage, when workers or the public are injured, it is easy to make the boss pay since, running a successful business and possessing distrainable goods, his solvency goes without saying. But things are different when the employer is harmed: the worker's poverty, and even more his tendency to disappear, prevents seizure of his property. Doesn't the workers' great mobility, indeed their propensity to vagabondage – an inheritance of the initiatory journey of journeymen under the *Ancien Régime* – leave bosses at the mercy of their workers, or of their being enticed away by other businesses? The bosses conclude that they must therefore be given a supplementary power to compensate for this threat arising from the unstable and elusive character of the working class.

The *livret ouvrier*, the *conseils de prud'hommes* – and above all the system of factory regulations – will be the State's answer to these complaints. With the *livret* (law of 7 Frimaire, Year XII), the boss can be sure that the worker will only leave him in the agreed ways since he will not be able to get employment elsewhere without his *livret*, which is kept by the boss for as long as the contract is in force. Furthermore, according to the terms of the law, 'any worker travelling without his *livret* will be deemed a vagabond and can be arrested as such'. To the employers' advantage, the *conseils de prud'hommes* (law of 1805) reconstitute a jurisdiction similar to that of the *jurandes* of the *Ancien Régime*. In fact, employers are in the majority here (five of them against four foremen) and the master's word is by itself decisive in disputes over hiring and wages (article 1781). To this there is added the decree of August 3rd 1820 which considers the employer so much a superior, a master, that it puts the police and prison at his disposal: 'Any offence tending to disturb order and discipline in the workshop, any serious lapse by apprentices in relation to their master, can be punished by the *prud'hommes* with imprisonment not exceeding three days.' Finally, for the system of *factory regulations*, Chaptal entrusted the jurist Costaz with drafting a legal project aiming to arrange things so that 'the person who directs work is obeyed exactly in everything relating to it'. The project specifies that 'since it is futile to claim ability to provide for every detail of production with regulations emanating from the public authority (. . .) taking account of the variety of occupations, the best course is to authorise those responsible for directing work to regulate everything relating to it'.

Throughout the nineteenth century these three institutions constitute paternalism's arsenal. One way or another they traverse the whole century, faltering during revolutionary periods and then recovering immediately afterwards. The *livret* will only be definitively abolished in 1890.[10] The composition of the *conseils de prud'hommes* and way in which their officials are appointed vary with different political regimes, but they only very gradually shed their paternalistic dimension by becoming equally representative of both sides and democratically elected. Factory regulation constitutes the central component of bosses' power in the enterprise, and it is around it that paternalism is really organised. In fact, by means of factory regulation the economic contractual relation between worker and boss is doubled with a sort of contract of employer's tutelage over the worker. Due to the fact that the boss is completely free in drafting these regulations, he can include – as is usually the case – a whole series of disciplinary and moral requirements which go far beyond the register of production to the extent of directing the worker's attitudes and mores, his social and moral behaviour, outside the enterprise.[11]

The point of briefly recalling the conditions for the appearance of paternalism and the content of its arsenal is to bring out the point of impact of social right on the structures of production at the end of the nineteenth century. The worker's subjugation in the nineteenth century factory stems, as we have seen, from the State's delegation of power over the worker to the boss, from its recognition of the full and absolute *responsibility* of the boss for organising everything relating to productive activities in his enterprise. The supremacy accorded to the bosses in the *conseils de prud'hommes* and the State's recognition of factory regulations drawn up solely by the bosses puts them in the position of legitimate guardians of their workers. Hence the oft-denounced character of the bosses' power as a veritable seigneurial justice, the boss being at once judge and policeman in his enterprise, with the ownership of modern means of production hardly differing from feudal land ownership and the resultant domination of those who work it. In other words, if the notion of responsibility handicaps the worker who is a victim of the organisation of work, for he is the one who has to prove a fault committed by the boss, it serves equally as an alibi for the employer's power in the particular organisation that he seeks to give to production. It is fundamental to paternalist power in the enterprise.

The reason given for the employer's exclusive responsibility, the pretext for the particular force given to his power, is the *singular* character of each enterprise. The State's delegation of power is supported historically on the recognition of the specific characteristics of each process of production, on the fact that at the time of drafting the Civil Code it seemed impossible for a central authority to lay down regulations applicable to every place of production in their diversity and particularity.

It is precisely the support given to disciplinary norms and the employer's power by the particular characteristics of every production that social right will break up by decreeing general norms relating to hours, conditions of work, health, and to the safety, age and employment of workers. Because of the very homogeneity of the cover it proposes for social risks incurred by the working class, the insurance technique requires that *general norms* be decreed which are valid and applicable everywhere. With the diffusion of these obligatory norms, the power of the bosses henceforth appears not so much delegated as *challenged* by the State, since it is suspected of being out of step with the demands of hygiene and protections for the worker introduced by social right. Thus, with social right, the boss is called upon to apply rules not of his own making but whose authority stems from the solidarity of the whole of society and the necessary generality of sanitary norms, and which can only have the effect of reducing the arbitrariness of his power.

Thus, the increasing proccupation with safety and prevention, linked to the politics of insurance and social legislation, inscribes a line of disintegration at the heart of the employer's paternalist power by casting legitimate suspicion on its arbitrary character.[12] Not, admittedly, that workers' revolts and union struggles count for nothing in this erosion of the employer's power. We know that at the end of the century these struggles often take factory regulations – their humiliating content and the practice of fines – as their target. But the advent of legislation protecting labour provides these struggles with a decisive point of support for counterposing the State's normalising interventions to its arbitrary delegation of power to the boss. Social right thus breaks up the paternalist system. To convince oneself of this, one needs only to follow the debates on the question of factory regulations conducted between 1880 and 1920 by the main jurists and economists of the period.

On one side one finds the paternalist school with Hubert Valleroux its principal leader in France. In *le Contrat de travail* (1906) Valleroux calls on 'legislators and government to maintain the Employer's authority in its entirety, for this authority is necessary and indispensable and it will seen that the laws either effectively passed or in preparation tend to weaken it'.[13] Why this insistence? Because, he explains, the real and concrete conditions of work have little to do with contractual law. According to Valleroux, a well run business requires the employer to envelop the entire life of his employee in a network of measures of foresight, education and discipline which puts his whole person in a relation of strict dependence on that of his employer. So, in Valleroux, the idea of the contract, legitimate in itself, is gradually absorbed by that of the employer's legitimate authority in the name of his unlimited responsibility. The worker entering a factory is in a situation akin to that of a child vis-à-vis his father or a student vis-à-vis the schoolmaster, where he must submit to an already existing and higher power. Is not the reason for the employer's power of the same order? Is it not the generative capacity of biological, cultural or economic life that confers on these authorities – family, school, enterprise – an indisputable right to formulate the law appropriate to the activities for which they are responsible? And, he adds, plagiarizing the bosses he seeks to defend, if these conditions do not suit them, the workers can always go elsewhere now that the *livret* has been suppressed.

On the other side is the contractual or 'exchangeist' school whose spokesmen are Yves Guyot (1895), Paul Bureau (1902), and Molinari (1893).[14] Not only are these authors in favour of social laws for humanitarian reasons, but they see in the system of factory regulation being called into question the means of finally bringing to a close the era of social violence inaugurated at the beginning of the century.

What, they ask, is the cause of all these strikes, insurrections and revolutions which have stained the nineteenth century with blood and threatened our free societies with a future of stifling state intervention? Is it really the principle of the contractual code? Or is it not rather its insufficiency, its purely theoretical proclamation and non-application in reality? Paternalist theories justify themselves on the basis of the same point of departure as the communist theories they claim to combat insofar as they postulate an absolute antagonism between capital and labour. If the latter are right, then it is true that there is nothing to counterpose to the Statist constriction of society they foretell save a fretful regression to semi feudal positions. But what if, instead of reading the theoreticians of the Revolution, one undertook to listen to the actual protagonists of these revolutions? What do they really say, against what do they fight? Against the glaring disproportion between rich and poor certainly. But also, and especially, against their unquestionable humiliation and oppression by the bosses, against the employers' authority and the arbitrariness of their decisions. 'Thus, what one calls the social question or the worker question is first and foremost a question of authority.'[15] And, 'all this results from the labour contract by which, in exchange for something quite definite and limited, the wage, the worker lets the employer exercise numerous and indefinite rights not only over his work but over his person' (ibid.). Does the real danger come from the contract then, or from authority? 'Everyone sees in workers on strike the spirit of subjects in revolt who have briefly escaped from a master's tutelage: a spirit of revolt which would be psychologically inexplicable if between employers and employees there are really only the simple bonds of one of those conventions that, in any other circumstance, can be calmly and without anger suspended or broken' (ibid.).

The vigour of the debate between paternalists and contractualists attests the force of the blows struck by social right against the employer's power as it had functioned until then. But what concretely did it produce? To what extent did it transform relations between bosses and workers and go beyond the direct opposition between capital and labour?

Social right undermines the military form that the employer's power availed itself of in the name of the full and absolute responsibility of the boss in his own domain. But does this inevitably ruin him by removing along with his discretionary power the well-springs of the liberal economy, as prophesied by the paternalist school? Rather, it could be said that it liberates him, giving him the possibility of installing a completely different way of managing labour, freeing him from the endless preoccupation with watching over and punishing a restive working class and thereby enabling him to enter into a contract with this class which is less tainted by domination but more concerned with productivity. One man, Taylor, was responsible for providing the bosses with this sound advice. Or rather, in France, his admirers, who appear on the scene immediately after the first social laws are passed and who broadcast the message of a *rationalisation of work* in proportion to its *normalisation* through social right.

In his first work, Taylor explains the advantage the boss can gain from the disintegration of his paternalist power, if he knows how to come to terms with it. Hasn't the obstacle to increasing profit always been the poisoning of relations of production by relations of power? All the tension between workers and bosses is really due to the latter's attempt to reduce wages by every means and, in the main, to their exploitation of the system of factory regulations to reduce wage increases by imposing fines and to raise productivity, they think, with the most militarised organisation of production possible. Now what do they really gain by this if not a permanent tension with their workers and the latter's utmost determination to reduce productivity? 'It is safe to say that no system or scheme of management should be considered which does not in the long run give satisfaction to both employer and employee, which does not make it apparent that their best interests are mutual.'[16] But how is this ideal situation to be achieved? For Taylor the answer is obvious: by offering better wages to workers. Certainly. But how can better wages be paid when workers are determined to reduce productivity and to resist the pressures on them of the disciplinary order? The answer is again obvious: by transferring discipline from hierarchical supervision *to the machine itself*. And this can be done by exploiting the move to normalise conditions of work instead of futilely opposing it and letting it be used as a weapon against productivity. Normalisation fixes criteria for the employment of the labour force on the grounds of its health and protection. It states the conditions under which particular jobs can be undertaken by particular types of individual. Its target is the disproportion between the effort required for a job and the person who must do it. It therefore attests a concern for the adaptation of man to the machine. Fine, says Taylor, this is the way to have done with military discipline in production at the same time. We will try to establish the minimum time in which a job can be done on a machine and set it at that speed. We will select the most capable man, the man best adapted to job and speed, and assign him to that machine, to that minute but precise portion of production.

Instead of a *surfeit of supervisory discipline* – permanent supervision, punishment by fines and deductions from wages, all costly ways of exercising power because of the resistance they provoke – instead of this whole military minded arsenal, Taylor proposes looking for man's *optimum adaptation* to the machine. This involves starting out by accepting and going along with the requirement of normalisation accompanying social right so as to hitch it to a concern for industrial rationalisation. It is a question of rationalisation since the machinic system will control work, invisibly as it were, as a result of incorporating into the machine's tempo a rational calculation of the time and movements necessary for completing a task. It is an *economic rationality* since a single and sole preoccupation with the economy of time and movements presides over this new organisation of work. As a consequence, supervision can be extended and resistance appears as an irrational symptom rather than as an insurrection against an oppressive order, a repressive hierarchy. Indeed, in relation to this new economic rationality the worker finds himself designated as the *human factor* of this organisation, as a simple factor and no longer determinant agent, and as a factor always *susceptible to irrationality* according to how well he adapts to a rationally regulated work. Thus it is a question of reducing human irrationality as far as possible by selecting, adapting and normalising individuals so that they are best suited to the laws of this economic rationality.

For Taylor, transferring discipline from hierarchical supervision to the machine and rationalising productivity aim to free relations between boss and worker from the harmful effects introduced by the issue of power. Rationalisation makes it possible to pay better wages and so put this relation on the level of solely contractual negotiation. But do we really see such a positive settlement here? Is the contractual school's dream in fact realised through normalisation: a situation in which, freed from the paternalist constraints on their relations, capital and labour can at last be freely exchanged and a dispassionate rivalry established between them under power which will belong to the one showing the greatest concern for production, in the properly understood interest of both partners?

In fact, on the workers' side, we witness the constitution of a posture symmetrically opposed to what Taylorism holds out to the employers. For the normalisation of conditions of production provided by the insurance technique can also be used to call the requirement of productivity into question and as a means for challenging the contractual relation.

Normalisation provides support for the pursuit of maximum productivity if one gives a minimal interpretation to safety norms out of a concern for compatibility with economic rationality. But normalisation can also be given a maximal interpretation, by orientating norms towards increasing the protection of workers' health and welfare rather than solely towards the optimal use of the labour force, thereby inscribing them in a *social rationality*. The norms aim not only to reduce risks but to prevent them. Now, where do these risks come from if not from the exclusive concern with productivity that prevails in the organisation of work? And this obsession with productivity that leads to the minimum consideration of conditions of safety and welfare in everyone's work, where does it come from if not from the employer's individualistic profit motive? From the point of view of social rationality, it is therefore the *economic factor which contains a dangerous element of irrationality*, the very element which arises from the individualistic logic of the enterprise, from its indexation on profit for some rather than on the welfare of all.

Thus, social rationality does not bring about the revival of an individual contractual relation but the maximum frustration of the individual contract and the arbitrariness of profit. Since the individual profit motive is the source of irrationality in production, social rationality aims to reduce this irrationality by always putting the principle of the collective to the fore. By inscribing their struggles in the rationality of the social with its concern for the protection and advancement of disadvantaged categories, trade unions can thereby make their voice heard by the public powers and demonstrate the inequality of the competing parties, the weak position of workers in relation to employers, and the need to counteract the profit motive of some with the collective concern of others. A good example of this is given by the collective agreements which begin to be made after the First World War. In principle they closely follow the formula of the insurance contract used to deal with the issue of accidents at work, but this is now applied to the question of wages. Just as the injured worker is no longer personally required to demonstrate the employer's fault but automatically benefits from cover, so the worker being hired no longer personally negotiates his salary but straightaway gets a wage fixed for all workers in the same circumstances in a given branch of industry. *Status*, comprising all those protections recognised by the State or conferred by it on the party reckoned to be weakest in the framework of a contractual relation, thus compensates for the *contract* and limits the margin for manoeuvre it allows.

Insurantial normalisation guided by social right therefore allows employers to put an economic rationality to work which relieves them of disciplinary problems, reduces the element of direct confrontation with workers, gives free rein to the requirement of productivity and puts relations between entrepreneurs and workers on the sole level of wage negotiation, since workers no longer have any hold over or possible rational objection to the organisation of production. But, at the same time, this normalisation allows workers' unions to make the employers' requirement of productivity the target of a movement seeking to expose the irrationality of the profit motive installed behind it, consequently authorising ever increasing demands for protection at the expense of productivity and for the element of status at the expense of the contract.

III Towards the Welfare State (l'État-providence)

Thus, through its impact on the paternalist structures of the enterprise, social right brings to an end the situation of the worker's direct subjection to the boss installed under the cover of the contractual fiction officially governing their relations. But in doing so it inscribes both of them in the two antagonistic logics of social rationality and economic rationality. The effect of the normalisation of relations of production is not so much to suppress the relation of power between workers and employers as to redistribute it as a function of the minimal or maximal interpretation each seeks to give normalisation. Normalisation therefore only effects a *transposition* of the conflict hitherto directly opposing labour and capital to the level of these two abstractions – the social and the economic. The evolution of the debate on the social question after the First World War attests this transposition. No longer, as throughout almost the whole of the nineteenth century, will formulae be sought for reconciling the organisation of labour with capital through a philanthropic conception of the enterprise, nor yet will the elimination of capital's weight on labour be sought through the development of producer cooperatives. The search for and dream of the best model for organising relations of production is finished with. The problem of the moment is elsewhere. It is more abstract, since it concerns the need for the best possible articulation of these two entities, these two logics of the social and the economic. It has also been raised to a higher level, so to speak, since the problem posed by this articulation directly concerns *the State*.

Just after the First World War significant forces organise around these two abstractions of 'the social' and 'the economic' seeking exclusive recognition for one or other rationality. The workers' movement detached itself from the anarcho-syndicalism for which the strike was a kind of revolutionary gymnastics and which refused social reforms as so many distractions or fire-guards seeking to delay the general strike. Workers' demands now aim to defend and enlarge the sphere of the social. The participation of the majority union with Léon Jouhaux in the organisation of the war economy, and the concretisation of new social rights on that occasion, leads the workers' movement to put itself forward as responsible for the general interest of society in the name of the extension of social rationality. Similarly, one sees the paternalist enterprise of the previous century give way to cartels and monopolies, to gigantic and anonymous industrial combines, the spread of which really does seem to obey a solely economic rationality of increasing productivity, to the point that they look more and more like States within the State.

Faced with these forces – unions and monopolies – both in their different ways claiming to incarnate modern rationality, the State's position and role will seem increasingly problematic. Its neutrality had been seen as desirable as a guarantee of social peace, and its interventions to this end were justified solely in terms of solidarity. But, in following this course, it was localised in a kind of extrinsic position vis-à-vis society and its conflicts. Now, is not this neutrality and distance synonymous with impotence when, with the growth of union organisations and the expansion of cartels and monopolies, these forces appear to determine the life of society much more than State action? How can the State prepare the future and guarantee society's progress when it has no serious hold on the forces which seem to be in the process of directing the future along dangerously antagonistic paths?

It is precisely in these terms that what may be called the 'question of the State' is posed in the twenties.[17] The State may be neutral, but it is weak, too weak, and it must overcome this weakness in one way or another. Either the State must be associated with those forces which put its social mission and promise to ensure social progress to the fore, denouncing the autonomy of the economic in relation to the State as leaving a dangerously free field to the individualistic profit motive and anti-social egoism which presides over the organisation of production. Or it must be associated with the forces which appeal to economic rationality and the prior need to advance this for it to be possible, only later, to have the resources at one's disposal that will enable social progress. Supporters of this view say that if the State wants to rise to the level of its function as guarantor of progress, then it must impose its authority on the unions which threaten to usurp its function and prejudice its objective by claiming to do its job better than itself. The entire debate of the inter-war years is organised around these two theories by which each of the antagonistic forces in society express their claim to prevail. Both call on the State to come down in favour of one or other of these partisan logics, at the expense therefore of its republican neutrality. The future success of Keynesian doctrine, which will make it possible for the State to articulate the economic and the social centrally rather than allowing either to predominate over the other, can be understood on the basis of this dangerous oscillation of the State's role between these two rival tendencies. It is its ability to effectively preserve the republican State's neutrality that explains its value. But the form of this effectiveness will also reveal its price.

The first solution to the problem of the State consists in extending its power from the purely political to the economic and social spheres by doubling Parliament, elected by citizens, with one or several small parliaments directly representing producers and consumers. Sydney Webb's term, *industrial democracy*, which was taken up in France by men like Hyacinthe Dubreuil, Maxime Leroy, Albert Thomas and, later, Georges Gurvitch, was the name given to this idea of extending democracy and the political management of society to the management of economic and social life.[18] The first three of these belong to socialist trade union thought. They are in its majority current which, with Léon Jouhaux, decided to play the 'social' card rather than that of the Revolution pure and hard. However, they retain anarcho-syndicalism's distrust of parliamentary democracy and this leads them to revive a mixture of the ideas of Proudhon and Saint-Simon, with their respective celebrations of producers and of industry. The fourth, a jurist and sociologist, bases his criticism of parliamentarism on a development of social right, especially as theorised by Léon Duguit.

The point of departure of this current of 'industrial democracy' is the acknowledged failure of parties. 'Citizens rally less and less round parties. They rally round great economic or social forces. A citizen is for or against monopolies as his grandfather was for or against the Charter.'[19] And these forces 'which juridically remain outside the wheels of State, struggle for pre-eminence without finding in government the means for facilitating agreement between them'. Consequently, 'they must be brought into government'.[20] Thus, these forces must be reconciled with each other, and the State's relation to them modified. Reconciling them to each other is possible, it is claimed, if one agrees to see the social and the economic, correctly understood, as permitting a kind of struggle which simultaneously serves the general interest, provided one accepts the idea that the economic constitutes only the means, while the social designates the end of progress.

The social, with its concern for solidarity, obviously reduces the individualistic egotism tied to profit. But so does the economic also since, with the industrial rationality provided by the American Taylor and the French Fayol, one can hope to reduce the irrational consequences of the profit motive on the organisation of production. In order to realise the general interest, all that is needed is to guide the development of these two tendencies in such a way that the first, social solidarity, benefits from the second, industrial rationality, until, in Albert Thomas' phrase, 'the social wins out over the economic'.

But how is this to be brought about? How can one make the meaning of the general interest triumph in the management of economic and social life? The answer given is that of extending political capacity to producers, consumers and entrepreneurs as such, rather than as abstract citizens. As Gusdorf argues, following Duguit, since the source of right is in society and not the State, the expression of society as such, that is to say on the real basis of production, must be organised according to a necessarily de-centralised formula and Parliament must be made the place where the real movement of society and not the conflict of abstract opionions is registered. The formula for rallying social and economic forces has already been sketched out during the First World War with the 'National economic Council' in which Albert Thomas participated. All that is needed is to enlarge this formula and above all to decentralise it so that, starting from the concrete forces making up society, the expression of the general interest is imposed on the political representatives of an indiscoverable general will, on that parliamentary class the ephemeral coalitions and ceaseless divisions of which favour the rise of 'economic congregations' and the triumph of individualism at the expense of society. It is hoped to redistribute the power of the State to effective social agents through the development of small economic and social parliaments and, above all, to make the meaning of the general interest, the spirit of the 'social', prevail over the development of the economy. The social, thus credited with political power, could reduce the irrationality of the economy.

But how can it be guaranteed that redistributing political power to social forces will result in greater harmony in the conduct of society? How can one be sure that such an operation will not hand the State over to the partisan and divergent choices of different categories of producers, to the narrow corporatism of some and the excessive demands of others? How, especially, can one not fear that the anarchic situation thereby created will open the door to communist subversion which, far from working towards the pursuit of the general interest on this new basis, will see only a springboard for conquering a State which has renounced its force in advance?

In fact, in the solution they put forward, the supporters of industrial democracy are at once taken at their word and wrong-footed by the communists and by the trade union minority which split from the CGT of Léon Jouhaux to join them. Yes, they say, it is indeed necessary to extend political power to the producers, but without believing for all that some gradual harmonisation can be hoped for between these two entities, the social and the economic. These two registers constitute only the amplified terms of a central contradiction betwen capital and labour and certainly not the form of going beyond or even softening it. According to the communists, in the context of capitalism industrial rationality is and can only be an instrument of profit, a supreme exasperation of the logic of exploitation. It brings with it a total proletarianisation of workers to which fragmented work and the alienation it creates, the worker's estrangement from production, amply attests. This modern pact, which aims to dispossess the worker of any hold on production in return for a more easily negotiable wage remuneration, must be refused. More precisely, this logic must be pushed to its ultimate limits where the relation between workers and bosses as a pure relation of power, of the latter's oppression of the former, will again become apparent. Thus, the extension of workers' rights is only of value insofar as these rights are able to thwart this capitalist logic and are inscribed in a frontal contradiction with it. The point is not simply to subordinate the economic to the social, but indeed to destroy the first by exploiting the second.

It is against the subversive potential of industrial democracy that all the *neo-corporatisms* of the inter-war period are directed. These can be grouped together under the now unfortunately famous formula of *authoritarian democracy*. Not that the proponents of this current, in other respects very diffuse, are all spiritual Pinochets. Far from it at times. But they all feel that society cannot be saved except by reinforcing State authority – it being necessary to understand authority here in a sense opposite to that of power. In a way, the idea behind the redistribution of State power among social groups with de facto responsibility for the general interest had been to extend the State's power. Increasing the State's authority involves its concentration in a strong executive which is seen as being the sole depository of the idea of society.

These neo-corporatist ideas emerge within a nebula which includes neo-socialists like Marcel Déat and Henri de Man, the new right of the period (Arnaud Dandieu and the 'Ordre Nouveau' group), and, in part at least, the journal *Esprit* and the early theories of François Perroux.[21] Without in any way seeking to lump these neo-corporatist tendencies together with the totalitarianism produced by their equivalents elsewhere, one cannot avoid observing a considerable similarity in their point of departure. For all of them, the basic evil lies in the recent divorce of the worker from his work, in that moral rupture which leads to the demoralisation of society. By bringing the worker's interest to bear exclusively on wages, this divorce is seen as generating a process of desocialisation and a reinforcement of individualism. Since the individual's satisfaction is now to be sought only outside work, he is pressured into demanding the extension of the private sphere of wages and consumption at the expense of the public sphere. The worker thereby loses his singularity as organic producer and merges into an anonymous mass of atomised individuals whose social isolation, like its correlate, the fusing of identity in a blind mass, lends itself to political manipulation by those who hold the system of production solely responsible for their fundamental dissatisfaction.

The neo-corporatists thus engage in a double denunciation of the 'American' model which engenders this individualism and of the communist model which readily exploits its consequences. The remedy they all propose is basically the same, albeit with endless variations in its dosages. Since the tragedy arises from the divorce between the worker and work, social right and industrial rationality, the social and the economic, and since it now seems futile to hope for their spontaneous harmonisation in some distant future, given the likelihood of the intervening time-span being exploited by a strategy which sets one element against the other and aggravates their division in order to provoke a fatal explosion: why not work straightaway for the immediate reconciliation of worker and work? How is this to be done? By imbricating the worker's statutory demands in the demand for a renovated command-structure in the enterprise. A *community of labour* could thereby be recreated where each would know his place in the enterprise, draw a legitimate professional pride from it, and agree to submit to a no less legitimate *authority*. And over this society made up of restored communities would reign a State confident in its strength, certain of its authority, and knowing how to exercise it to maintain the good order of society without being burdened with the excessive caution of the purported neutrality within which it had been confined, that paralysis designed to limit it to its necessary minimum. In the words of Dandieu and Aron in *la Révolution nécessaire*: 'For us, the idea of revolution is inseparable from the idea of order. When there is no longer order in the social order, it must be sought in Revolution and the only revolution we envisage is the Revolution of Order'.[22]

Since the problem is the State's lack of hold over the course taken by society, say the proponents of this view, this grasp will be secured by increasing its authority, by rigorously concentrating it and extending its expression to the economic and social sphere. An *extension of its authority* and not a *dismantling of its power* as demanded by partisans of industrial democracy. Officially, the State's position consists in trying to balance relations between the social and the economic. Instead of this we see these relations disrupted, particularly under the conflicting intrigues of trade union forces. By increasing its authority the principle of order will reign over partisan interests. This time the formula is for the political decreeing its law to the economic and the social, reducing their division from outside and by force, subordinating the social to the economic in the name of the latter's subordination to the political.

But how, when the space for discussing ideas and interests is so narrowly circumscribed, can the danger be avoided of this path ending up in a new despotism with the principle of authority prevailing over its democratic foundation? This route shuts the door on subversion, but is not this only to create a dangerously congealed order? It reduces the neuralgic gap between the economic and the social, but is not this at the price of a dangerous autonomisation of the political? Especially as we have the examples of Italy and Germany to show us where this temptation may lead.

In this admittedly rapid evocation of the question of the State in the inter-war years, it is possible to recognise, like a prolonged and caricatural echo, the polemic between Duguit and Hauriou before the First World War. Whenever the impossibility of founding the State solely on political sovereignty is shown or demonstrated anew, it comes to appear as pure power, threatening and threatened at the same time: *de facto or transcendent power, simple power of constraint or legitimate authority; constraint that must be justified by socialising it or authority that must be validated by concentrating it*. Between these two tendencies, the idea of progress provides a rhythm for one and a goal for the other. It sufficiently links them together for the State to seem not to lean too much towards anarchy nor too much towards authoritarianism. It becomes discredited as soon as the two tendencies it contains unloose their restraints and nourish political illusions in which democracy vanishes along with the State's neutrality. In any case, in the twenties and thirties it seemed that to be able to govern the State needed a greater hold on society than could be secured by its foundation on electoral sovereignty alone, and that it tragically lacked the means necessary for carrying out its function as guarantor of society's solidarity.

Perhaps this enables us to better understand the tremendous welcome given to Keynesianism at the end of this period. The primary reason for this is that the 'general theory' makes it possible to forge a link between the economic and the social which, in principle, entails no subordination of one to the other since it proposes to link them together by a *circular mechanism*. In fact, the theory makes the social the means of 'reinflating' the economic when the latter is at risk of being affected by weak demand, and also of standing in for it, as it were, through the artificial but effective injection into society of an increased capacity to buy and employ. Equally, the economic, thus maintained in a constant state of good functioning, is the means for sustaining the pursuit of a social politics which provides safeguards for workers that keep them in a state of availability for work, rather than leaving them to the possibility of sinking below a threshold of poverty which makes them unfit to resume work when economic activity picks up again. The republican State's neutrality can thereby be preserved: it is not necessary for it to opt for the economic or the social nor therefore show any preference at all for the forces which take shape behind these instances. It can and must content itself with *articulating* them effectively.

Another reason for the attraction of Keynesianism doctrine is that it offers the democratic State a way to escape the unfortunate alternative either of making society seize up under the increasing pressure of authority or of letting it break up into its component parts as a result of the redistribution of State power to a multiplicity of actors pursuing contradictory strategies. Between these two temptations the General Theory opens up a middle way which is to improve the governability of society through its *regulation by time*. In fact, the theory provides an ability to anticipate crisis phenomena by acting on the signs by which crises are foreshadowed, and to get out of crises by recourse to the combined action of levers which are able to reduce the margin of fluctuation between periods of equilibrium and disequilibrium. It provides the principle of a *government of variables* in which the tendencies of social and economic life can be read, its crises forestalled and equilibria arranged for. The first economic theory to take time into account, Keynesianism offers the republican State a way of controlling the course taken by society while remaining in a position external to society.

In order to preserve the ideal on which it is founded, the Republican State must guarantee the progress of society. It is because of its manifest failure in this task that the Republic found itself endangered in the inter-war period. With the Keynesian-inspired solution put in place at the end of the last war, this problem may in some ways be considered resolved. Henceforth, the State possesses the means for securing the course taken by the progress it guarantees. At any rate, it gives every proof of its success and especially, with the brand new panoply of all these new measures, the outward signs of governing society by the simul-taneous manipulation of economic and social variables the know-ledge of which it ostentatiously and perhaps naively masters with statistical and planning bodies. Even better, it could be said, the *progress it only externally and very often inadequately guaranteed*, is now practically given over to its charge. No doubt the only way to guarantee progress was to take charge of it, to become *positively responsible* for it. But doesn't this lead even more to an inversion of the relations between State and society? No doubt the State is always neutral vis-à-vis social conflicts, but so as to embody the destiny of society from the vantage point of its position external to them. The Welfare State does not take part in the ideological options dividing society, but it takes charge of the levers of its destiny, giving the State control over the future of society *and depriving society of that control to the same extent*.

We asked how, to what extent and at what price, the Republic was able to overcome the contradictions affecting its instrument *par excellence*, the language of right on which was founded its promise of a society reconciled with itself. As a result of the contradictory interpretations to which this language of right was susceptible, the republican State, in its first historical version, found itself paralysed, trapped as it were, by the double requirement to reorganise society in conformity with the hopes put in the proclamation of the right to work on the one hand and, on the other, to refrain from intervening in society in the name of the defence of the rights of the individual, the security of property and personal freedoms.

The means for intervening were discovered at the end of the nineteenth century in what we called the homogeneous language of statistics, as employed by the technique of insurance applied to social problems. Just as the classical language of right is absolute in principle and contradictory in its effects on society, so the language of statistics is relative in its terms and homogenising in its effects. For the absolute character of the opposition between the right to work and property rights, it substitutes the relative calculus of risks and chances. It counters the division between workers and capitalists with a mechanism of common compensation, with collective amends for injuries suffered within the framework of the collectivity that they form. The social rights which follow from the use of this technique are not absolute, but relative and circumstantial. They do not require the State to embark on a partisan transformation of society but engage the collectivity in compensating for its own shortcomings and excesses.

Viewed in its *impact* on social relations, this solution will break up the system of workers' subjection to their employers in the form that this had been contrasted with the proclaimed equal sovereignty of all members of society. It breaks the employers' paternalist power at root, at the point where it supports itself on the singularity of the enterprise so as to organise production according to methods of domination which sidetrack the labour contract into a contract of dependence. The universality of norms shatters the arbitrariness of the employer's personal power. A new balance is thus given to relations between bosses and workers with the disintegration by social right of the paternalist government of the enterprise. But this is according to an arrangement which nonetheless does not create a new harmony and a calm transparency of their respective positions. For, some support themselves on this normalisation in order to extend the sphere of the State's protection of the worker, while others exploit it to establish a rationalisation of production with the sole end of increasing productivity.

The political *price* of this operation begins to be confronted in the inter-war period with the growth of organisations appealing exclusively to either this social or economic rationality. Both trade unions on one side and cartels and monopolies on the other claim to impose their law on the evolution of society and to contain within themselves, each more than the other, the vocation of realising the general interest. And all of this takes place on the basis of a State which seemed to be more impotent than neutral. It is resolved to pay this price in the face of the increasing dangers of fascism or communism which, by exploiting these two antagonistic rationalities, hope to impose their forcible reconciliation in the form of the subjection of one to the other or vice versa. The price consists in making society's destiny the State's positive responsibility by centrally articulating the economic and the social in accordance with the Keynesian formula, which has the advantage that it connects them up in a circular way as it were, thus maintaining the

State at equal distance from the rival forces seeking to impose their destiny on society. But the other consequence of this is that society is dispossessed of a direct hold over the course it takes and the State no longer appears as only a power protecting society's solidarity but as the positive manager of its progress, the agent of its destiny.

Thus what the State as guarantor of progress only succeeded in theorising, the Welfare State achieves, but by inverting the place it occupies in relation to society. Formerly it had been a question of reinforcing the solidarity of society so that it could pursue its own progress. Now the State must aim to guide progress and become positively responsible for it so as to gain the means for securing the social promotion of society and eradicating the sources of evil, poverty and oppression which prevent it from corresponding to its ideal. Society is no longer the *subject of its evolution* so much as the *object of a promotion* devised over its head and aiming to bring freedom to each and security to all.

Essentially, at the basis of this reversal of relations between State and society we find an operation which *elides the notion of responsibility* in the field of social relations.

By suppressing reference to responsibility it was possible to find an effective remedy for social problems, a way to de-dramatise them while providing them with a relative solution. By implicating the whole of society in the mechanism of amends for *de facto* harms suffered by individuals it was possible to avoid imputing responsibility to some, and particularly to entrepreneurs, for the suffering of others. It was shown that it was possible to forgo a reorganisation of society while compensating for the distress created by its existing organisation. The relativity of a compensatory procedure was substituted for the absolutism of a just order. But doesn't this very relativity of risks and chances which replaces the absolute character of wrongs and merits contain in embryo the principle of an inflation of expectations and demands? If it is *relatively* to each other that social categories can insist on their right to compensation for handicaps or harms suffered within the division of labour, where can a limit be found to the increase in these demands? We no longer say that 'it is the employers' fault' but that 'it is society's doing (meaning: fault)'. And what isn't it necessary to do to compensate for the shortcomings of society? How far must the promotion of the social be taken?

Similarly, by suppressing or reducing the previous effects of the notion of responsibility in the organisation of work it was possible to avoid the confrontation of labour and capital. By decreeing universal norms in the sphere of relations of production it was possible to break at root paternalistic kinds of oppression justified by reference to the employer's singular responsibility for everything and everyone relating to his enterprise. The need to make the economic and the social compatible could be substituted for the direct confrontation of capital and labour and the immediate violence deriving from it. But this could only be done by transferring that necessity to the State, by making it *responsible* for the evolution of society.

There is a considerable price to be paid then for this clever move which, by the elision of responsibility, made it possible to find a practical solution to social problems and to escape from liberal certainties as well as from socialist blackmail. We began to become aware of this price at the beginning of the sixties. It is that, having eliminated responsibility from the sphere of social relations, the disposition of State and individuals is such that the former has to make *allocations* to everyone as the price of the *promised* progress for which it is responsible, while individuals settle for being permanent *claimants* from the State as compensation for the grip on their *evolution* of which it has *dispossessed* them. And it is that between State and individuals, so it comes to be said, there is no longer a society.

Notes

1   On social economy in general, see Gaëtan Pirou (1834). On the new school, Charles Gide (1905), and by the same author, a history of the new school in the form of a course at the Collége de France taught in 1927 and 1928 (1932). Also, see C. de Greef (1921).

2   Émile de Laveleye (1877).

3   Lujo Brentano, translated from the German in (1885). A. E. F. Schäffle (1889), translated by Malon in 1880.

4   *Congrès international des accidents du travail et des Assurances sociales*, (1889) Paris.

5   The new school's promotion of the insurance technique can be seen most clearly in the records of the *Congrès international des accidents du travail et des Assurances sociales* which took place in Paris in 1889, Berne 1891, Milan 1894, Brussels 1897, Paris 1900, Dusseldorf 1905, and Vienna 1905. During this period the meetings in question have a pronounced polemical character and the political and theoretical issues opened up by this new technology, or rather, the way in which it succeeds in overcoming the classical ideological criticisms of State intervention, can be seen. After 1909 the Congresses take on a much more technical character.

6   On insurance technology and its impact on the notion of responsibility, see Tabouriech (1888). Saleilles (1897), in particular, analyses the reduction of the role of responsibility in nascent social right. The theorists of the application of insurance to social problems are particularly Maurice Bellom (1892–1901) and Édouard Fuster (1907). Fuster edits the *Bulletin des assurances sociales* from 1909, which follows on from the *Bulletin du comité permanent des congrès des accidents du travail et des Assurances sociales*, published since the first Paris Congress in 1889.

7   Émile Cheysson (1898).

8   Claudio Jannet (1888).

9   On the Le Chapelier Law and the context in which it was passed, see Marc Sauzet (1892), written as a series of articles published in *Revue d'économie politique*, Paris.

10   See Marc Sauzet (1890).

11   On the system of factory regulation, its history and the legislative debates surrounding it, the most illuminating work is certainly Desroy du Roure, *l'Autorité dans l'atelier, le Règlement de l'atelier et le Contract de travail*, Paris. From a more juridical angle, see Bodeux (1882) and Lalle (1906).

12   Ganger (1900).

13   Valleroux (1906).

14   However, these authors pursue different options within the same exchangeist or contractualist framework. For the pure liberals, Guyot and Molinari, it is a question of challenging the enterprise's disciplinary organisation in order that they individually achieve *self-government* (Molinari's term). For Bureau, who is inspired by the christian social thought deriving from Le Play, it is the collective form of the labour contract that is important insofar as it restores balance to relations with capital.

15   du Roure, *op. cit.*

16   Taylor (1911).

17   An introduction to these debates can be found in Barthélemy (1928).

18   *Industrial Democracy*, Sidney and Beatrice Webb's major work, was published in England in 1898. It is taken as a reference point for Maxime Leroy in his search for a form of government supported on the productive forces which was outlined before 1914 in Leroy (1907) and (1908). His line finds a special audience after the war and the Tours meeting, Leroy (1921), (1922), and (1924). Leroy's search is then taken up by Hyacinthe Dubreuil who seeks to reconcile Taylorised productivity with a restoration of the productive spirit in the working class, Dubreuil (1931) and (1935). Albert Thomas' writings are above all circumstantial and published within the framework of the ILO, of which he is one of the leaders and the principal organiser between the wars. Finally, from Georges Gurvitch we cite only (1932).

19   Leroy (1935) *op. cit.*

20   ibid.

21   The original inspiration for this whole tendency is certainly Henri de Man's critique of Marxism is (1927), his inquiry into the worker's relation to work in (1929), and his bringing together of socialism and nationalism in (1932). He is the inspiration for Marcel Déat in (1930), as also for the 'Ordre Nouveau' group, and especially for its two leaders, Dandieu and Aron, in three books which created a considerable stir at the beginning of the thirties (1932a), (1932b) and (1933). Francois Perroux develops an analysis of the enterprise close to these authors and to the journal *Esprit*, which, at the same time, initiates a re-evaluation of the notions of community and authority (1938).

22   Aron and Dandieu (1933) *op. cit.*

References

Aron, R. and **Dandieu, A.** (1932a), *Décadence de la nation française*, Paris.

Aron, R. and **Dandieu, A.** (1932b), *le Cancer américain*, Paris.

Aron, R, and **Dandieu, A.** (1933), *la Révolution nécessaire*, Paris.

Barthélemy, J. (1928), *la Crise de la démocratie représentative*, Paris.

Bellom, M. (1892–1901), *les Lois d'assurance ouvrière à l'étranger*, Paris.

Bodeux, M. (1882), *Études sur le contrat de travail*, Paris.

Brentano, L. (1885), *la Question ouvrière*, Paris.

Bulletin du comité permanent des congrès des accidents du travail et des Assurances Sociales. Bulletin des assurances sociales.

Bureau, P. (1902), *le Contrat de travail, le Rôle des syndicats professionels*, Paris.

Cheysson, É. (1898), 'Les accidents du travail' in *la Réforme sociale*, April 16, Paris.

Congrès international des accidents du travail et des Assurances sociales (1889), Paris.

Déat, M. (1930), *Perspectives socialistes*, Paris.

de Greef, C. (1921), *l'Économie sociale d'après les méthodes historique et au point de vue sociologique. Théorie et applications*, Brussels.

de Laveleye, É. (1877), *De la propriété et de ses formes primitives*, Paris.

du Roure, D. *l'Autorité dans l'atelier, le Règlement de l'atelier et le Contrat de travail*, Paris.

Dubreuil, H. (1931), *Nouveaux standards. Les sources de la productivité et de la joie*, Paris.

Dubreuil, H. (1935), *la République industrielle*, Paris.

Fuster, É. (1907), *la Statistique de risque professionel*, Paris.

Ganger, E. (1900), *Sécurité des ateliers et Accidents du travail*, Paris.

Gide, C. (1889), *Congrès international des accidents du travail*, Paris.

Gide, C. (1905), *Économie sociale*, Paris.

Gide, C. (1932), *la Solidarité*, Paris.

Gurvitch, G. (1932), *l'Idée de droit sccial*, Paris.

Guyot, Y. (1895), *le Travail et le Socialisme, les Grèves*, Liége.

Jannet, C. (1888), *l'Assurance obligatoire*, Paris.

Lalle, H. (1906), *la Question du règlement de l'atelier*, Paris.

Leroy, M. (1907), *les Transformations de la puissance publique*, Paris.

Leroy, M. (1908), *le Loi. Essai sur la théorie de l'autorité dans la démocratie*, Paris.

Leroy, M. (1921), *Les Techniques nouvelles du syndicalisme*, Paris.

Leroy, M. (1922), *Vers une république heureuse*, Paris.

Leroy, M. (1924), *le Socialisme des producteurs*, Paris.

Man, H. de (1927), *Au-delà du marxisme*, Brussels.

Man, H. de (1929), *Joy in work*, London.

Man, H. de (1932), *Nationalisme et Socialisme*, Brussels.

Molinari, G. de (1893), *les Bourses de travail*, Paris.

Perroux, F. (1938), *Capitalisme et Communauté de travail*, Paris.

Pirou, G. (1934), *les Doctrines économiques en France depuis 1870*, Paris.

Revue d'économie politique, Paris.

Saleilles, R. (1897), *les Accidents du travail et la Responsabilité civile*, Paris.

Sauzet, M. (1890), *le Livret obligatoire des ouvriers*, Paris.

Sauzet, M. (1892), *Essai historique sur la législation industrielle en France*, Paris.

Schäffle, A. E. F. (1889), *The Quintessence of Socialism*, London.

Tabouriech, (1888), *Des assurances contre les accidents du travail. Assurance collective et de responsibilité civile*, Paris.

Taylor, F. W. (1911), *Shop Management*, New York.

Valleroux, H. (1906), *le Contrat de travail*, Paris.

Webb, B. and **Webb, S.** (1898), *Industrial Democracy*, London.

7 Expertise and the state

Terry Johnson

The policies of 'deregulation', of secondary significance during the Thatcher government's early drive toward privatization, became, with the reorganization of the National Health Service and the reform of the legal profession, politically significant in Thatcher's last term of office and remains a central – if somewhat modified – plank of Majorism. The emergence of Thatcherite 'deregulation' policies have been explained in largely ideological terms; that is, as a product of neo-classical economics – a return to the primacy of market forces and a commitment to competition, cost-effectiveness and consumer choice. This was un-doubtedly the dominant rhetoric of the privatization programme overall. However, once such rhetoric is applied to 'deregulation' as it affected an increasingly wide range of institutions, including the professions, it loses force and coherence as a full explanation of government policy.

The rhetoric of individual choice and the market, as applied to the professions, was already established in 1979 when the government disbanded the Regional Planning Councils. This act initiated a process through which the Thatcher government progressively dismantled the institutions of professional planning pieced together by successive Conservative and Labour governments from the 1940s onward; so reneging on what had been a major plank in the post-war consensus. One outcome of the flight from planning was the marginalization of professional planners and a depreciation of their claims to expertise. As we now know, this early exercise in professional disestablishment had the added effect of politicizing environmental and spatial issues by removing them from the arena of 'neutral' professional judgment. Politicization was the effect attending a sequence of 'deregulation' policies, including those affecting optical services, the stock market and broadcasting, and leading to the major confrontations between the professions and government associated with the reorganization of secondary and higher education and the health service, and the reform of legal services.

The general implications of government policy towards the delivery of expert services only emerged with clarity in the third term of the Thatcher government. As the pieces of the jigsaw fell into place – the Education Reform Bill (1988), the Health Service's White Paper *Working for Patients* (1989), the Lord Chancellor's Green Papers on Legal Services (1989), the White Paper *Broadcasting in the '90s* (1988), the Monopoly and Mergers Commission report on professional advertising (1989) – it became clear that an unprecedented shake-up in the organization and control of expert services was under way, with effects that threatened to rival those of the privatization of the state-run industries.

What is clear today, however, is that despite the rhetoric of 'deregulation' employed by the government, there has been little 'deregulation' in practice. Markets in professional services may have been reconstructed; they have not been freed. The state has been rolled back, only to be reconstructed in another, equally pervasive form. In effect, government policy has, consciously or not, initiated changes in the way in which expertise has been incorporated into the state for more than a century, and in so doing has opened the door to changes in professional jurisdictions, the relations between professions, and relations within professions. Finally, it has had the effect of creating conditions for the further internationalization of expertise, particularly in the context of the single market of the European Community. In order to develop these arguments further, it is first necessary to place the whole discussion in a theoretical context drawn from Foucault. In particular, we will look at what Foucault means by governmentality, in order to establish that this concept provides a basis for our analysis, leading to the conclusions reached above.

Foucault and governmentality

The object of this section will be to argue that the emergence of the modern professions has been integral to what Foucault calls governmentality (1979b). Briefly, Foucault's concept of governmentality rejects the notion of the state as a coherent, calculating subject whose political power grows in concert with its interventions into civil society. Rather, the state is viewed as an ensemble of institutions, procedures, tactics, calculations, knowledges and technologies, which together comprise the particular direction that government has taken; the residue or outcome of governing. One strand in the plethora of such outcomes has been the institutionalization of expertise in the form of the professions.

According to Foucault, governmentality is a novel capacity for governing that gradually emerged in Europe from the sixteenth century onwards. This capacity was associated with the parallel invention, operationalization and institutionalization of specific knowledges, disci-

plines, tactics and technologies, which were themselves the conditions
for an extension of the governing capacity. The period from the
sixteenth to the eighteenth century was, he argues, notable for the
appearance throughout Europe of a series of treatises on government:
on the government of the soul and the self; on the government of
children within the family; and on the government of the state (Foucault
1979b: 5–9).

This re-thinking of the various forms of governance was, in turn,
associated both with the early formation of the great territorial,
administrative states and colonial empires, and with the disruptions of
spiritual rule associated with the reformation and counter-reformation in
Europe. Together, these discourses on government were precursors to
the disciplines of morality, economics and politics which were so crucial
to the constitution of the modern nation-state.

Among the critical transformations in political thought identified by
Foucault was that relating to the juridical conception of sovereignty.
Specifically, he identifies a revolutionary break with the Machiavellian
assumption that the power of the prince was ideally deployed in securing
his own sovereignty, and a change to the view that governing was no
more than the 'right disposition of things' leading to the 'common
welfare and salvation of all' (Foucault 1979b: 12). This novel discourse
increasingly conceived of popular obedience to the law as the sole
source of legitimate rule (i.e. sovereignty and law were rendered
synonymous), and also made it possible to identify – in the capacity to
make 'dispositions of things' – the means of governing; those tactics and
knowledges developed in order to regulate territories and populations.
Statistics, for example, was a emergent system of knowledge with
attendant techniques that revealed that populations had their own
regularities; rates of death, disease, cycles of scarcity, etc. These newly
observed regularities of structure were irreducible to the family as the
object of rule. Thus, claims Foucault, the art of government gave way to
a science of government:

> It was thanks to the perception of the specific problems of popula-
> tion, related to the isolation of that area of reality that we call the
> economy, that the problem of government finally came to be thought,
> reflected and calculated outside the juridical framework of sover-
> eignty. (Foucault 1979b: 16)

That form of government which came to have population as its object of
rule, and political economy as its principal form of knowledge, was an
ensemble of institutions, procedures, analyses, calculations, reflections
and tactics that constituted *governmentality*, a 'very specific albeit
complex form of power' (Foucault 1979b: 19); the form of government
that came to characterize modernity. It is clear from Foucault's studies

foucault's study Panoptican – shows the discipline central to the maintenance of government.

of the clinic and the penitentiary that the bearers of these knowledges/disciplines, the experts, became crucial in the development and maintenance of this governing capacity, and that the institutionalization of expertise in the form of the independent professions was integral to the emergence of the modern state.

Governmentality and the rise of the professions

In developing the concept of governmentality, Foucault was concerned with expertise insofar as it empowered a radical extension of the capacity to govern. From this point of view, the history of the professions becomes an important aspect of the transformation of power associated with the emergence of governmentality as the 'disposition of things'. The carrying out of these complex governing tasks inheres in such knowledges/disciplines as those identified by Foucault in *Discipline and Punish: The Birth of the Prison* (1979a) as constituting the 'normalising gaze' of nineteenth-century institutions of mass observation and control, represented by the panopticon. Novel forms of expertise in the fields of public hygiene, mental health and mass surveillance emerged in concert with developing government policies and programmes such as those relating to the asylum, and were intimately involved in the construction of governable realms of social reality.

The rapid crystallization of such expertise and the associated establishment of occupational corporations were, then, directly linked to problems of governmentality, such as the classification and surveillance of populations, the normalization of the citizen-subject, the discipline of the defined deviant, etc. The parallel establishment of the officially recognized jurisdictions of medicine, surgery, psychiatry, law, accountancy, etc., were the result not only of occupational strategies of advancement, but also of government programmes and policies.

Equally important for Foucault's view of the state–profession relationship is his conception of power as a social relation of tension, rather than an attribute of the subject. Given this conception, power can never be reduced to an act of domination, nor does the analysis of power start from a consideration of the conditions in which an individual is able to impose his or her will. According to Foucault, the relationship of power peculiar to the modern liberal, democratic state emerged with the shift from divine to popular legitimacy. That is to say, in the modern era legitimate political power has resided in the obedience of subjects, and it is Foucault's central concern with the formation of the obedient subject that explains his focus on the role of discipline/knowledge in his analysis of modernity. He argues that the characteristic outcome of power is not a relationship of domination but the probability that the normalized subject will habitually obey. It is the obedience of the citizen-

Monday

subject that reproduces the legitimacy of power in the modern state. Consequently, the actions of subjects – the self, the body – become the objects of new disciplines and technologies, which are, in turn, the products of expertise in the form of the personal-service professions.

Foucault's concept of 'normalisation' focuses our attention on the mechanisms through which the objectives of governments are geared to the reproduction of the self-regulating subject; to the alignment of the personal and collective conduct of subjects. Governmentality is, in short, all those procedures, techniques, institutions and knowledges that constitute an ensemble empowering such political programmes and policies. The modern professions emerged as part of that apparatus of governmentality; an emergent pattern of cognitive and normative changes – the 'great transformation' – that not only generated the popular legitimations underpinning liberal, democratic government, but also induced what Stanley Cohen (1985) has called a profound shift in the 'master patterns of social control'. This shift included the construction of new deviancy control systems, the institutional expression of which were the 'austere' and 'rational' bureaucratic organizations created for the classification and segregation of the poor, the criminal, the mad, the sick, the young, etc. It is from Foucault that we derive the revisionist history of the asylum which rejects the essentialist view that the building of the asylums in the nineteenth century was a necessary response to the individual pathologies of an increasingly anomic, urban, industrial environment, or that the medical profession was the sole source of expertise available to staff these new institutions. What has become clear is that the classification of the mad, and the typologies of mental illness, were a product of government policy associated with the problem of pauperism in an increasingly urban, industrial society, and that official recognition of the medical mad-doctor was the outcome of jurisdictional and political struggles (Scull 1979). The emergence of psychiatry as a medical specialism was, like the asylum itself, in part a product of government policy, constituting part of that ensemble of techniques and procedures that we now call the state. The implication of this conclusion is that Foucault sets out not to provide an alternative theory of the state, but to analyse a particular form of governing, which may characterize either state or non-state institutions (Barry 1992). The professions were, then, inextricably fused in this 'transformation' of the strategies and technologies of power. They were, in part, both the progenitors and the beneficiaries of this complex network of governmentality.

The question that Foucault fails to pursue at any length is: how and where does this expertise get stored, produced and embodied? Abbott (1991) has suggested that there are three types of role and rule figuration that may be involved in the social structuring of expertise. It may be variously embodied in commodities, including self-help manuals, training texts or expert systems; in organizations, with the detailed division of tasks and the ordering of their performance according to bureaucratic rules and procedures; or in individuals, highly trained and socialized in accordance with an agreed ethical and disciplinary code. We are here concerned only with the third type; that is to say, professionalism, as the dominant form of institutionalized expertise in the second half of the nineteenth and early twentieth century.

Expert services, as they emerged in alliance with government policies in the fields of health, business, welfare, law, etc., depended, as Larson (1977) argues, on the production of a distinctive commodity inextricably bound to the person and personality of the producer – the professional practitioner. While Foucault's analysis focuses on the normalization of the self-regulating subject-client as the object of governmentality, we are concerned with the expert professionals, who render:

> aspects of existence thinkable and calculable, and amenable to deliberate and planful initiatives: a complex *intellectual* labour involving not only the invention of new forms of thought, but also the invention of novel procedures of documentation, computation and evaluation. (Miller and Rose Chapter 5, p. 77, this volume)

In short, in the course of the nineteenth century, professionalism became as much a condition for the exercise of political power as were the burgeoning formal bureaucracies often, mistakenly, identified as constituting the sole apparatus of the state (see Miller and Rose Chapter 5, this volume). Expertise became incorporated into the process of governing, but it did so in the institutionalized form of independent, neutral colleague associations, controlling recruitment and training, providing codes of conduct and procedures of discipline. However, such market monopolies were increasingly underwritten by government in the form of official recognition or licence. In developing this argument, then, we are seeking to open up a new domain of Foucauldian analysis, linking the process of professionalization directly to the process of state formation. In so doing it raises several fundamental questions regarding the structure of expertise today – in particular, are the 'deregulation' policies of the Thatcher government a response to or a condition for a radical change in the state–profession relationship?

Professions and the state: the case of deregulation

From a Foucauldian perspective, both state and professions are, in part, the emergent effects of an interplay between changing government policies and occupational strategies. This is a view that undermines the dominant conception of the state–profession relationship in sociology, wedded, as it is, to a notion of the state as a pre-constituted, calculating subject whose interventions are inimical to the development of autonomous professionalism. Sociologists of the professions commonly identify state intervention in Britain as beginning with the collapse of *laissez-faire* in the nineteenth century. Starting from this mythic point of the separation of state and society, the history of the British professions is seen as a process with only two possible outcomes – autonomy or intervention. Foucault rejects any attempt to present these competing accounts as adequate histories. Rather, he views them as constituting inadmissible alternatives to history; the realization of preconstituted essences; an evolution foretold in its origins.

It is particularly important to rid our thinking of the distorting effects of this autonomy/intervention couple when considering Thatcherite 'deregulation' policies, which were themselves politically justified by a neo-liberal discourse and the goal of 'rolling back the frontiers of the state,' so 'freeing' the market in professional services. As I have argued above, the reality of the state–profession relationship since the beginning of the nineteenth century at least has been an intimate relationship between professionalization and state formation; so much so that government regulation has been crucial for the formation of markets in professional services, and in securing the conditions for autonomous practice. Recent government policies have not severed this historical relationship. Despite the political rhetoric, government policy towards the professions since 1979 has involved neither 'deregulation' nor increasing intervention, but a re-articulation of the state–profession relationship; a shift in the focus of government concerns regarding expertise; structural shits in ocupational autonomy. So-called 'deregulation' policies have turned out to involve varieties of re-regulation, even in those cases where they have had the effect of destabilizing the established jurisdictions of professional occupations.

With little risk of exaggeration, we can identify the high point of professionalism in Britain as coinciding with the post-World War II Labour government – despite conventional interpretations of the effects of the launch of the National Health Service in 1948. This was a period in which the goal of professionalization was seriously and optimistically pursued by teachers, social workers, librarians, planners and a legion of new, technically based experts. Such optimism was the product of seemingly successful strategies in eliciting both public approval and official benefits, insofar as professionals were increasingly located in new, 'corporatist' structures as 'neutral' experts, with the task of implementing the social and political goals adopted by the wartime National Government and its Labour successor. Paradoxically, an important event in this general process was the achievement by medical consultants in negotiating an effective controlling position in the

National Health Service (that is, within the financial parameters set by government).

The heyday of professionalism was short lived, however. Frustration began to mount among claimant professionals in the 1950s and 1960s. The dream of establishing themselves in the mould of medicine and law began to fade as more and more services were incorporated into bureaucratic settings, as the trade union functions of the associations were prioritized in their relationship with government, and as technical advances led to a more detailed division of labour and increasingly routinized work. Also, from the 1960s onwards, mounting public scepticism regarding the benefits of professionalism began to sour relations in the wake of 'planning blight', of the failures of the legal and health services, and of the dangers perceived as inherent in science, following ecological disasters of various kinds. The expansion of higher education and the rise of the feminist movement, with its hostility to the male professions, were important underpinnings of such loss of faith. It was this pronounced shift in public opinion that undoubtedly strengthened the resolve of governments in both Britain and the United States to confront the professions in the 1980s.

In the case of Britain, the strength and timing of the onslaught on the professions can be explained, in part, by the resurgence of classical liberal views, which from Adam Smith onwards had been deeply hostile to all forms of 'club, corporation, clique, cabal, and cartel'. However, the stimulus to reform throughout the advanced capitalist world had its roots in what has been called the financial 'crisis' of the modern state, arising out of the cost explosion associated with welfare provision in the context of rapidly aging populations.

As suggested above, the resultant policies have had the effect of destabilizing the established jurisdictions of a number of professions. They have modified or promise to change long-standing work practices, in law, medicine and higher education. They have transformed relationships between cognate occupations, including those between solicitors and barristers, solicitors and estate agents, bankers and estate agents, accountants and solicitors, etc. As the effects of such policies work through the system they also reconstitute networks of expert/official discourse, creating new institutional forms such as medical audit and academic appraisal. A further effect of the policies has been to shift the established boundaries between 'neutral' expertise and politics, so re-politicizing issues once safely consigned to the expert's domain. Let us look at these effects in a little more detail.

First, the disruption of established jurisdictions, with consequent effects for cognate occupations. A simple case in point is the proposal to allow solicitors to enter into multi-discipline partnerships, which not only has obvious consequences for the practice of law, but also has the potential to restructure the practice of accountancy and of estate agency in relation to allied legal services. In the case of law, the already existing trends towards large-scale partnerships and multi-disciplinary services are likely to be stimulated further by the Thatcher reforms, including the freeing up of professional advertising, so that the organization and control of legal and cognate services may well involve their incorporation into a more closely woven, commercial, corporate network. One of the consequences of such developments may well be to reduce the traditional significance of the division between barrister and solicitor, already blurred by the reforms relating to advocacy in the higher courts and recruitment to the bench, while increasing the status gap between lawyers providing corporate services and those whose futures would seem to lie in the salaried work-sites of multi-disciplinary, high-street service groupings and the proliferating agencies of public advice.

The pattern of medical jurisdictions established by the formation of the National Health Service in 1948 entailed the subordination of general practice to an elite of hospital specialists, sheltered from demanding patients by the GPs (general practitioners), yet protected from the discriminatory consequences of GP referral by the provision of a guaranteed salary and access to private practice. Bevan achieved his political goal not merely by 'stuffing the mouths' of consultants with gold, but by firmly establishing their elite status and authority within medicine. Recent reforms, ushered in by the Griffith proposals of 1983, the White Papers on primary medical care (1987) and on working for patients (1989), have the potential to reverse the earlier outcome, largely as a by-product of the policy to reduce health service costs by decentring the hospital consultant within the service as a whole.

The redrawing of the general practice contract and the establishment of large-practice budget holders with the resources to shop around for hospital services are reforms which, while threatening to regulate GPs more closely, at the same time promise to increase their relative status and independence. For example, while government attempts to increase efficiency are inherent in the reform of remuneration in re-establishing a 'market' relationship with the patient through a per capita fee structure, in the introduction of the limited list for prescribed medicine, in the attempt to establish consumer sovereignty through the Patients' Charter, in introducing medical audit into the primary health team, and in strengthening the management role of the Family Practitioner Committees, their effects will, almost certainly, be countered by the establishment of budget-holding GPs.

The capacity of general practice budget holders to shop around the hospital system effectively reintroduces the constraints of referral into the pseudo-market of the independent trust hospitals, so undermining the autonomy of the consultant specialists. The foundation of trust hospitals not only exposes the consultant elite to the vagaries of GP referral, it also threatens to erode the established status of hospital specialists further by increasing the relative authority of general managers, in line with the political goal of managing scarcity through an explicit rationing system of audited health-care provision, rather than leaving the rationing process implicit in the clinical decisions of individual doctors, as in the past. In the rationalization of health-care allocation there is a displacement effect, shifting the crucial decisions from the clinical to the managerial level.

These policies are, then, likely to reinforce a trend towards the relative inflation of GP incomes and status within the profession; a process already set in train by contractual changes ushered in by the General Practitioners' Charter of 1965, which led to a rapid increase in time-saving, status-enhancing partnerships and health-centre practices, the creation of the Royal College of General Practice, and the allied search for a secure knowledge base for general practice. The control over resources enjoyed by the new budget-holding partnerships could attract more graduates to general practice at the expense of hospital specialization in the future. Whatever the specific outcome, these government reforms are disrupting established jurisdictions within the medical profession, and are likely to shift the nodal points of professional autonomy away from the hospital specialist and towards the generalist practitioner, implying a shift in the articulation of state and profession in a process of expanding governmentality.

As mentioned above, this shift in relations between state and professions has its more dramatic effects in the displacement of existing boundaries between the spheres of politics and neutral expertise. According to Starr and Immergut (1987), the general sphere of politics in modern society has the capacity to expand and contract. In periods of social change, including political reform, arenas of decision making once considered realms of neutral, objective fact may be reconstituted as politically contentious. That is to say, matters of purely technical concern – to be resolved by recognized experts – erupt into 'political controversy'.

For example, the systems of financial and medical audit developed in respect of general practice and hospitals in the National Health Service have become hot political issues, centred on the competing criteria of 'cost' and 'care'. Cost criteria, it has been argued by the medical profession, are likely to distort the clinical judgments of GP budget holders, particularly in respect of the elderly and the chronically ill, who would become a drain on practice budgets funded in accordance with an undifferentiated per capita rate. Thus, what were once accepted as technical matters best determined within the confines of the GP's consulting room became, in the process of reform, burning political issues.

Equally, during the controversy leading up to the Courts and Legal Services Act (1990), even the most fundamental constitutional principles became issues of political contention, with the law lords claiming that the proposed reforms presaged not only an end to the independent bar and bench, but the destruction of the constitutional autonomy of the courts and a weakening of the doctrine of the separation of powers. The Lord Chief Justice himself referred, in the House of Lords, to the major Green Paper of 1989 as 'an insidious threat to freedom' (*The Independent*, 8 April 1989). While the eruption of controversy may, as in this case, prove a temporary phenomenon, on occasion such reforms involve a permanent shift in the boundaries, so redefining the role played by neutral experts in governmental processes. One such example is the medical audit, which violates professional principles regarding the inadmissibility of external evaluation by rapidly bringing into being a new occupation of 'auditor advisors', staffing the Medical Audit Advisory Groups attached to the regional health authorities.

These restructurings of occupational jurisdictions and boundaries between expertise and politics are, according to Foucault, always associated with the fact that governmentality has as its object of rule the subject; the 'normalisation' of the citizen-subject. Government-initiated change has, in these recent reforms, been securely linked with the political commitment to the 'sovereign consumer'. In the case of reform in the National Health Service, this translates into a shift in behaviour from the primary obligation of the sick to seek medical advice, as a means of social control, to a new set of obligations, including the stress on prevention, the obligation to care for the self by adopting a healthy life style, the commitment – shared with the new GP – to community care. The changes initiated in state-expert governing structures are, then, the product of new policy goals, which include, as part of the process, changing the way the citizen-subject normally relates to health-care provision.

To return to Starr and Immergut (1987), changing government objectives has the effect of shifting the boundaries between what was regarded as contentious and what was accepted as neutral. To put it in another way, the arenas of professional neutrality and autonomy are transformed, not only as a product of changing occupational strategies, not only as an effect of technical change, but as a result of changing government objectives and policies. As government objectives alter, transforming the boundaries of politics, so too do professional jurisdictions and the established powers and functions of the state. The point is central to Foucault's view of governmentality:

Since it is the tactics of the government which make possible the continual definition and redefinition of what is within the competence of the State and what is not, the public versus the private, and so on;

thus the State can only be understood in its survival and its limits on the basis of the general tactics of governmentality. (Foucault 1979b: 21)

The processes described by Starr and Immergut are just these tactics of governmentality. They are the policy-triggered politicizations and depoliticizations, which constantly 'disturb established rights and powers' (Starr and Immergut 1987: 222) of experts, as well as those boundaries that conventionally and legally demarcate divisions between the public and the private, between the technical and the political, and, it follows, between the professions and the state. Such boundaries are maintained even when, as observation shows, they are characterized by continuous movement. In short, those outcomes of governmentality we call the state, including those bodies of experts and expertise that both make it up and yet are allowed autonomy from it, are always in process of *becoming*.

Conclusions

The Foucauldian perspective suggests that those cognitive and normative elements that operate to establish the boundaries between associations of professional experts and the state must be viewed, in terms of process, as means or weapons in the struggle to define the boundaries of the technical and political; as the means of negotiation used by politicians and officials as well as professionals in generating those discourses that define the possible realms of governance. Professional men and women have, for example, routinely mobilized their claims to expertise and technicality as means of establishing and sustaining an arena of independent action. The doctors use their claim to diagnostic inviolability as a weapon in the effort to influence government policy. The outcome of the battle between the Royal Colleges and the British Medical Association on the one hand, and the British government on the other, over the reform of the National Health Service is merely one phase – albeit a radical one – in this continuous political process, determining not only the future of that service but also the future lineaments of medical expertise and the future powers and capacities of the state.

Since the emergence of modern, liberal, democratic government, expertise, in the institutional form of professionalism, has become a key resource of 'governmentality'; that is, of the technical and institutional capacity to exercise a highly complex form of power. Governmentality has been associated with the official recognition and licence of professional expertise as part of a general process of implementing government objectives and standardizing procedures, programmes and judgements. Also, because governments depend on the neutrality of expertise in rendering social realities governable, the established professions have been, as far as possible, distanced from spheres of political contention. Such a process is one of the major conditions of professional autonomy. However, because government policies and policy objectives change over time, these boundaries are in constant flux, having the effect of refashioning jurisdictions, breaking down arenas and neutrality, and constructing new ensembles of procedures, techniques, calculations and roles, which reconstitute the lineaments of the state itself.

Once we recognize the symbiosis of professionalization and state formation, it also becomes clear that any government that pursues policies with the effect of politicizing established areas of expertise and destabilizing existing professional jurisdictions also risks undermining the entrenched conditions that sustain legitimate official action. It is clear that the Thatcher government retreated from its full confrontation with the legal profession once the law lords had made it a constitutional issue.

The concept of the state that emerges from this discussion includes, then, that multiplicity of regulatory mechanisms and instrumentalities that give effect to government. This state itself emerges out of a complex interplay of political activities, including the struggle for occupational jurisdictions. The state forms, in the context of the exercise of power, systems of technique and instrumentality: of notation, documentation, evaluation, monitoring and calculation, all of which function to construct the social world as arenas of action. It is in the context of such processes that expertise in the form of professionalism has become part of the state. Expert technologies, the practical activities of professional occupations, and the social authority attaching to professionalism are all implicated in the process of rendering the complexities of modern social and economic life knowable, practicable and amenable to governing.

The professions are, then, involved in the constitution of the objects of politics; in the identification of new social problems, in the construction of the means or instrumentalities for solving them, as well as in staffing the organizations created to cope with them. The professions become, in this view, socio-technical devices through which the means and even the ends of government are articulated. In rendering a realm of affairs *governable*, whether it be education, law or health, or even in shaping the self-regulating capacity of subjectivity among citizens, the professions are a key resource of governing in a liberal, democratic state. Governments throughout the Western world have, in recent years, confronted the established professions in an attempt to control the welfare cost explosion inherent in the aging of populations. These reforms involve a radical shake-up of professional jurisdictions and established privileges as well as a re-articulation of the state–

profession relationship. The long-term issue is whether these changes also threaten professionalism as the dominant means of institutionalizing expert services.

References

Abbott A. (1988) *The System of the Professions*, Chicago, University of Chicago Press.

Abbott, A. (1991) 'The future of the professions: occupation and expertise in the age of organisation', unpublished manuscript.

Barry, A. (1992) ' "Free market" or "super state": harmonization, technology, and the government of Europe', paper presented at the conference 'The Anthropology of Europe: After 1992'.

Cohen, S. (1985) *Visions of Social Control*, Cambridge, Polity Press.

Foucault, M. (1979a) *Discipline and Punish: The Birth of the Prison*, Utah, Peregrine Smith.

Foucault, M. (1979b) 'On governmentality', *Ideology and Consciousness* 6, 5–22.

Larson, M.S. (1977) *The Rise of Professionalism: A Sociological Analysis*, London, University of California Press.

Scull, A.T. (1979) *Museums of Madness*, London, Penguin.

Starr, P. and **Immergut, E.** (1987) 'Health care and the boundaries of politics', in C.S. Maier (ed.) *Changing Boundaries of the Political*, Cambridge, Cambridge University Press.

8 Personality as a vocation
The political rationality of the humanities

Ian Hunter

Abstract

In responding to periodic government demands that it provide a rational justification for its activities as a public utility, the humanities academy typically appeals to the absolute ethical and intellectual values of liberal education. This paper investigates the nature of this response and its relation to the governmental field. The historical, ethical and political claims involved in the appeal to liberal education are discussed and rejected. It is argued that the cultivation of personhood has neither a single ('complete') form nor a privileged home in the university arts faculty. Weber's sociology of ethical orders is used to frame a discussion of intellectual cultivation as a specific vocation or discipline of life. From Foucault's conception of 'governmentality' the paper draws an account of a sphere of political rationality dependent on the historical deployment of particular intellectual and political technologies. The problem of the political rationality of the humanities is then discussed in terms of the unplanned historical convergence of the disciplines of cultivation and the technologies of government.[1]

Almost any educated person could deliver a lecture entitled 'the goal of the university'. Almost no one will listen to the lecture voluntarily. For the most part, such lectures and their companion essays are well intentioned exercises in social rhetoric, with little operational content. Efforts to generate normative statements of the goals of the university tend to produce goals that are meaningless or dubious. (Cohen and March, in OECD, 1987a: 30)

1. Introduction

In July 1988 the Australian Government's Department of Employment, Education and Training released a White Paper (Dawkins, 1988) outlining significant changes to the funding, structure, management and operations of the nation's higher education system. The objective of these changes was to

Published in *Economy and Society Volume 19 Number 4 November 1990* harness universities and colleges to the problems of national productivity and national debt. This was to be achieved through an overall expansion of the system and a selective prioritising of those sectors deemed most relevant to 'knowledge-based' and 'value-added' industrial production: engineering, computer and information sciences, business studies and economics, Asian studies (ibid.: 17). The means of implementing the new policies comprised an increasingly familiar – if politically incongruous – mix of regulatory and de-regulatory strategies. Measures to prioritize strategic research, unify different sectors of the system, establish uniform budgeting procedures and attach funding to output and performance measurement appeared alongside proposals to encourage academic entrepreneurship, give greater autonomy to university managements and admit 'market forces' by part-charging students for their education.

Such policies and measures are not of course unique to the Australian context. There are strong parallels in the Thatcher Government's educational reforms of the 1980s, albeit with important differences of political emphasis and strategy. And the transnational character of the thinking informing such policies is readily apparent in the education policy analysis of the OECD. (See, for example, OECD 1982, 1987a, 1987b.) As we shall see in more detail below, such policy measures represent a characteristic modern form of governmental rationality and action.

Typically the response to such initiatives is nuanced and politically uneven. The Australian reform programme has been supported at various points and to various degrees by the Australian Council of Trade Unions, business groups, 'femocrats', the college sector, university managements, scientific and technological organisations and even, to a limited extent, by the Federation of Australian University Staff Associations. The multi-valent character of the White Paper's proposals – encompassing such goals as national prosperity, equity for disadvantaged groups, managerial efficiency, public accountability – has allowed a wide variety of groups to translate their interests into those of the Government and thereby form part of an extended governmental network surrounding the universities.

Against this background of wider response the character of the one site of implacable refusal and resistance stands out in sharp relief. It is the humanities academy – in which for present purposes we can include the humanistic social sciences – that has formulated the single radical rejection of the reform programme. It has done so by invoking a quite different goal for higher education: liberal cultivation of the intellect. To the Government's proposal to gear higher education to social and economic needs and purposes the humanities academy replies that it is the custodian of a goal whose completeness and universality identifies it with the absolute end of humanity as such – the culture of the 'whole' person and the disinterested pursuit of knowledge.

This response sets the stage for a drama of political opposition which is perhaps as inconclusive as it is familiar. On one side, in a statement accompanying the Australian reforms, we find the minister expressing his confidence 'that we will find in the academic community generally a real concern for the future economic performance of the country and a desire for change in the role of the higher education system in responding to national needs'. He continues:

> Our universities and CAEs are the main source of the highly educated men and women so essential to our economic growth. They provide the scientists, engineers and technologists we need to develop and maintain a modern industrial structure, as well as the teachers needed to expand the skill base of the workforce and to educate the next generation. We must also recognise the crucial contribution made by our economists, historians, philosophers and others in the humanities as Australian society works its way through the complex range of issues arising from the shift in our national economic circumstances. (Dawkins, 1987: 2)

On the other side, it is quite clear that the minister's confidence is radically (and no doubt knowingly) misplaced, at least as far as the humanities academy is concerned. For the latter, culture and knowledge are 'ends in themselves' and this makes them final for all other ends, including 'national needs'. In responding to the Government's Green Paper (the draft version of the White Paper) the Australian Historical Association, for example, has this to say:

> Despite the general assurances . . . concerning the continued importance of humanities and social science education, we find the general emphasis of the paper unduly narrow and instrumental. It contains much about the means of achieving national goals, but little about the contribution which humane learning, and history in particular, can make to the debate about national priorities. There is much about the forms of technical training necessary to secure improved levels of productivity, for example, but little about the equally important ways in which wide-ranging curiosity-led teaching and research contribute to the maintenance of a general culture of innovation and creativity. It is natural, and perhaps necessary, that in times of economic restraint educational resources should be concentrated upon those activities which give promise of immediate economic benefits. But it may be self-defeating in the long-run if, in so doing, the government leaves unwatered the seedbed of creative and critical thought. (Australian Historical Association, 1988: 30)

For a purer statement of the thinking underlying such opposition we can cite a second response.

> To begin with, the humanities refuse to value knowledge and understanding only in pragmatic or utilitarian terms, but see them as values in their own right. What justification is given is in terms of the moral, imaginative and intellectual development of individual scholars and the students they teach and the enrichment of society's cultural life. It is easy to see how at odds this

is with the green paper's emphasis on the contribution knowledge can make to Australia's international competitiveness. (Brett, 1988: 32)

And, to remind ourselves that this discourse is by no means nation-specific, we can note a similarly embattled reaffirmation of the values of humane learning from the United Kingdom.

> Liberal education saw itself as being about the formation of character, the learning of values – moral, ethical, aesthetic – 'the inner being' as much as the outer. It believed that education could only be called such when it engaged and involved the full range of human activities and potentialities. (Light, 1989: 33)

Here we are confronted by a collision between two discourses whose mutual incomprehension is matched only by their internal coherence. On the one hand, the governmental discourse seeks to constitute universities as legitimate objects of governmental intervention. It does so by conceiving of their educational activities in terms of the formation of skills and knowledges with calculable, hence plannable, economic outcomes. On the other hand – in its appeal to a series of putatively untranscendable oppositions between culture and utility, critical and instrumental reason – the defence of the humanities seeks to establish their institutional autonomy by rendering their ends opaque to all purposive rationality. Here it is assumed that the goals of 'full' personal development and disinterested truth seeking, invested in liberal education, place the humanities beyond the calculable outcomes of 'vocational' training, hence beyond the governmental rationality premised on such calculation.[2] Pushed to its extreme, which is not in fact very far from its centre, this defence ends by identifying the automomy of the humanities with their ineffability.

> Within liberal education there is typically an emphasis upon personal freedom, but equally crucially a stress upon the autonomy of the educational process, its necessary freedom from the more direct forms of State or local control. Within this more libertarian conception education can encompass the free-thinking, even the antinomian and the anti-authoritarian. But more importantly its province is the ultimately unaccountable. (ibid.: 40)

Needless to say significant intellectual and political penalities are incurred in trying to calculate one's situation and prospects by proclaiming their incalculability. There is a sense in which the standard defence of the humanities leaves their practitioners incapable of reasoning about their actual determinants and functions. Identifying the humanities with the complete cultivation of the person and the disinterested pursuit of knowledge may indeed render them autonomous of government. But it also threatens to render them autonomous of history – where what has counted as 'complete' and 'disinterested' has varied with the instruments of knowledge and cultivation, and the circumstantial (even governmental) uses to which they have been put.

It is not my purpose, however, to reject the defence of the humanities from the standpoint of governmental reasoning. Indeed, it will be argued below that the project to render social reality transparent to governmental calculation cannot be accepted at face value either; dependent as it is on specific political and intellectual technologies whose successful deployment is by no means guaranteed.[3] My object is not therefore to undertake a philosophical adjudication of the two discourses as if they inhabited the same domain of reason. Rather it is to offer a genealogy of their currrent impasse, tracing it to the unplanned convergence of two formerly distinct departments of existence and ways of life.

In discussing the historical relation between the 'cultivated man' and the 'expert' Weber provides a characteristically succinct introduction to the circumstances that initially distinguished the two ethics.

> The term 'cultivated man' is used here in a completely value-neutral sense; it is understood to mean solely that the goal of education consists in the quality of a man's bearing in life which was *considered* 'cultivated', rather than in a specialized training for expertness. The 'cultivated' personality formed the educational ideal, which was stamped by the structure of domination and by the social condition for membership in the ruling stratum. Such education aimed at a chivalrous or an ascetic type; or, at a literary type; a gymnastic-humanist type, as in Hellas; or it aimed at a conventional type, as in the case of the Anglo-Saxon gentleman. The qualification of the ruling stratum as such rested upon the possession of 'more' cultural quality (in the absolutely changeable value-neutral sense in which we use the term here), rather than upon 'more' expert knowledge.
>
> Behind all the present discussions of the foundations of the educational system, the struggle of the 'specialist type of man' against the older type of 'cultivated man' is hidden at some decisive point. The fight is determined by the irrestibly expanding bureaucratization of all public and private relations of authority and by the ever-increasing importance of expert and specialized knowledge. This fight intrudes into all intimate cultural questions. (Weber, 1948: 243)

No doubt Weber's distinction between a form of power exercised through the cultivation of a prestigious personality and that dependent on expertise in the arts and ends of government is too schematic as it stands. None the less it offers a potentially fruitful reorientation to the relations of mutual incomprehension holding between today's 'cultivated men' and government planners.

Is it the case that the modern humanities are the heirs of earlier charismatic cultivations of personhood, while government has become dependent on 'the ever-increasing importance of expert and specialized knowledge'? If so then to expect calculable economic outcomes from the humanities may turn out to be no less misguided than to defend them as the key to 'complete' personhood. It is possible to propose, then, that if we are to understand the current disposition of the humanities towards government it will be necessary to formulate a new object of investigation: the historical deployment of the disciplines of liberal cultivation and the nature of their historical relation to the forms of expertise characteristic of modern government. This paper represents an initial attempt at such a formulation.

2. Liberal education

We have noted that the specification of the humanities as the vehicle of liberal education has two aspects: the complete cultivation of the person and the disinterested pursuit of truth. Elaborating on the notion of complete cultivation Judith Brett, for example, provides this account:

> The humanities are concerned, as their name implies, with the development of that which is most distinctively human in us. How this is described will vary: our formation in language; our preoccupation with meaning; our dependence on symbols; our creation of culture.
>
> This essential humanness is discovered and developed through the study of the thought, ideas, language, symbols, culture, and ways of life of other people, and these are reached through their books, letters, official documents, paintings, buildings, music, and whatever other material remains are available. (Brett, 1988: 32)

Bernard Williams provides us with a representative defence of the second aspect, in claiming that the humanities are the essential vehicle of 'social understanding'.

> In Boston, there is a rather grand and mysterious painting by Gaugin called *Where do we Come From? . . . What are we? . . . Where are we Going?* Everyone always has difficulty with the last question . . . What is certain, I take it, is that there is no hope for answering the last question unless we have some ideas for answering the first two; . . . The most basic justification of the Humanities as on-going subjects is that our insights into the first two questions essentially involve grasp of humane studies, in particular because the second question involves the first. Any understanding of social reality must be based in understanding its history, and you cannot read its history without insight into its cultural products and those of other times. (Williams, 1987: 186)

While these two aspects of the humanities differ – representing respectively an ethic of personal cultivation and a discipline of knowledge – it is typically assumed that they are mutually reinforcing: the humanities and their liberal education are both a humanising knowledge and a knowledge dependent on humanisation. We will leave this assumption to one side for the moment.

The defence of the humanities in terms of the liberal education involves three sorts of claim, the first being the ethical claim noted above: that a liberal education is what makes us 'distinctively human' and is the key to understanding ourselves and our society. This specification of the liberal education was first explicitly formulated in the early nineteenth century and it is not difficult to track Brett's and Williams's accounts back to Arnold's and Newman's. Not only does Arnold appeal to the many-sided development of liberal cultivation as a bulwark against the instrumental 'machinery' of governmental reforms, he also treats culture as the privileged medium in which an 'essential humanness is discovered and developed'.

> What we want is a fuller harmonious development of our humanity, a free play of thought upon our routine notions, spontaneity of consciousness, sweetness and light; and these are just what culture generates and fosters. Proceeding from this idea of the harmonious perfection of our humanity, and seeking to help itself up towards this perfection by knowing and spreading the best that has been reached in the world. . . .
>
> But what we are concerned for is the thing, not the name; and the thing, call it by what name we will, is simply the enabling ourselves, whether by reading, observing, or thinking, to come as near to the firm intelligible law of things, and thus to get a basis for a less confused action and a more complete perfection than we have at present. (Arnold, 1932: 162–3)

The ethical absolutism of this species of cultivation – which claims to bypass the 'machinery' of mundane knowledge and action through its unmediated access to the being of humanity – is made clear in Newman's comment that:

> that alone is liberal knowledge which stands on its own pretensions, is independent of sequel, expects no complement, refuses to be *informed* (as it is called) by any end, or absorbed into any art, in order to present itself to our contemplation. (Newman, 1959: 134–5)

At the same time, when seeking to enshrine it as the fundamental discipline of the university, Newman identifies liberal knowledge with 'a gentleman's knowledge'.

> I consider then that I am chargeable with no paradox when I speak of a knowledge which is its own end, when I call it liberal knowledge, or a gentleman's knowledge, when I educate for it and make it the scope of the university. (ibid.: 136–7)

This of course returns us to Weber's cautionary remark that ideals of cultivation are rooted in the social personas of prestigious social groups; and it provides a glimpse of the problems posed by the historical variability of ethos for the ethical claims of the humanities. We will return to these issues below.

The second element of the defence is historical or philosophico-historical. Here it is claimed that the university organised around its arts faculty was and is the essential social embodiment of the liberal education. No doubt there is a degree of nostalgia involved in this claim as the arts-centred university did not survive the nineteenth century. None the less it is an integral part of the defence. In criticising the 'utilitarianism' of the Green Paper, Brett (1988: 32), for example, speaks of 'the traditional role of the universities in providing a "liberal" education'. After reaffirming the interdependence of universal knowledge and complete cultivation in Newman's account, Leinster-Mackay (1979: 32) tracks the liberal education to its origins along the well-worn path to medieval Oxford, Paris and Bologna. C. A. J. Coady constructs his version of the claim by crediting the humanities with fulfilling 'the traditional ideal of a liberal education', the cultivation of attitudes appropriate to a 'comprehensive' and 'critical' understanding. History quickly becomes apology:

> Universities provide the natural, though not exclusive, home for these attitudes in a society like Australia and it is part of the justification for training people in the professions and other occupations within universities that they may absorb some of these civilising influences. (Coady, 1988: 17)

But perhaps the most uncompromising modern formulation of the philosophico-historical claim is to be found in Kenneth Minogue's *The Concept of a University*. According to Minogue Newman's liberal education has its origin in the contemplative life of early medieval monasticism. Springing fully formed from the monastic mind, 'universities are the impulse to contemplation issuing into a social institution'. This origin explains and justifies the autotelic and disinterested forms of cultivation and knowledge that form the 'concept' – though not necessarily the reality – of the modern university.

> We have already seen that the academic world grew out of religion, and religion very commonly adopts an attitude of piety towards at least some parts of the world. To try to control or manipulate (certain aspects of) God's handiwork is an impiety. The academic world would seem to have inherited this kind of piety with regard to everything that exists. It renounces passionate involvement, as did its monkish ancestors, and gets in return a freedom to roam wherever its inclination leads. (Minogue, 1973: 96)

Here we can clearly see the dual philosophical role performed by the figure of origin. The origin (of liberal education in the medieval university) is both the point at which an ideal or essential function is actualised and the point at which modern actuality is idealised or essentialised, through attachment to its originary 'idea'.

The third and final step in the defence of the humanities involves a philosophico-political claim. If liberal education is the vehicle of full humanity and universal knowledge, and if the arts-centred university is the institutional embodiment or natural home of liberal education, then such a university cannot in principle be subordinated to government in terms of social purposes. To the contrary, the university must set the ethical and intellectual horizons of social life. The standard political arguments for academic freedom and institutional autonomy thus turn out to be based on ethical and philosophical claims regarding the unsurpassable and indispensable human-ising functions of liberal education. It was on such grounds that Newman dismissed the idea that the functions of a university education might be gauged in terms of its social utility and argued instead that its ends were co-terminus with the ends of life itself.

> If then a practical end must be assigned to a university course, I say it is that of training good members of society. Its art is the art of social life and its end is fitness for the world . . . a university training is the greatest ordinary means to a great but ordinary end. (Newman, 1959: 191)

A similar argument is implied in Bernard Williams' defence of the institutional autonomy of the humanities. According to Williams a democratic society aspires to be 'transparent in its workings' so that its operations can be governed by the understanding of its citizens. Williams regards the humanities as the institutional embodiment of 'social understanding'. This means that they form an unsurpassable intellectual horizon for the government of society and thereby win the right to a privileged and autonomous existence.

> If it is right that the Humanities as subjects make an essential contribution to the understanding of society . . . then questions of who should be taught how much of the Humanities are essentially connected with questions of how open or transparent society should seek to be . . . the conclusion is not only that it is vital that the Humanities should be pursued as ongoing subjects but that access to them, and some kind of knowledge of them, are things that should be as widely spread as they can be. (Williams, 1987: 188)

Such are the ethical, historical and political claims underlying the defence of the humanities. In what follows I argue that these claims are unsustainable in their presented forms. As a result the humanities cannot be defended as the embodiment of the humanising mission of liberal education. We can begin with that set of claims whose virtue is to include statements of fact and thereby allow of reasonably direct adjudication, the historical.

2.1 History

Leaving open for the moment the question of what might count as a liberal education, is it the case that the arts-centred university has been the institutional embodiment or 'natural home' of activities going under this name? In fact there are quite straightforward historical reasons for answering this question in the negative. In striking exemplification of the divorce between the defence of the humanities and the results of their research, it has been known for a considerable time that between the seventeenth and twentieth centuries liberal education was typically pursued outside the university and university education was not liberal.

Sheldon Rothblatt's *Tradition and Change in English Liberal Education* amasses a considerable amount of evidence in support of the following conclusion:

> In the eighteenth century a liberal education did not assume, and certainly did not require, residence at a university. One of the outstanding features of liberal education in the Georgian period is the many institutional forms that it could take. A liberal education could be offered in boarding or grammar schools, or in Dissenting academies and private educational establishments, or it could be acquired by the wealthy on a grand tour of the continent. Locke thought a tutor would provide it, and while his influence lasted tutorial instruction was one major source of liberal instruction. (Rothblatt, 1976: 75)

The many middle-class men and the few women for whom a liberal education was deemed an asset typically acquired it in educational settings quite unlike Oxford and Cambridge. Conversely, recent scholarship also suggests that the education provided by the universities in this period was anything but liberal. The fact that all kinds of education were organised around classical studies tells us very little, as the forms taken by those studies and the functions they served were so various. For the same reason we should resist the temptation, offered by terms like *literae humaniores* and 'humanism', to assume a common core for liberal and university education.

Rothblatt (ibid.: 78–82) shows that, despite the success of Renaissance humanistic scholarship elsewhere, the Oxbridge curriculum stayed scholastic and medieval. It remained centred on Aristotelian logic and rhetoric and removed from both liberal cultivation and the inductive sciences throughout the seventeenth and eighteenth centuries. Moreover, even where the new Renaissance scholarship did transform the arts curriculum, as in some of the leading continental universities, its 'humanism' had little in common with what is meant today by 'the humanities' or 'the development of that which is distinctively human in us.' In the first place, as we can learn from Grafton (1981), Renaissance humanism was dedicated to forms of philological analysis and commentary on classical texts quite unlike the methods of modern philosophy, history and literary criticism. Secondly, it has been clear since Baldwin's (1944) pioneering reconstruction of grammar-school education, that the humanistic teaching of the classics was organised around the doctrines and practices of *imitation* – of the rhetorical form of the classical texts as well as their ethical contents. Hence it has little in common with a post-Romantic humanism centred on the values of originality and personal experience. (We should recall that Renaissance scholarship was 'humanist' in basing itself on the study of non-divine texts, but not in treating these texts as creative expressions of an author's personal humanity.) Finally, as Oestreich (1982) and Grafton (1983) have shown, when Renaissance humanist scholarship was incorporated in university curricula it was not 'liberal' in the sense of being opposed to practical purposes or administrative ends. To the contrary; commenting on Justus Lipsius, one of the foremost humanists of the sixteenth century, Grafton has this to say:

> As a professor in the new Protestant university of Leiden and the older Catholic one of Louvain, Lipsius built from classical ingredients exactly the equipment his aristocratic students needed to survive in an age of religious war. In the philosophy of the Stoics Lipsius found a simple guide to life, one that would enable the young aristocrat to put off fear and anger, to master his passions and then to discipline himself and his soldiers. In the detailed study of Roman antiquities Lipsius found a perfect guide to the most pressing problems of state-building and army-formation. Above all, in the detailed accounts of Roman military organisation and technology given by Polybius and others Lipsius found not old but new knowledge – a full set of instructions for building a shatteringly effective military machine. (Grafton, 1983: 65)

No doubt these capacities do not belong among those that modern humanists would accept as distinctively human, and they probably do not come within the ambit of Arnold's 'sweetness and light'. None the less, they were an important objective of Renaissance humanism and the early-modern arts faculty, where these happened to coincide. For better or for worse the humanistic scholarship of the early-modern university was not liberal in the modern sense, and the historical claim that the humanities academy is the original, traditional or 'natural' home of liberal education falls without much pushing.

2.2 Ethos

In the light of these remarks, what are we to make of the claim that is fundamental to the standard defence of the humanities: the ethical claim that the liberal education is responsible for a cultivation of the person so complete and a pursuit of truth so detached as to constitute an 'essential humanness'? It should already be clear that the central weakness of this claim lies in the historical specificity and variability of the formation of human attributes. This is what makes all talk of 'complete', 'disinterested' or 'essential' humanity very difficult to make sense of.

Most accounts of liberal education are cast in terms of the role of liberal studies in forming the fully cultivated 'whole' person. The difficulty is that what counts as 'wholeness' or complete cultivation is specified in different and often incompatible ways at different times and in different circumstances. The same goes for what Weber calls the 'pedagogy of cultivation'. Consider, for example, a manual of liberal education typical of those used in the seventeenth and eighteenth centuries; Cleland's (1948) *The Institution of a Young Noble Man*. It recommends that in addition to the mastery of rhetoric and the reading of polite literature – designed to school the manners, form the taste and develop the sociable arts of conversation – the liberally cultivated gentleman should have some familiarity with fencing, dancing, riding, and perhaps falconry and hunting. These were necessary to provide the body with the demeanour, bearing and grace required by the rituals of court or the mercantile balls and salons. Here the possession of a liberally formed person was a key to getting on in society.

No doubt the inclusion of these bodily arts seems quaint from the perspective of today's liberal studies. But are we to say that seventeenth and eighteenth-century liberal education and the person it formed were in comparison less complete? Why? Might we not be tempted to say that the supplementation of the literary with the bodily arts produced a *more* complete cultivation? But this would be equally misleading. The problem lies in the notions of 'complete person' and 'essential humanness' themselves. These notions imply that human attributes and the statuses to which they attach are organic and synthetic; and that at the end of the synthesis lies the goal of an ideal or full humanity: the many-sided character, whole person, and so on.

It is just as plausible to suggest, however, that in observing different ideals of cultivation we are looking at goals of development internal to the ethics of different social groups – internal to what Wittgenstein calls different 'forms of living' and Weber different 'conducts of life'. According to Weber not only is the 'cultivated man' only one amongst several possibilities contained in the historical repertory of personhood, but it is a possibility itself subject to profound sociological variation.

> The pedagogy of cultivation . . . attempts to educate a cultivated type of man, whose nature depends on the decisive stratum's respective ideal of cultivation. And this means to educate a man for a certain internal and external deportment in life. In principle this can be done with everybody, only the goal differs. If a separate stratum of warriors form the decisive status group – as in Japan – education will aim at making the pupil a stylized knight and courtier, who despises the pen pushers as the Japanese Samurai have despised them. In particular cases, the stratum may display great variations of type. If a priestly stratum is decisive, it will aim at making the disciple a scribe, or at least an intellectual, likewise of greatly varying character. (Weber, 1948: 426–7)

It is possible to propose, then, that the differences in ideals of cultivation that we have already noted – between the armed humanism of Lipsius and the contemplative humanism of Newman and Arnold, between the liberal education of the *courtigiano* and that of the modern English teacher – represent differences in the 'internal and external deportments' of particular social groups. In Weber's account these different ethical physiognomies are not united in a universal form of subjectivity or 'person'. Instead, each is particular to the *Lebensführung* or conduct of life of a specific social group and the circumstances in which it becomes socially 'decisive'.

Needless to say, in following Weber down this path we are deviating from the great philosophical anthropologies launched by Kant and Hegel. According to these anthropologies the cultivation of personhood has an absolute and universal form. This is determined either by 'man's' dependence on a supersensible (transcendental) substratum of intellectual categories and moral imperatives, or by his development towards a total form through the successive splittings and reconciliations of the World Spirit. Moreover both Kant (1986: 264–7) and Hegel (1979: 158) were tempted to identify this absolute culture of the person with the ethical ideal of their own stratum, the enlightened scholar. It is not my concern here to engage directly with this style of philosophical anthropology. I mention it only to mark the difference between its universalist and totalising conception of culture – so central to the modern humanities – and the argument of the present paper. Suffice it to say that, given the differences between the goals and techniques of cultivation already noted, the burden of proof must lie with those who believe that these different ethical deportments – from the Samurai to Oscar Wilde – are somehow subsumed as aggregative moments or stages in the synthesis of the absolute person.

Moreover this allocation of the burden of proof finds strong prima facie justification in the researches of non-philosophical anthropologists. In two remarkable essays Marcel Mauss assembles a wealth of anthropological evidence in support of the argument that human attributes – internal and external deportments – are the products of specific hence variable forms of social organisation and cultural technique. In his essay on the body Mauss (1973) argues that bodily dispositions and abilities – spitting, dancing, digging, swimming, jumping, giving birth, marching, eating, squatting – are in fact complex assemblages of actions, requiring the transmission and mastery of specific 'techniques of the body' in order to be performed and acquired. Mauss's account in no way excludes the biological and anatomical. Indeed, some techniques – for example, those for teaching children to open their eyes underwater when learning to dive and swim – are dedicated to the social harnessing of specific biological reflexes. At the same time, Mauss's insistence on the importance of ethical authority and 'prestigious imitation' in the training process recalls Weber's sociological observations on the role of 'decisive' status groups in establishing styles of social cultivation and deportment.

Mauss's (1985) partner-essay, on the category of the person or self, is no less wedded to a view of human being as a variable amalgam of biological donations and cultural-technical fabrications. Departing from modern usage, Mauss uses the term 'individual' to refer to the unstructured, biological and psychological human being as 'raw material'. The notion of person on the other hand is construed as a specialised artefact of social organisation and cultural technique. It encompasses those instituted articulations of capacities, statuses, rights, duties, virtues and traits through which societies organise the deportments and relationships of their members. Mauss uses this distinction in order to discuss a number of peoples and cultures in which not all individuals have (or are) persons and in which those who do, do not possess personhood in a 'personal' manner. In these predominantly clan-based societies persons are special configurations of statuses, capacities, rights and traits which are not invested in the first instance in individuals. Rather the attributes of personhood are attached to trans-individual entities or institutions – totems, naming systems, masks, ritual genealogies, spiritual ancestors. And these institutions are responsible for a distribution of personhood to individuals on a variety of bases – birth (real or ritual), combat, spiritual possession, status, gender, ancestor incarnation, and so on.

We of course think of our persons – our rights, duties, capacities, virtues, traits – as inalienable, as rooted in the conscience and consciousness of every individual. The leading tendency of Mauss's essay, however, is to relativise this conception of the 'person as self'.[4] This conception is treated as a special case, peculiar to the modern West, of the cultural forms in which personhood is elaborated and borne by individuals. In Mauss's view the person as self is an historical creation and he ascribes its elaboration particularly to specific institutions of law and morality. It was Roman law, argues Mauss, that first dissolved the distribution of personhood on the basis of clan genealogies and gave it a new though still delimited generality, on the basis of the citizen's role in the republic. And it was Stoic and Christian morality – Puritanism in particular – that was responsible for attaching the status and attributes of personhood to an inner soul and for developing the ethical techniques of individual self-monitoring and control: conscience and consciousness.

So, unlike the universal person of Kant and Hegel, Mauss's person as self is neither an emanation of the timeless metaphysical categories of subjectivity nor an anticipation of the final moment of historical self-consciousness, in which the subject recollects and transcends all its determinations. Instead, this remarkable mode of human being was brought into existence as a result of the historical development of particular legal and moral institutions. And it is this light that we should view the deep differences that exist between alternative forms of ethical comportment, or ways in which individuals cultivate their persons. The Puritan personality, formed through the application of techniques of self-watchfulness in private pursuit of the 'signs of grace', thus represents a particular construction of the person. The personality of the courtier or gentleman, organised around an array of bodily and mental techniques for the presentation and management of a stylish and sociable public self, represents a quite different construction – as is shown by the Puritan's unremitting hostility towards this figure. Of course, the Puritan personality has itself been subjected to scornful critique (for its lack of wholeness!) from the perspective of the Romantic persona: a persona organised by the deployment of techniques of aesthetic cultivation and dedicated to the refinement of sensibility. Needless to say, these options by no means exhaust the field and do not form a natural hierarchy.

It is possible to suggest, then, that what counts as being a person is dependent on historically contingent and variable cultural institutions and techniques. If so, then it is no longer possible to take seriously the ethical claim that the humanities are responsible for an 'essential humanness', through their cultivation of the 'complete' person. The fact that ideals and organisations of the person are always dependent on the deployment of definite and limited bodily and ethical techniques means that they are too historical and variable to have an essential or complete form. Moreover, the variety of institutions and circumstances responsible for such deployments – caste training, religious regimen, aesthetic culture, military discipline, court ritual, professional training – suggests that humanising cultivation is only contingently invested in the humanities as subjects. Perhaps it is time for the humanities to cultivate some ethical modesty.

2.3 Politics

It should be immediately clear that once the historical and ethical claims involved in the defence of the humanities have fallen so too does the standard claim to social and political autonomy. We have seen that the arts-centred university is not the natural home of liberal education. Further, liberal education is only one among several historically available cultivations of personhood. Hence, it makes no sense to treat the humanities academy as the essential vehicle of a form of cultivation whose complete or unsurpassable character warrants the academy's immunity from governmental intervention. In fact, far from being an unsurpassable 'end in itself', the liberal cultivation of personality is characterised by a multiplicity of ends. Its goals have included civility, taste, good manners, wisdom, sociability, a refined sensibility, bodily grace, aesthetic 'wholeness', eloquence and others, depending on the use of particular techniques of cultivation and the circumstances of their deployment. Indeed, we might be tempted to say that it is not the absence but the multiplicity of social purposes that characterises liberal education; not the opposition between culture and utility but the utility of cultivation.

Consider in this regard one of the central purposes of eighteenth-century liberal education, the propagation of 'civility'. According to Norbert Elias (1982: 251–92) the techniques of shaming, ethical control, and body management associated with notions of civility and mannerliness first appeared in late-feudal courts, where they were responsible for the physical and psychological transformation of a warrior aristocracy into courtiers. The dissemination of these techniques to other social groups and milieus through schooling and courtesy books provides the historical setting for the eighteenth-century liberal education described by Rothblatt.[5] Let us say that the literary arts, bodily disciplines, and techniques of self-management and presentation that comprised this education had as their object the formation of personality in the form of civility. This was a specifiable combination of polite learning, agreeable manners, taste, bodily grace, conversational suppleness and sociability.

Now, there can be little doubt that in the transition from court to salon the arts of civility were transformed and came to serve a new end: the gaining of place and favour in a commercial society whose reward structure was significantly tied to the rituals of social intercourse. And Rothblatt is certainly justified in commenting that:

> Liberal education was concerned with definable ends and with visible qualities of character. The proof was a liberal education lay in behaviour, expressed as style, taste, fashion, or manners. . . . Polite education was utilitarian. It softened class differences in such a way as to enable some degree of social mobility to take place. (Rothblatt, 1976: 26)

So, while the liberal education had civility as its object rather than specific vocational expertise, and while it did indeed take as its goal the cultivation of the whole man, it was by no means beyond practical ends and the 'whole man' was in fact a highly specialised cultural artefact. To this extent the liberal education was itself vocational.

The impact of this conclusion on the post-Romantic understanding of liberal education is, needless to say, shattering. And the work of scholars like Rothblatt and Grafton shows the extent of the gulf between the standard defence of the humanities and some of the more recent historical discoveries made within them. None the less, I wish now to argue that this conclusion must remain a preliminary one. It is not that it contains an error but that it leaves room for further misunderstandings. Without retreating from our argument on the vocational character of liberal education, it is necessary to supplement it, if we are to understand the relation between the liberal and the governmental.

Consider, in this regard Rothblatt's comment that 'Polite education was utilitarian'. As long as this is taken to refer to the practical character of the outcomes of liberal education and their role in a specific social milieu, no problems arise. We are, however, predisposed to push the statement much further than this. In fact, at this juncture we seem to be drawn irresistably towards two important misunderstandings.

On the one hand, we are tempted to treat the vocational character of liberal education as a sign of its subservience to a general social function (social mobility in a class society) or of its foundation in a general political principle (utility). No doubt this path is taken in order to convert what is otherwise the description of a specific cultural milieu into a general theoretical explanation. But the result is that the political rationality of liberal education comes to be understood in terms of forces acting on or through it, in accordance with general sociological functions or political principles.

On the other hand, we are also tempted to interpret liberal education's vocational character as a sign that it has been imposed on humanity in some extrinsic manner, in lieu of a more authentic form of development. Here one is inclined to pay too little attention to, and put too little store by, the historically available forms of cultivation for a different reason: we continue to imagine their ethical subordination to a more organic hence complete form of human development promised to us by history.

Interestingly enough, the sociological reduction of liberal education and the Romantic belief that its true form is ideal thus turn out to be quite complementary. Hence, it is not uncommon to find the same author succumbing to both temptations at the same time; that is, explaining a practice of cultivation in terms of its functionality or utility for a particular structure of society, while simultaneously treating this practice as an historical stage in the evolution of a more complete – typically aesthetic – culture. I do not wish to discuss here the degree to which Rothblatt's own account is drawn down these two convergent paths. For the moment I simply want to indicate prima-facie reasons for refusing to interpret the vocational character of liberal education either as a sign of its extrinsic sociological or political determination or of its ideal form waiting over the historical horizon.

In the first place, it is not clear that during the eighteenth century Britain possessed a highly developed social sphere organised around politically calculable ends that liberal education might or might not serve. At this time Britain was a geopolitical space where the professions still functioned as autonomous guilds; where there was no national education system; where important public positions were dispensed through patronage rather than competitive-entry examination; and where the extension of government into social life through the deployment of new bureaucratic technologies had hardly begun. Under these circumstances it is probably anachronistic to describe eighteenth-century liberal education as 'utilitarian' in the sense of being integrated into a politically calibrated set of social purposes. In other words, the functional integration of liberal education into a social sphere and the degree to which its utility might be calculable may themselves be matters of historical contingency dependent, for example, on the deployment of specific governmental technologies and forms of calculation. If this is so then the political rationality of liberal education is not something determined in a general way, by sociological function or political principle. It is something that will have to be described as a matter of more or less, in terms of the variable deployment and scope of the instruments of government – instruments whose success is bringing the institutions of liberal education within the range of political calculation is a purely practical affair.

Secondly, although civility was the practical and vocational goal of liberal education, this does not mean that it was imposed in some artificial or extrinsic manner by 'society'. A two-centuries old discourse on alienation has made us extremely resistant to the view that the cultivation of self might support practical and vocational ends without sacrificing personal authenticity and 'wholeness'. Yet it seems clear that civility constituted a goal of development and a focus of ethical commitment no less (and no more) essential or human than ideals such as (Puritan) conscientiousness, aesthetic self-stylisation or, more recently, existential self-problematisation. We can recall Weber's location of these ideals as internal to the ethics of autonomous social groups or conducts of life. The central point whose consequences must be grasped is the dependence of the goals of cultivation on the practical deployment of specific and variable ethical techniques. Recognition of this dependence allows us to affirm the practical and vocational ends of liberal education without concerning ourselves with the false problem of loss of authenticity or 'wholeness'. But it also gives us a further reason to acknowledge that, for all their practicality and mundanity, these ends are not reducible to a functional social purpose or a general political rationality working through them. The same dependence on contingent ethical technique that denies universality to the goals of liberal education also establishes their intransivity to general social functions and political principles.

Hence, for all its importance as an antidote to the standard defence, Rothblatt's account only takes us part of the way in our discussion of the political rationality of the humanities. For ease of exposition we can focus the limits of this account in a terminological point. While arguing that liberal education is 'vocational' Rothblatt does not clarify the relation between the two senses of the word in which this may be true. Is liberal education vocational in the sense of filling an occupational niche in society, or in the sense of being a 'calling' or vehicle of ethical passion and commitment for its practitioners? Floating in the uncontrolled space between these two senses it is hardly surprising that liberal cultivation should be by turns explained away in terms of its utility and idealised away in terms of an essential humanness.

Our conclusion regarding the vocational character of liberal education must therefore remain preliminary pending the resolution of two further problems. First, we must clarify how the disciplines of liberal education succeeed in focusing ethical passion and commitment despite the practical and limited character of their ends. Second, we must learn to discuss the political rationality of liberal education as a purely contingent phenomenon; that is, as something dependent on the historical emergence of administrative technologies and forms of calculation capable of attaching such education to the 'governmental' sphere. These are the tasks directing the next stages of our discussion.

3. Personality as a vocation

Max Weber's well-known lecture 'Science as a Vocation' provides most of the assistance necessary to resolve the first of these problems. Addressing an audience of German university students in 1919 on their choice of career, Weber is concerned with knowledge as a vocation (*Beruf*) in both senses of the word: as an occupation and as a 'calling' or focus of ethical commitment. Unlike today's addresses on the 'goals of the university' and the 'future of the humanities' Weber's lecture is not an exercise in apologetics. Rather, it is an intellectually uncompromising argument to the effect that there can be no general or overarching rationale or justification for the various professions of knowledge, and that as a result academics must acquire an ethical modesty matching the intellectual limits imposed by their disciplines.

Weber (1989: 3–8) begins by painting a grim picture of the academic career structure. This, he says, is dominated either by professional charisma and patronage (Germany) or by bureaucratic control and market forces (America). In either case career success is heavily mortgaged to irrational forces and surprisingly dependent on sheer luck, particularly in the area of recruitment and appointment: 'No university teacher likes to be reminded of discussions about appointments, for they are rarely pleasant.'

But it is Weber's second object, his discussion of 'the inner vocation for science', that illuminates our present concerns. This discussion is contextualised not only by Weber's portrait of the academic career structure but also by a withering attack on Romantic self-cultivation whose 'idols are "personality" and "personal experience" (*Erleben*)'. Weber remarks that 'One tortures oneself with efforts to "experience" because this belongs to the proper style of life of a "personality", and if it does not succeed one must at least pretend to have this gift of grace' (ibid.: 11). Such attempts to discover personality and 'meaning' through the authentic and incalculable experience of life 'for its own sake' are futile, however, given the historical spread of 'science'. (The word translates the German *Wissenschaft* or organized knowledge, under which Weber includes human sciences such as history, aesthetics and sociology, as well as the natural sciences.) Modern knowledges are based not in personality and experience but in methods, techniques and practices. And their deployment has brought ever larger tracts of life within the sphere of the calculable, subjecting them to purely technical goals of progress. It is in this context that Weber introduces the question of whether knowledge itself constitutes a vocation.

> Does 'progress' as such have a recognizable meaning that goes beyond technical ends, so that devotion to it can become a meaningful vocation? However, the question of the vocation *for* science – thus, the problem of the significance of science as a vocation for the person who devotes himself to it – is already another question: namely, what is the vocation of science within the totality of human life and what is its value? (ibid.: 14)

Weber's answer is multi-faceted. He begins by arguing that science as such as no vocation, in the sense of an overarching importance or value lying beyond its institutional existence, in terms of which it might be justified. All knowledges presuppose the validity of the 'rules of logic and method' used by them and this is unproblematic, as long as truth is understood in technical terms as the outcome of a methodically organised practice of knowledge. But these same knowledges also presuppose that what they know is 'worth knowing' or has value beyond its technical ends; that is, is valuable 'for its own sake', for the refinement of existence, the saving of lives, the operation of democratic society, and so on. And these sorts of presupposition will not work as justifications for science, says Weber, for two reasons.

In the first place, together with specific methods and techniques, they constitute the conditions of existence of particular knowledges. Hence, such presuppositions are accepted without further justification as a condition of entry to the knowledge. While they permit access to regimes of rationality they are not themselves open to a higher-level rational adjudication. So, medical science presupposes the value of preserving life, even when this entails horrendous suffering and degradation for the life being preserved. Jurisprudence can tell us what judgements are available given the ensemble of norms, precedents, statutes and procedures that constitute the legal system; but it cannot hold the ensemble itself up to meta-legal judgement. Similarly with the aesthetic and cultural sciences: they presume the value of aesthetic self-cultivation associated with a particular practice of cultural analysis but – as we can see with a vengeance today – this value lacks self evidence beyond the practice that supports it.

Secondly, because these presuppositions and valuations fall outside the spheres of organised reason that they help make possible, they are not open to 'scientific' advocacy. 'Such advocacy is meaningless in principle,' argues Weber (ibid.: 22), 'because the different value systems of the world stand in conflict with one another'. Using religious metaphor he draws an analogy between the incommensurate ethical commitments of particular knowledges and the mutually exclusive worship of different gods: 'destiny not "science" prevails over these gods and their struggles. One can only understand what the divine is for one system or another, or in one system or another' (ibid.: 23). And it is this unavailability of the values of knowledge to knowledge – their existence in the non-rational domain of practical reason and commitment – that establishes the ethical and intellectual limits of the vocation of the scholar. 'Thus the matter has reached its limit as far as discussion in a lecture room by a professor is concerned, although the great problem in *life* is naturally far from being solved. But this is an area in which powers other than universities have their say' (ibid.). We will return to Weber's somewhat manichean view of these powers below.

None the less, while arguing that 'science' itself has no vocation or general justification, Weber also argues that particular sciences can still constitute vocations – that is, occupations capable of focusing ethical commitment – for the individuals who practise them. For this to happen, however, the individual must give up the pursuit of both authentic 'personal experience', and general justifications for science and accept the personality made available by the ethic and techniques of a particular discipline. 'Ladies and gentlemen! Personality is only possessed in the realm of science by the man who serves only the *needs of his subject*, and this is true not only in science' (ibid.: 11).

Once this fundamental ethical and intellectual reorientation has been achieved *then* it is possible for the methodised knowledges or sciences to appear as vocations in both senses of the word. Then they can inculcate the ethos of acknowledging 'inconvenient' facts. They can transmit 'knowledge of the techniques by which life . . . can be controlled through calculation' as well as the 'methods of thought and the tools and education necessary for it' (ibid.: 25). Finally, and most significantly, without adjudicating in the realm of values, they can permit this realm to be 'clarified'. Social science, for example, while not allowing us to judge between competing social ends, can clarify their internal dependence on a specific *means* or social technology and on an 'ultimate' (because unjustifiable) ethical commitment. This represents both the contribution and the limits of the contribution that methodised knowledge can make to clarity. It can tell us:

> Figuratively speaking, you will serve this god *and you will offend every other* if you decide in favour of this standpoint. For you will necessarily arrive at such-and-such ultimate, internally meaningful *conclusions*, if you remain true to yourself. (ibid.: 26)

It should be clear however, in view of Weber's initial argument, that these justifications that allow science to function as a vocation for its practitioners do not provide a vocation or reason for practising science in the first place. Indeed, the ethical pertinence of such justifications is a *result* of that fundamental commitment to the ethos of a particular discipline of knowledge which Weber views as an ungrounded decision. In summary:

> Admittedly, the assumption which I am presenting here derives from the one fundamental fact – that life, as long as it is to be understood in its own terms, knows only the unending struggle between those gods. Put literally, that means the incompatibility of the ultimate *possible* attitudes towards life and therefore the inconclusiveness of the battle between them. It is thus necessary to *decide* between them. Whether, under these circumstances, science is becoming a 'vocation' for somebody, and whether science itself has a vocation which is objectively worthwhile are once again value-judgements about which nothing can be said in the lecture-room. For a positive answer is a *pre-condition* of teaching. (ibid.: 27)

The academic can *display* the vocational ethos of a particular discipline of knowledge but cannot *defend* this ethos, which is grounded only in decision and practice.

Is this why the defence of the humanities sounds so hollow and unconvincing? Why it is divorced from the knowledge formed inside the disciplines that compose the humanities? Why it is turned to only for ceremonial or apologetic purposes, when the academy is no longer attending to the 'needs of its subjects'? In short, is the defence in terms of the values of liberal education an attempt to present in the form of a rational and conditional acceptance a commitment to an ethos and an ethical technology arrived at only through unconditional decision or initiation? These questions can be answered affirmatively, although not without qualifying Weber's account in at least one significant regard.

Weber's analysis certainly clarifies the first of the problems posed at the end of our discussion of liberal education: namely, the problem of reconciling the ethical dimension of goals like 'civility' with the fact that such goals serve limited practical ends and do not form part of a complete cultivation of the person. Here Weber argues that because ethical goals are only available as the result of the practice of particular disciplines, it is meaningless to talk of a 'complete' personality organised around the general (non-specific) goal of 'personal experience'. Indeed, rather than detracting from their ethical worth, the definite, limited and practical character of the disciplines of cultivation is precisely what enables them to focus the passions and form the persons of their practitioners. The meaningfulness of knowledge and cultivation as disciplines for the lives of their practitioners is inversely related to the attempt to find meaning for them in general or in the world.

> Science today is a 'vocation' conducted through specialist disciplines to serve the cause of reflection on the self and knowledge of the relationships between facts, not a gift of grace from seers and prophets dispensing sacred values and revelations. Nor is it part of the reflections of wise men and philosophers on the *meaning* of the world. That is an inescapable fact of our historical situation, and we cannot avoid it, if we remain true to ourselves.
> (ibid.: 27)

The ethical character of cultivation thus does not lie in the goal of a true self whose completeness constitutes a synthetic ideal for all the particular disciplines of cultivation. It lies instead inside the particular disciplines whose ethical techniques form the kinds of self to which it is possible to be true.

Weber also provides significant assistance in negotiating the difficult relation between the local and practical character of the ends of cultivation and their intransitivity with regard to general social function and political rationality. Ends such as conscientiousness, civility, or the balanced sensibility are not justifications for or explanations of the disciplines of liberal explanation. The reason being that the ethical intelligibility and pertinence of these goals is the *result* of a prior commitment to or induction into these very disciplines. It is possible in Weber's terms to discuss disciplines in terms of their goals after one has committed oneself to the practical mastery of particular disciplines. It is not possible, however, to provide a general rationale for the practice of cultivation in terms of it serving a social function or political logic lying outside it; in terms, for example, of its necessity for the reproduction of class relations or the flowering of democracy. As attempts to offer a rationale for the disciplines of cultivation by attaching them to overarching functions and purposes, these explanations confront the same obstacle as attempts to justify liberal education in terms of its humanising mission: the apparently impermeable barrier that Weber erects between the scientific ethos that exists inside the methodising disciplines and the surrounding world of practical and political life. In this world, says Weber, 'words are not means of scientific analysis but means of winning over the attitudes of others politically. They are not ploughshares for loosening the soil of contemplative thought; they are swords against opponents, instruments of struggle' (ibid.: 20).

The impermeability of this barrier does indeed present difficulties, not least for the second task we have set ourselves: the clarification of the relation between the 'internal' goals of the humanities and their 'external' political administration. If Weber is right then this relation is not itself subject to scientific clarification. We would thus be left with a humanities academy irrationally committed to indefensible disciplines of cultivation and a government intent on reforming the academy using political rhetoric purely as an 'instrument of struggle'. This outcome is by no means a *reductio ad absurdum* of Weber's argument, however. Indeed, as an empirical description it possesses a high degree of plausibility. There are, none the less, real difficulties with the way in which Weber draws the distinction between the inside and the outside of knowledge.

Traditionally of course this distinction has been discussed in terms of a fundamental difference between the world of politics and value judgements and the world of science and facts. It should be clear, though, that in Weber's formulation this difference is as far from being fundamental as it is from being non-existent. For Weber, entry to the realms of demonstrable truth is not guaranteed by the nature of facts or the mind. It is the contingent result of a non-rational acceptance of the ethos and disciplines of a group of methodical behaviours and techniques. For this reason, Weber's drawing of the boundary between science and politics, the inside and outside of knowledge, is not a description of a fundamental theoretical distinction. Instead, it takes the form of an *ethical exhortation* to his student audience – a call to duty and a plea for the forms of restrained and methodical intellectual behaviour that we call 'scientific'.

In this regard, Weber's answer to the question of what might restrain scholars from using the methods of *scientia* for political and ethical advocacy is utterly clear-eyed.

> I would state as a premiss that some very respected colleagues are of the opinion that it is not possible to achieve this self-restraint and that, even if it were possible, it would be a whim to avoid it. Now one cannot demonstrate to anyone scientifically what his duty as an academic teacher is. One can only demand of him the intellectual integrity to see that the establishment of facts, the determining of logical and mathematical relations or the internal structure of cultural values, is one thing; while answers to the questions of the *value* of culture and its individual components of how one should act in the cultural community and in political associations are another. He must see that these are completely heterogeneous problems. (ibid.: 20–1)

The difficulty is that the succesful making of this demand for self-restraint – hence the consequent recognition of the fact-value distinction – is itself an act of ethical and political persuasion taking place within the disciplinary ethos that makes scientific conduct possible and desirable. In other words, Weber may well be right to differentiate the forms of reasoning achieved by methodised (scientific) conduct from those associated with attempts to provide ethical or political justifications for such conduct. But this difference cannot take the form of a fundamental theoretical distinction between knowledge and value-judgement, or science and political advocacy. There are two considerations.

The first is one that Weber is well aware of; it concerns what we might call the 'ethico-technical' character of the objective disciplines. Weber does not assume that the capacity for establishing demonstrable and repeatable truths is given in the nature of 'man' or the mind. The methodical interrogation of nature requires first the methodising of the being who interrogates. And this is in turn contingent on the deployment of a systematising ethos and techniques whose initial 'ascetic' uses are practical and ethical rather than scientific. Weber's comment on the emergence of systematic experiment as a tool for 'reliably controlling experience' is illuminating.

> Experiments had been conducted early; for instance, in India physiological in connection with the ascetic techniques of the Yogi; in Hellenic antiquity mathematical experiments for military purposes, and in the Middle Ages for the purposes of mining. But it was the achievement of the Renaissance to have made the experiment the principle of research as such. In fact the pioneers were the great innovators in the field of art – Leonardo and men like that. Above all the musical experimenters of the sixteenth century with their experimental keyboards were characteristic. From these circles, the experiment entered science, especially through Galileo, and it entered theory through Bacon. (ibid.: 16)

Devices for controlling experience, repeating and objectifying it, emerge from highly diverse departments of existence where they serve a variety of practical, ethical and political functions. Consider, for example, Marcus Aurelius' advice on how to fix and objectify perception:

> When an object presents itself to your perception, make a mental definition or at least an outline of it, so as to discern its essential character, to pierce beyond its separate attributes to a distinct view of the naked whole . . . Nothing so enlarges the mind as this ability to examine methodically and accurately every one of life's experiences. (Marcus Aurelius, 1964: 59)

The hortatory and practical character of this advice clearly places it among those other Stoic techniques for establishing consistency of conduct and individual control of the faculties. (Precisely the techniques identified by Mauss as a key element in the emergence of the category of self.) The aptitude for science, or the methodical use of the intellect, far from being theoretically divorced from ethics, is in an important sense the product of ethical discipline and technique.

The second factor undermining any fundamental distinction between science and the ethico-political is one that Weber leaves out altogether. It concerns the rationality of the political itself. Weber discusses the consequences of the rise of methodised knowledges via his famous notion of 'the disenchantment of the world'. As these knowledges spread they bring ever larger tracts of existence within the sphere of technical control and the calculable, resulting in the shrinkage of magic and the irrational. The problem is that in 'Science as a Vocation' Weber leaves (normative) political knowledge and administration completely beyond the expanding pale of rationality, in the domain of the irrational and incalculable, peopled only by false prophets and demagogues. This is of course congruent with his argument that it is impossible to adjudicate the various ethical components of life and that politics is therefore merely persuasive or coercive.

Recent work by Michel Foucault and his collaborators – Foucault (1979, 1981), Donzelot (1979a, 1979b), Lash and Whimster (1987) – suggests a new approach to this problem, however. This work has begun to provide us with an account of how the practice of politics was itself brought within the sphere of the calculable. Under the headings of 'governmentality' and the 'theory of police' this work describes the historical emergence and deployment of an array of political technologies, discourses, techniques of calculation and forms of social supervision. The effect of this deployment was the gradual transformation of the exercise of political power into a 'rational activity' in the Weberian sense; that is, into an activity responsible for subjecting a department of existence to technical control through the methodical deployment of particular instruments of calculation and intervention.

As with other areas of 'science' the transformation of government into a zone of systematic calculation and control was conditional on systematising the intellectual and ethical conduct of those who governed. Commenting on the teaching of politics in early-modern Dutch and German universities, and in particular on the use of classical Stoic texts as ethics manuals, Gerhard Oestreich has this to say:

> The major concept in politics was *prudentia civilis* or *prudentia politica*. This embraced the whole area of the training of princes and the education of their advisers, the new bureaucracy and, not least, the military. At the same time it took in all the institutions of the early modern state. Political ethics, like prescriptions for private morality, gave direct precepts for practical conduct. At the universities education was directed not to the transmission of knowledge, but to the training of men for active life. Jesuit and Calvinist teachers alike, at schools and universities, insisted on the constant revision of what had been learnt and on the training of the will, the aim being the attainment of *virtus socialis*, active involvement in social life. (Oestreich, 1982: 162)

It appears that the exercise of power was not exempt from those rationalising developments that Weber holds responsible for the emergence of other scientific domains.

It is thus possible to argue a 'Weberian' critique of Weber's dichotomy between the rational and the political. And something like this is implied in the following remark by Foucault:

As for all relations among men, many factors determine power. Yet rationalisation is also constantly working away at it. There are specific forms to such rationalisation. It differs from the rationalisation peculiar to economic processes, or to production and communication techniques; it differs from that of scientific discourse. The government of men by men – whether they form small or large groups, whether it is power exerted by men over women, or by adults over children, or by one class over another, or by a bureaucracy over a population – involves a certain type of rationality. It doesn't involve instrumental violence. (Foucault, 1981: 253–4)

In short, politics is not an irrational universe surrounding the rational activities of the sciences – a universe characterised by the 'unending struggle' between contradictory and indefensible ethical presuppositions. Rather, it is itself one such rational activity, carved out when the exercise of power and those who exercised it were subjected to the methodical disciplines of an emergent technology of government.

Weber's attempt to establish a hard and fast dichotomy between science and the ethico-political is thus eroded from both directions. On one side, the objective disciplines are dependent on the ethos and ethical discipline of their practitioners, and this transmits ethical normativity to the heart of the sciences, as we can see in the instances of medicine, jurisprudence, aesthetics, sociology, and so on. On the other side, through the deployment of systematic forms of political calculation and intervention, government has itself acquired an objective character. And this has resulted in various formerly more autonomous 'components of culture' – including the universities – themselves being opened to technical calculation and control.

We are now in a better position to grasp the second topic of our discussion, the historical character of political rationality. We have already noted the strong similarity between Foucault's history of the 'governmentalising' of politics and Weber's account of the 'rationalising' of other areas of human activity and endeavour. In light of this we can suggest that the sphere of government is rational in the same sense as other scientific domains. In other words, its rationality does not lie outside it in the form of general values or principles that justify adherence to it. The goals that governmentality proposes for itself – maximising the prosperity and security of the state, optimalising the health, good order, productivity and well being of its citizens – are not rational justifications for the governmental sphere. They are values whose ethical pertinence is available to individuals only after their induction into the disciplines of government. In short, to speak of the rationality of government is to refer to the manner in which its subjects are rendered methodical and its objects calculable through the deployment of systematising instruments and disciplines.

For this very reason, however, the objectives of government cannot be entertained or dismissed at will. If government is only rendered calculable through the deployment of definite and limited political and intellectual disciplines then these set limits to the forms of political will and imagination that they empower. At the same time it must be acknowledged that there are other forms of politics than the governmental. In particular there is the organised competition for power through the system of political parties and elections. Dependent on the political mobilisation of populations around charismatic leaders and platforms, the system of electoral party politics has overlapped the machinery of governmental politics in an unplanned and fluctuating manner. None the less the forms of political expertise character-istic of bureaucratically managed states were historically autonomous of the party politics with which they have become entwined, and remain significantly autonomous today. Risking a degree of simplification, then, it is possible to say that the governmental disciplines are the central determinants of the calculable pursuit of politics. They have not existed for all time, however, and they exist today only as contingently deployed techniques, institutions and forms of calculation. This is what it means to talk of the historical character of political rationality.

The consequences for our discussion of the political rationality of the humanities should be clear enough. Political calculability is not something that the academic disciplines have possessed in all historical circumstances – in those of the seventeenth and eighteenth centuries, for example. It is something that was formed when new administrative and intellectual technologies began to link up previously dispersed departments of existence and centres of power – including the universities – into a ramified governmental network. We would therefore expect the 'governmentalising' of the university to take the form of a piecemeal and contingent extension of the instruments and ethos of political calculation to academic institutions and disciplines.

4. Governing the humanities

To break the spell of the fantasmatic and disabling oppositions between cultivation and utility, the liberal and the vocational, science and politics, we must learn to come to terms with both the technical character of the humanities and the instrumental character of government. In the light of the preceding discussion it should be clear that the technical character of the humanities lies not in their 'external' subordination to technical purposes but in their 'internal' dependence on definite and limited ethical and intellectual techniques of cultivation. It should be equally clear that to speak of the instrumental character of government is not to refer to its subordination to extrinsic social ends or political purposes. Rather, this signifies the fact that government in modern states is dependent on the deployment of specific instruments – of recording, calculation, intervention – which has transformed the exercise of power into a 'rational activity'. Let us say that the form in which the humanities academy has been governmentalised is contingent on a series of exchanges between the ethical and intellectual techniques of today's liberal education and the governmental technologies responsible for bringing education within the sphere of political calculation.

As far as the technical character of the humanities is concerned, I have discussed this in detail elsewhere (Hunter, 1988), so I will be brief here. Perhaps the most important consequence of the dependence of the cultivation of personhood on definite and limited ethical techniques is one that we have already discussed: it means that there is no synthetic form of the person (the 'complete' personality) or ideal formative domain ('personal experience'). Weber's contempt for the Romantic cult of personality and his critique of attempts to provide rational justification for the rationalising knowledges stem from the same source: his recognition that the various goals of cultivation and objectives of the sciences are not the *reason for* the deployment of particular technologies of cultivation and methods of knowledge but the *result of* such deployment, which is itself without further justification. Consequently there is no essential form of the person or ideal form of cultivation to which the humanities academy might lay claim to defend its autonomy. Other ways and places in which persons are formed – in armies, monasteries, medical schools, families, battleships, clan systems, courts, legal systems – are neither worse nor better than the humanities academy on some scale of 'humanity', only different. (Needless to say, this does not prevent us from making relevant ethical and political judgements on other, more local and pragmatic, scales).

It is for this reason that, as we saw in the first part of the argument, the liberal education has no essential form, and the university arts faculty has not been its historically inevitable vehicle. Between the sixteenth and nineteenth centuries something called liberal education was carried out in a variety of milieus outside the university. And where, as in certain continental arts faculties, something called humanism was taught it bore little relation to what we call liberation education. Indeed, it was often supporting a variety of ends associated with the transformation of politics into a science by reducing government to method and methodising the conduct of the governors. Hence, if we are to understand the history of the humanities academy we must give up the story of its ancient origin as the institutional actualisation of an ideal cultivation of the person. Instead, we must develop a description of the quite recent historical circumstances in which a specific set of ethical and intellectual techniques left the sphere of voluntary self-cultivation and achieved a more systematic deployment via residency in the corporate 'shell' of the university.

We can observe in passing that these circumstances of emergence have created an inescapable instability in the humanities disciplines, between their 'ascetic' and 'scientific' deployments. We have noted Weber's argument that the methodological interrogation of nature was dependent on methodising the faculties and conduct of the interrogators, and that this was in turn dependent on 'disciplines of the self' whose initial deployment was ethical and ascetic rather than scientific. One of the leading features of the modern humanities is their incorporation of specific ascetic disciplines. In the 'critical' (Romantic) teaching of literature and history, for example, texts are not the objects of a methodised knowledge. They are devices attached to practices of reading and writing whose object is the problematisation and stylisation of the reader's 'divided' or otherwise 'incomplete' self. If this begins to indicate the way in which such practices differ from philological or 'object-oriented' forms of literary and historical scholarship it is also a significant index of the tasks of moral formation now performed by the humanities.

Finally, the 'technical' basis of liberal cultivation is responsible not only for its variable and 'migratory' character but also for the contingency of its historical 'spread' or penetration of social space. We have rejected the idea that cultivations of personhood have a universal (because essential) form, and recognised instead their dependence on the deployment of definite and limited techniques of cultivation.[6] But this means that the degree of generality of specific forms of cultivation must be discussed in terms of the institutional systematisation of their deployments or 'apparatuses'. Should we be surprised to learn, then, that the current generality and social significance of the liberally cultivated personality, far from being opposed to the sphere of the governmental calculation, is indeed one of its by-products – the result of the dissemination of the techniques of cultivation through the school and university systems? We shall return to this possibility directly.

Before doing so we should clarify what is meant by the 'instrumental' character of government. The central phenomenon to be grasped here is the 'rationalisation' of the exercise of power that followed the historical deployment of calculable political technologies. Foucault (1981: 240–54) discusses the following developments, amongst others: the appearance (at the beginning of the seventeenth century) of discourses defining government not in terms of legality and justice but as an 'art' or set of techniques for specifying and augmenting the strength, productivity and security of the state and for securing the good order and welfare of its citizens; the deployment of statistical survey and associated forms of recording and calculation which were capable of rendering an ever-widening array of areas – health, criminality, poverty, ignorance, production and consumption – into objects of administrative calculation and intervention; and the invention during the eighteenth and nineteenth centuries of a new array of political technologies – mass school systems, prisons and asylums, centres of bureaucratic adminis-tration, public health systems, social insurance – able to transform the life of the population in accordance with the objectives of government. These and other parallel developments are catalogued in Small's (1909) great com-pendium, *The Cameralists: The Pioneers of German Social Polity*. 'Government' in Foucault's lexicon thus does not refer to an historically specific vehicle for an eternal will to power. Instead, it refers to an historically specific form of power: one that emerged when the form and objectives of statecraft were brought within the sphere of the calculable through the development of new political and intellectual technologies.

Perhaps the central casualty of this shift in perspective is a particular conception of the state. This is a conception in which the state is pictured as a vehicle through which sovereign power is exercised according to a general will or principles (to protect capitalism, realise the good life, secure the greatest good of the greatest number) and is forever encroaching on an essentially different realm – civil society, priviate life, the 'public sphere' – where power resides in close proximity to rationality, cultivation and community. The history and theory of governmentality problematises both sides of the picture. If the forms and objectives of the exercise of power have become dependent on specific intellectual and political technologies, then government cannot be a vehicle for the sovereign will or principles of the state. Rather 'the state' will represent a particular historical configuration of the technologies of government. It is in this context that Rose and Miller speak of the 'governmentalization of the state' as an historical phenomenon emergent during the eighteenth century.

> States began to be transformed from limited and circumscribed central apparatuses to embed themselves within an ensemble of institutions, procedures, analyses and reflections, calculations and tactics that sought to shape and enhance the strength of the nation through a calculated supervision and administration of the forces of each and all. (Rose and Miller, 1989: 4)

At the same time, if the state was only the inheritor of political powers and rationalities formed in the technologies of 'government', then neither was it set apart from community, private life or the 'public sphere' through the coercive or manipulative pursuit of sovereign power. In flagrant disregard of the borders between state and civil society, coercion and consent, the technologies and agents of government are widely dispersed in social space – across medical, educational, insurantial, managerial, therapeutic, bureaucratic, ethical, fiscal sites – forming many local centres of calculation and intervention.

What this means is that power is not exercised by some agents who possess it for their own ends against other agents who lack it. Rather, the goals and exercise of power are effects of the deployment of those intellectual and political technologies that render reality calculable as an object of administration. The articulation of these technologies around specific objectives constitutes a political programme and it is the programme, argue Rose and Miller, that establishes parameters for the viability and intelligibility of political principles and ideals.

> programmes are something more than merely the formulation of wishes or intentions. . . . They first of all lay claim to a certain knowledge of the sphere or problem to be addressed – knowledges of the economy, or the nature of health, or the problem of poverty are essential elements in programmes that seek to exercise legitimate and calculated power over them. But further, programmes presuppose that the real is programmable – they make the objects of concern thinkable in such a way as to be

understandable, enabling their ills to be diagnosed, their cures prescribed, evil averted and good ensured. Government thus depends upon rendering the field to be governed into thought as a domain subject to certain determinants, rules, norms and processes that can be acted upon and improved by authorities. (ibid.: 11)

Two consequences follow for our understanding of governmental power. First, there is no single point from which this power can or should be resisted. A general 'oppositional' politics is unintelligible if the field of calculable political objectives and programmes is co-extensive with the governmental field. Second, at the same time, the exercise of power in this field is neither uniform nor guaranteed. If governmental power is indeed formed across a dispersed array of institutions, sites, techniques of calculation, then its exercise is not automatic but contingent on the composition of the array into a functioning network.

> The 'power' of a government, a Department of State, a local authority, a military commander or a manager in an enterprise is thus conditional upon their capacity to compose and stabilise an assemblage of forces by means of which their objectives and injunctions can be translated into the actions and calculations of others. . . . Translation is successful only to the extent that one agent manages to impose a particular way of thinking and acting upon another, assembling agents in a network because they have come to understand their interests according to a certain language and logic, the dependencies and relations required of them, enrolling them because they have come to identify with others and to construe their goals and their fate as in some way inextricable. (ibid.: 15–16)

Thus, in Rose and Miller's analysis, power is not an explanation for a government's success in composing such a network. It is something explained as an effect of particular strategies of composition, which may or may not succeed.

In the light of these remarks on the rationality of government and the technical character of the humanities, we can conclude by proposing four topics for future discussions of the place of the humanities in the governmental sphere.

4.1 The governmentalising of liberal education and the liberalising of government

The disciplines of the modern humanities took their place in the university not as prodigals returning to their natural home, nor as emissaries of a state bent on exploiting their moral powers for its own ideological ends. Instead, their appearance was tied to an historical event that occurred quite outside the academic sphere: the governmental construction of a school system whose object was the education of the entire population. This event was the direct result of the developments mentioned above – the gradual deployment of an array of political and intellectual technologies which rendered the productivity and welfare of populations calculable and governable. The emergence in the early nineteenth century of a programme which linked national well-being to the intellectual and moral education of the 'popular classes' was due neither to the idealism of radical reformers nor to the logic of state power. It was the result of the massing of a whole series of social surveys, reform campaigns, architectural innovations, evangelical movements, pedagogical theories and ethical imperatives. Above all, it was the product of the deployment of an array of powerful 'disciplinary' techniques – of observation, normalisation, optimalisation. These transformed the physical health, intellectual abilities and ethical bearing of whole populations into objects of political measurement and intervention. The agents of this new governmental technology were not philosophers or plutocrats, prophets of culture or minions of capitalism; they were pedagogues, doctors, social reformers, statisticians, bureaucrats, feminists, worker's associations, religous societies – in short all those whose interests were 'translatable' into the new political rationality of governmental education.

The result of these developments was the appearance of an unprecedented conception and apparatus of education: a system of institutions in which the social attributes of the population could be rendered governable through calculated management of the milieus, disciplines and relationships responsible for forming the person. It was this governmentally conceived and executed 'pedagogisation' of the social sphere that was responsible for the migration of the disciplines of liberal cultivation first to teachers colleges and then to universities, during the latter part of the nineteenth century. The old philologically based classical arts faculties were thus reorganised around a new core of ethical and intellectual disciplines, concentrated in the teaching of 'English' and history. The role of these disciplines was indeed 'liberal', in being focused on the formation of personality not the objectification of knowledge. Of course, the personality formed was no longer invested in the civilised figure of the gentleman or the cultivated persona of the aesthete, but in a series of new personnages – first the sympathetic teacher and administrator, then the guidance counsellor, welfare officer and therapist – without whom the strategy of educating the population through 'moral management' could not function. These personages have come to form a stratum for whom the cultivation of personality is a vocation in both senses of the word.

In other words, the current importance of liberal studies in the university is a direct result of their role in forming the special personalities and personnel required by the education system. While thus being governmentalised, however, the disciplines of liberal education have in their turn contributed to the liberalisation of government. Their deployment means that the pedagogical government of the population is not carried out through the coercive inculcation of dogmas, but through the unintrusive supervision of the techniques and milieux in which individuals form themselves as persons.

4.2 The porosity of the university shell

In fact the reorganisation of the university arts faculty around the new disciplines of the humanities – disciplines whose 'personalising' form is in no sense at odds with their governmental function – is a local instance of a wider field of events. From the middle of the nineteenth century the classical, clerical and collegial organisation of the old universities was penetrated by a variety of new forces. Often moving at a tangent to each other, these forces have colonised existing elements of the university or implanted new ones. In linking these elements to extra-mural programmes, interests and enterprises they have stripped the assets of the old university and left it – in Coleman's (1973) description – as a corporate 'shell', open to a variety of investments. In young countries like Australia this process provided the formative milieu of the university.

Without attemping to be exhaustive, it is possible to take note of the following instances: the establishment of centres of research, development and teaching attached to the agricultural and mining industries, either as independent institutes (Australia) or incorporated in state universities (America); the attachment of specific academic disciplines to governmental programmes in the areas of public health, medical research and defence, through the targeted provision of research funding; the ethical, intellectual and political autonomisation of schools of medicine and law, deriving from their role in producing expert personnel for prestige professions; the appearance of a whole scatter of research institutes, in fields ranging from social policy to space research, criminology to genetic engineering, whose attachment to a variety of external sources of funds and objectives leaves them largely independent of the university shell; and, in Germany and America in particular, the development of research schools, removed from undergraduate teaching, and dedicated to forming the expertise and personnel required by an array of scholarly professions.

So, while they were by no means duplicated in these other instances, the events which saw the 'liberal' reorganisation of arts facilities around the personnel requirements of popular education, were far from isolated. The corporate shell of the university has proved capable of focusing a wide variety of forces and initiatives. Meeting with little resistance, these penetrate the university on a variety of tangents and continuously redistribute its contents across a variety of functional fields. And along each of these lines of penetration the academic disciplines have been connected to the governmental field through specific bridgeheads. Whether through concerns with national security or social justice, public health or equal opportunity, professional personnel or 'liberal' personalities, lines of communication and translation have been established between the ethics and expertise of the scientific vocations and the technologies and programmes of government. In short, despite all talk of disinterested research and complete cultivation, the university in general and the humanities in particular have not proved impervious to the 'demands of society'. To the contrary, they have proved quite porous. And, far from constituting an ethical and theoretical cockpit from which all of social life might be guided, the university is in fact a shell for a divergent array of programmes, functions, knowledges, norms and objectives whose calibration and interrelation occurs only through 'governmentality'.[7]

4.3 The contingency of government

Nevertheless, even if the various elements of the university – including the humanities – lack the autonomy promised by the transcendence of social purpose, and even if the interrelation of these elements is intelligible only in terms of governmental calculations and objectives, this does not mean that they are in danger of becoming mere tools of an extrinsic political will or principle (the state, capitalism, utility, instrumental reason). As we have seen, government is not the expression of a general political will or principle. It is the historical consequence of the deployment of a limited ensemble of techniques, institutions and forms of calculation in which a particular range of political goals and programmes can be formulated. For this reason, even though academic activities lack the transcendent character necessary to preserve them from the horrors of usefulness, their 'governmentalising' has not been achieved by rendering them transparent and subordinate to a sovereign political power or logic. The process is far more piecemeal and uncertain than this, in being dependent on the practical execution of a series of measures whose success is by no means predictable.

First, academic activities have been linked to governmental objectives through specific *problematisations*. The adequacy of the educational provision was called into question by linking it initially to the problems of crime and poverty, then to the problems of national efficiency and productivity, and recently to the public funding and accountability of universities themselves. Second, these linkages are dependent on the deployment of particular *instruments of calculation*. It was the deployment of statistical analysis that first made the social and moral costs of inadequate education calculable and manageable; and today the form in which educational problems are conceived and assessed remains dependent on specific instruments for the inscription, storage and interrogation of information. Finally, these connections are maintained through a range of *administrative and managerial techniques*. Religious schools were first subjected to state supervision by tying their funding to inspection, and as governments have increased their share in the funding of universities they have deployed a range of techniques – of load calculation, cost accounting, performance measurement – designed to achieve public accountability and supervision.

The Australian Government's recent White Paper seeks to problematise higher education by linking it to the problems of national productivity and national debt. It proposes to introduce new instruments for inscribing, storing and monitoring higher education's vital statistical signs and for calculating its cost and efficiency. And it seeks to deploy new administrative mechanisms by tying research funding to institutional performance and size, introducing performance and other accountability measures, and equipping academics with administrative expertise. While these measures place the proposed restructuring of higher education firmly in the governmental field, they by no means signal the presence of the implacable and deadening hand of state intervention. Rather, viewed in the light of Rose and Miller's analysis, they represent an attempt to compose a particular network of forces. The White Paper constructs a specific programmatic intelligibility for the field of higher education and floats goals and objectives into which a variety of interested parties might translate their interests. There are a number of reasons for insisting on the contingency of the governmental process.

First, there is the dispersed and highly ramified character of the higher education network itself. It includes not only the scatter of disciplines, knowledges, projects and activities that have installed themselves in the university shell – not to mention the surrounding institutions, professions and programmes to which they are attached – but a wide variety of interest groups: staff associations, quangos, student unions, professional associations, university councils, and the coporate vice-chancellors. Second, there is the obstacle posed by the statutory autonomy of the Australian university's corporate shell. While this shell has proved porous to all manner of extra-mural forces and functions its legal independence as an administrative agency prevents direct ministerial and departmental control, ensuring that supervision will take place at a distance, through 'governmental' means. Third, in the case of the humanities academy, there is the ethical and intellectual 'intransitivity' arising from its dependence on definite and limited ethical techniques and disciplines. These give rise to internal goals – the aesthetic sensibility, the self-critical intellect – whose 'translatability' into governmental norms and objectives is a contingent matter. Finally, and most importantly, there is the sheer contingency of the mechanisms of government themselves. A particular problematisation may or may not succeed in expanding the sphere of the calculable, depending how difficult it is to construct and operate, its success in enrolling a variety of interest groups, and so on. And new managerial mechanisms – for example, the tying of institutional funding to efficiency, and research funding to performance measures – may or may not create a new administrative environment for universities, depending on the degree of compliance they meet with, the spread of expertise required for their operation, and their cost efficiency.

To recall Rose and Miller, the success of such measures in composing the network of forces around a specific programme is neither guaranteed nor explained by recourse to 'state power'. Rather, such success – in its contingency and variability – explains the degree and scope of governmental power, such as we may happen to find it in particular circumstances.

4.4 The strategic character of ethico-political activity

Finally, the contingency of the governmental field notwithstanding, it is futile for the humanities academy to attempt to place itself beyond this field by appealing to absolute ethical and intellectual principles – complete cultivation and the disinterested pursuit of knowledge.

On the one hand, we learn from Weber that such goals are not justifications for the ethical and intellectual techniques of the sciences, only signs of their practical deployment. Moreover, our historical discussion of liberal education shows that what counts as 'complete' or 'disinterested' varies with the deployment of specific technologies of cultivation and with the historical circumstances under which they are deployed. The ethical and intellectual goals of the humanities do not transcend their practical deployment.

On the other hand, turning Weber against himself, we have also argued that the field of government itself has a rational and ethical character. The historical appearance of a specific set of political and intellectual technologies systematises the conduct of the governors and transforms the exercise of power into a rational art, just as Weber envisages for the other 'sciences'. This dependence of government on the ethical regimentation of its practices and practitioners explains why its objectives – to relieve poverty, diminish crime, improve morality, increase productivity, secure the well-being of the population – are so thoroughly normative. The techniques of government, we might say, transform ethical norms into objects of political calculation and administration.

Hence, not only are the goals of the humanities technical but the techniques of government are rational and ethical. Government confronts the humanities not as a coercive or philistine use of power but in the form of a series of rational and ethical programmes. Some of these, such as the improvement of national economic efficiency and productivity, can no doubt be subjected to the usual denunciations; others – expanding the number of university places, increasing the participation of women, intervening in irrational employment and promotions procedures, equalising per-student funding – cannot.

This is not to say of course that governmental initiatives are infallible and self-actualising. To the contrary, I have stressed their fallibility and fragility by pointing to the contingency of the problematisations, forms of calculation and political technologies that form particular programmes. It is to say, however, that it is the programme that establishes the parameters for political understanding and activity. We cannot understand the way in which the humanities are governed by discoursing on their responsibility for complete cultivation or the disinterested pursuit of truth. That is indeed the speech that all can give but few will listen to. Rather, understanding can be reached only by clarifying the piecemeal negotiations, translations and transformations that link the ideals and disciplines of the humanities to the ethics and technologies of government. This accounts for the inescapably provisional and strategic character of such understanding.

5. Conclusion

If the political rationality of the humanities is not inherent in their 'humanising' mission, then neither is it imposed on them by general political principles such as utility. Taken in tandem, the 'ultimate' (decisionistic) character of the disciplines of cultivation and the contingent character of political rationality, mean that we cannot understand the governmentalisation of the humanities in terms of their transparent subordination to political reason. But neither can it be understood as a coercive intervention doomed to failure by the unsurpassable character of their ethical or rational goals; that is, by the allegedly fundamental dichotomies between science and politics, cultivation and utility, personality and vocation. (The instruments and disciplines of the governmental sphere are no less ethical and rational than those of the academic disciplines and possess exactly the same kind of autonomy.) Instead, I have argued that this process takes place through the practical establishment of a series of 'bridgeheads' or relay-points permitting exchanges to take place between two initially disparate ethical institutions: the disciplines of cultivation and the technologies of government.

This is the historical and theoretical context in which we must view the relations between government and the humanities: as a series of specific points of exchange between a group of literary, philosophical and historical disciplines, organised around goals of aesthetic stylisation and intellectual clarification, and a political technology calculating the outcomes of education in terms of productivity and welfare, efficiency and equity. For this reason the place of the humanities academy in the governmental sphere can neither be read-off from its own ethical and intellectual goals nor directly derived from the governmental ends proposed for it. Instead, it must be described in terms of series of open-ended negotiations, resistances, translations and interventions flowing between the disciplines of the humanities and the methodology of government. Academics seeking to engage with this reality – who wish to, in Weber's (1948: 128) words, 'measure up to the world as it is in its everyday routine' – must learn not to look down on these exchanges but to live up to them.

Divison of Humanities, Griffith University
Brisbane, Queensland, Australia, 4111

Notes

1   This paper is a revised version of my contribution to a larger collaborative project on the political rationality of the humanities. Funding for this project provided by the Australian Research Council and the assistance of the Institute for Cultural Policy Studies at Griffith University are both gratefully acknowledged. In developing the present analysis I benefited greatly from the work and comments of my co-researchers, Denise Meredyth, Bruce Smith and Geoff Stokes. Comments by Barry Hindess, David Saunders and one of this journal's anonymous reviewers were responsible for significant qualifications to and clarifications of the argument. Finally I should like to thank Nikolas Rose and Peter Miller for permission to quote from their unpublished working-paper 'Rethinking the State: Governing Economic, Social and Personal Life'.

2   Here it might seem that I am neglecting the more pragmatic defence according to which the humanities are justified in terms of their role in producing generalist graduates possessing 'transferable skills'. Despite the fact that it tells us very little about what sort of abilities and dispositions the humanities actually produce in their students, this defence seems quite unexceptional. The difficulty that it presents for the concerns of this paper arises from its role as a sort of 'half-way house' between the defenders of liberal and vocational education. In this role it can neither display the ethical commitments nor reveal the intentions of the antagonists who meet in it. For this reason it is not treated as a topic in its own right.

3   In the Australian case, for example, commentaries on the Green Paper such as Davis (1988) have pointed out that the connection between educational input and economic outcomes, postulated in the governmental equation, is neither clear nor direct. There are real technical difficulties in calculating the needs of the labour market and co-ordinating the forms of expertise required by industry with those produced by the university. Moreover, there is no clear empirical connection between prioritising technological and production-oriented education in the universities and the improvement of national productivity and international competitiveness. In the case of two highly economically competitive nations, German universities give little emphasis to technological training because of the amount undertaken by industry itself; and Japanese universities give high priority to general liberal studies, for the same reason.

4   I say 'leading tendency' because there is a counter-current in the argument which treats the relation between modern Western and other elaborations of the person as one of evolution towards the highest possible form. This teleological current is the source of significant ambiguities in Mauss's argument; however, these are not dealt with further in this paper.

5   For an account of the role of print technology in these changes in the French context, see Chartier (1987).

6   Given our Romantic heritage it cannot be too often observed that the forms of cultivation – and this applies especially to aesthetic culture – are not a birthright but depend upon the practical mastery of specialised, often esoteric, techniques. Weber's remarks on the differential religious qualification of particular social groups can be readily applied to other forms of cultural qualification, such as the aesthetic.

> The empirical fact, important for us, that men are *differently qualified* in a religious way stands at the beginning of the history of religion. This fact has been dogmatized in the sharpest rationalist form in the 'particularism of grace,' embodied in the doctrine of predestination by the Calvinists. The sacred values that have been most cherished, the ecstatic and visionary capacities of shamans, sorcerers, ascetics, and pneumatics of all sorts, could not be attained by everyone. The possession of such faculties is a 'charisma,' which, to be sure, might be awakened in some but not in all. It follows from this that all intensive religiosity has a sort of status qualification, in

accordance with differences in the charismatic qualifications. 'Heroic' or 'virtuoso' religiosity is opposed to mass religiosity. (Weber, 1948: 287)

The peculiarity of our situation is that we live at a time in which the formerly virtuoso charismatic qualification of the aesthete has been widely distributed through the incorporation of its disciplines in a governmental school system.

7   Here the 'portmanteau' character of Foucault's term – its capacity to join the exercise of power to a mentality peculiar to government – is a useful reminder of the dependence of government on a specific kind of expertise and of the latter on the administrative field formed by the exercise governmental power.

References

Arnold, M. (1932) *Culture and Anarchy*, edited with an introduction by J. Dover Wilson, Cambridge: Cambridge University Press. (First published 1869.)
Aurelius, Marcus (1964) *Meditations*, trans. M. Staniforth, New York: Dorset Press.
Australian Historical Association (1988) 'History and Higher Education: A Response to Higher Education a Policy Discussion Paper', in the *Australian Historical Association Bulletin*, (July): 29–36.
Baldwin, T. W. (1944) *William Shakespeare's Small Latine and Lesse Greeke*, Urbana: University of Illinois Press.
Brett, J. (1988) 'Uphill Battle for the Humanities', *Australian Society*, (February).
Chartier, R. (1987) *The Cultural Uses of Print in Early Modern France*, Princeton NJ: Princeton University Press.
Cleland, J. (1948) *The Institution of a Young Noble Man*, New York: Scholar's Facsimile Reprints.
Coady, C. A. J. (1988) 'The Academy and the State', *The Australian Universities' Review*, vol. 31.
Coleman, J. S. (1973) 'The University and Society's New Demands Upon It', in C. Kaysen (ed.), *Content and Context: Essays on College Education*, New York: McGraw-Hill.
Davis, D. J. (1988) 'Flexibility and Future Labour Needs in the Light of the Green Paper: a Consideration of the EHW Factor', in G. Harman and V. Lyn Meek (eds), *Australian Higher Education Reconstructed?*, Armidale, Department for

Administrative and Higher Education Studies, University of New England.
Dawkins, J. S. (1987) *The Challenge for Higher Education in Australia*, Canberra: Australian Government Publishing Service.
—— (1988) *Higher Education: a Policy Statement* (the White Paper), Canberra: Australian Government Publishing Service.
Donzelot, J. (1979a) 'The Poverty of Political Culture', *Ideology and Consciousness*, 5: 73–86.
—— (1979b) *Policing the Family*, London: Hutchinson.
Elias, N. (1982) *State Formation and Civilization*, Oxford: Blackwell.
Foucault, M. (1979) 'On Governmentality', *I & C*, 6: 5–22.
—— (1981) 'Omnes et Singulatim: Towards a Critique of Political Reason', in S. McMurrin (ed.), *The Tanner Lectures on Human Value* II, Salt Lake City: University of Utah Press.
Grafton, A. (1981) 'Teacher, Text and Class Room: A Case Study from a Parisian College', *History of Universities*, 1: 37–70.
—— (1983) 'From Ramus to Ruddiman: The *Studia Humanitatis* in a Scientific Age', in N. Phillipson (ed.), *Universities, Society and the Future*, Edinburgh: Edinburgh University Press.
Hegel, G. W. F. (1979) *System of Ethical Life* and *First Philosophy of Spirit*, translated and edited by H. S. Harris and T. M. Knox, Albany: State University of New York Press.
Hunter, I. (1988) *Culture and Government: The Emergence of Literary*

Education, London: Macmillan.

Kant, I. (1986) 'What is Englighten-ment?', in *Philosophical Writings*, E. Behler (ed.), New York: Continuum.

Lash, S. and Whimster, S. (eds) (1987) *Max Weber, Rationality and Modernity*, London: Allen & Unwin.

Leinster-Mackay, D. P. (1979) 'The Idea of a University: A Historical Perspective on Some Precepts and Practice', *Vestes* (The Australian Universities' Review), 20.

Light, A. (1989) 'Two Cheers for Liberal Education', in P. Brooker and P. Humm, *Dialogue and Difference: English into the Nineties*, London: Routledge.

Mauss, M. (1973) 'Techniques of the Body', *Economy and Society*, 2: 70–88.

—— (1985) 'A Category of the Human Mind: the Notion of Person; the Notion of Self', in M. Carrithers, S. Collins and S. Lukes (eds), *The Category of the Person: Anthropology, Philosophy, History*, Cambridge: Cambridge University Press.

Miller, P. and Rose, N. (1990) 'Governing Economic Life', *Economy and Society*, 19: 1–31.

Minogue, K. R. (1973) *The Concept of a University*, Berkeley and Los Angeles: University of California Press.

Newman, J. H. (1959) *The Idea of a University*, New York: Image Books.

OECD (1982) *Policies for Higher Education in the Eighties*, Paris, OECD.

—— (1987a) *Universities Under Scrutiny*, Paris: OECD.

—— (1987b) *Structural Adjustment and Economic Performance*, Paris: OECD.

Oestreich, G. (1982) *Neostoicism and the Early Modern State*, Cambridge: Cambridge University Press.,

Rose, N. and Miller, P. (1989) 'Rethinking the State: Governing Economic, Social and Personal Life', unpublished working paper. For further discussion see Miller and Rose (1990).

Rothblatt, S. (1976) *Tradition and Change in Liberal Education: An Essay in History and Culture*, London: Faber & Faber.

Small, A. W. (1909) *The Cameralists: The Pioneers of German Social Polity*, Chicago: University of Chicago Press.

Weber, M. (1948) *From Max Weber: Essays in Sociology*, translated, edited and introduced by H. H. Gerth and C. Wright Mills, London: Routledge & Kegan Paul.

—— (1989) 'Science as a Vocation', in P. Lassman, I. Velody and H. Martins (eds), *Max Weber's 'Science as a Vocation'*, London: Unwin Hyman.

Williams, B. (1987) 'What Hope for the Humanities?', *Educational Review*, 39.

9 Archaeologizing genealogy
Michel Foucault and the economy of austerity

Phil Bevis, Michèle Cohen and Gavin Kendall

Abstract

Analysing the development and transformations of Michel Foucault's *Histoire de la sexualité* project, we find a pivotal series of 'monolithic' conceptions, organized around the *archaeus* of an 'austere economy'. We argue that three series of 'gaps' condition the particularities of the texts: Foucault's decisions are related strategically to psychoanalysis as a technology of the self.

Introduction

In this paper, we examine Michel Foucault's project of a *History of Sexuality*.[1] Through an attempt to lay the basis for an account of its development, we want to re-open a discussion of how it came to be transformed in the process of its execution. In raising the question of *how* these transformations occurred, we would like to apply some of Foucault's investigative and analytical procedures to his own work: the aim would be to establish the conditions of possibility for the process of re-vision whereby Foucault's gaze falls upon an apparently different series of problematics as successive volumes are written and published.[2] In short, what we propose might be seen as some sort of 'archaeology', an archaeology of Foucault's last major genealogical enterprise. Clearly, some of the transformations of the *History of Sexuality* are related to the changing strategies Foucault adopted for his ongoing project – realizing a genealogy of sexuality would need to work towards a radical break with the very deployments we presently take for granted. Nevertheless, we try to show how the organization of the project also related throughout its development to a series of considerations never explicitly evident in the texts themselves: an invisible hand seems to grip the tiller of his vessel *The History of Sexuality*, a fleshless hand which none the less bears the unmistakable stigmata of a Christian asceticism.

Published in *Economy and Society Volume 18 Number 3 August 1989*

The rationale for our work should not be understood as an attempt to evaluate Foucault's project as either 'right' or 'wrong', nor do we wish to imply that Foucault's choices in the conduct of his project were 'incorrect'; it is obviously possible to defend his decisions as to what are appropriate targets for consideration, and we recognize that every piece of work can make interventions only on a basis of strategic decisions. The published text is not the handmaiden of some final truth(s), the means by which dogmata might be established, so much as a grille which might open up new avenues for inquiry. Our assessment of Foucault's work will thus centre around two interrelated questions: first of all, how far does it satisfy its own conditions as a genealogy? – that is, how far does it provide a history of the present and give us a convincing description of the conditions of possibility for that present? Second, what scope for intervention does it facilitate? how far does it enable us to think differently? In particular, we are concerned over the restructuring, the *penser autrement*, of the relation between self, sexuality and truth: are there aspects of Foucault's work which either obstruct or facilitate such reconceptualizations? These questions in turn relate to problems over the conduct of a genealogy – what procedural steps can be justified and what steps are in themselves problematic?

To prepare for some of the arguments in this essay, it is necessary for us to make a digression at this point on archaeology and genealogy: we need to expand on how Foucault's treatment of these 'toolkits' gives rise to what we term a 'gap', itself the condition of possibility for Foucault's texts. The exact relation between genealogy and archaeology in Foucault's work has been the source of much dispute. However, it seems clear that Foucault himself regarded archaeology (or, as he sometimes called it, the 'critical task') not as a separate method of analysis from genealogy, but as one complementary with it. Genealogy is distinguished by a differing emphasis: it examines process while archaeology examines the 'moment', however temporally extended that moment might be. Genealogy offers us a processual perspective on the web of discourse, in contrast to an archaeological approach which provides us with a snapshot, a slice through the discursive nexus (cf. Foucault 1971b: 62–5; 1981: 70–1; Kremer-Marietti 1985: 194–7). The genealogical method has gradually been made evident through Foucault's later studies, as well as interviews and lectures (see particularly HSI and Foucault 1971a; 1975; 1977a; 1977b; 1977c; 1980a). Beyond this, Foucault (1978b) has suggested a three-dimensional approach, involving genealogy, archaeology and, in addition, *strategy*. This introduction of a third element into the frame is a still further refinement, which seems to represent an attempt to co-adapt archaeology and genealogy while prioritizing the latter; once it is argued that genealogy has primacy, archaeology becomes downgraded to a mere methodological tool, while genealogy enjoys the overseer status of the *technē* of investigation. The insertion of the strategic into the genealogical doubles the latter, which is now seen as constituting not only the investigation desired but also the investigation realized: genealogy thus takes on an ambiguous position as both the 'end' or 'point' of the project, as well as the texts that are actually produced. The doubling of genealogy thus entails a gap.[3]

It is partly within this 'gap', interior to the process of genealogical investigation, that the possibilities of Foucault's texts arise; but our contention is that the 'gap' also occasions a dislocation between HSI, which seems to lay the ground for a genealogical account of sexuality, and HSII and HSIII, which, as we hope to show, rather comprise a series of archaeological slices of the deployment of sexuality in antiquity and Christianity. We want to raise the question of the extent to which the project can be realized through such a tactical depiction of a series of slices; in other words, how can we be sure that these slices maintain a relevance for the contemporary deployment of sexualities? How can these stories of the sexual practices of antiquity be put to work? How do they unpack the problematics of the present? What we wish to address, then, is the 'gap' between the promise and the published work: is the 'gap' closed so that the work can be judged successful in its own terms? or is the 'gap' the insuperable divide which provides the conditions of impossibility for a *History of Sexuality*?

We will examine the 'gap' in relation to a problem of 'homogenization'. Extended historical periods such as 'antiquity', as well as discursive formations[4] such as 'Christianity', tend to be characterized monolithically, suggesting a notion of the deployment of sexuality which fails to acknowledge its heterogeneity; at the same time, a reliance on conservative accounts of historical periods feeds these 'homogenizing' tendencies, and perhaps imperils the political imperatives that are served by a history of the present.[5] To begin an examination of these issues, we shall play devil's advocate, and critically examine Foucault's work in relation to his source materials. We begin by looking at the way Foucault deals with the problem of sexuality in antiquity.

The sticky problem of antiquity: sexual practice in ancient Greece

Foucault's engagement with the problematics of antiquity takes place primarily in HSII and HSIII. In these volumes, Foucault attempts to specify a particular conception of sexuality (primarily male sexuality, but including homosexuality and homoeroticism), as characteristic of ancient Greek society. In order to do this he treats the fifth and fourth centuries BC in Greece as equivalent, eliding temporal and geographical limits and invoking what he unearths about Athenian practices as a description for all of Greece. In this manner, Foucault suggests a rather undifferentiated picture, for example, of life for women in fifth-century Greece, as one in which they were consistently subordinate, concerning themselves only with hearth and home. Yet it is not at all clear that this situation held in other Greek states, particularly Sparta;[6] there is, moreover, evidence to suggest that women's position in many spheres changed greatly in the Hellenistic period, enabling them to take on a different role even in Athens (cf. Pomeroy 1984). We need to ask why Foucault chose to sketch such an undifferentiated antiquity, and why his account omits crucial evidence that would allow a different story to be told. In the same way, we might examine what on the face of it seems a worrisome aspect of the project: Foucault's 'masculinist' bias in the construction of what is supposedly a history of sexuality generally, not just of male sexuality.

It might be contended that the evidence used is partly to blame, since Foucault chose to examine, for example, dietetics, a primarily 'masculine' discourse; but while it is clear that the cultures he was examining did treat women as second-class citizens (frequently not even as citizens), there was still some scope to redress the asymmetry. Even within the Hippocratic corpus, Foucault could have looked at some of the extensive gynaecological works which concern themselves with the radically different ways in which the woman's body was seen to function. Foucault in fact largely ignored this work, and while he does refer to Soranus, an important developer of these gynaecological writings and medical theoretician in his own right, the text is put to curious use: Foucault has Soranus stress the advantages of virginity and the dangers of intercourse. This first mention of Soranus arises in the context of an introductory discussion where Aretaeus is taken as exemplifying the way the Greek physicians of the first century elaborated a 'fear of the sexual act'; thus Soranus symptomatizes the elaboration of 'a very ancient fear' that characterizes the emergence of a concern over austerity. Soranus, however, was concerned primarily not with sex but with the hazards early pregnancy would entail for adolescent girls.

To take another point, Foucault's characterization of the homosexual relation in antiquity as unequal, dichotomized along the axes of activity/ passivity and man/boy, ignores the use made of such relations in some Greek states to produce soldierly solidarity: through fostering relations between young men of about the same age (particularly while being trained), soldiers were made more loyally bound to each other.[7] We also learn from Plutarch[8] that boys in Sparta were allowed the company of lovers of their own age, and it would seem likely that this too was because of its good effects on their military prowess. This imbrication of homosexual relations with the technologies of military loyalty was a powerful device in antiquity, and one much copied.[9]

In addition, Lloyd (1986) has argued that Foucault's reliance on texts alone as sources 'distorts' his account: so, the Greek authors' reticence on lovemaking techniques and positions may be counterposed to an examination of the evidence from vase painting, where a wide variety of sexual practices is explicitly depicted. Is it the silence of the texts or the loudness of the vases which most faithfully conveys the relation of the Greeks to austerity? Or is the whole issue of austerity one which demands a more subtle approach than can be achieved by balancing out evidences as if 'evidence' were unproblematic, its meaning simply given? Cohen (1987) is critical of Foucault (as well as of Dover, on whom Foucault is heavily reliant) for his substitution of the axis 'activity/passivity' as the Greeks' equivalent of the modern dichotomy 'homosexuality/heterosexuality', and catalogues a multiplicity of understandings of sexuality in Classical Athens, characterizing their complex culture somewhat unhelpfully as a 'patterned chaos'.[10]

This homogenization of what is an extremely complex series of deployments is due in part to the sources, both primary and secondary, on which Foucault relies. His selective use of primary sources tightens his account and suggests a rather unvariegated field of relations in the domain of the sexual. None of this is surprising, given the extreme difficulty of constructing an account from the ancient sources. Those sources which are most readily available are derived from or are sympathetic to Athens, and concentrate on the perceived 'Golden Age' of Athenian democracy, even though the sources themselves may date from a considerably later period: this pervasive tradition of re-writing the story of the classical period, with its insistence on the superiority of the Athenian cultural experience, is clearly not targeted by Foucault, whose work is permeated by this orthodoxy, at the expense of a story which might stress the multiplicity of practices in antiquity.

On the other hand, his use of secondary sources produces a different but comparable set of problems, since the conceptual categories and periodizations they utilize suit their own problematizations rather than serving the needs of Foucault's project. If conventional historical analysis aims to render familiar a past that is thoroughly strange, and achieves this through the lens of the present, Foucault's writing can be seen as turning this process entirely on its head: a genealogical account opens up new possibilities for the present insofar as that present is rendered strange. It does this by throwing into question some of the features of the present that have come to be taken for granted as somehow natural and basic – by speaking the unspeakable. If this is so, then genealogies and histories are not only quite different, but at odds with each other. In particular, the demarcation conventional history makes between what is internal and external to the analysis – what may legitimately be investigated and what is irrelevant – is thoroughly at odds with the genealogical emphasis on the dispersed nature of discursive practices that target sexuality in its deployment. Thus it might be expected that to risk reliance, as Foucault did, on historians such as Pomeroy (1975) and Dover (1978) could result in an easily (mis)understood and monolithic picture of sexuality in antiquity. While this reliance need not necessarily be fatal for his project, our argument is that it diverted attention away from the possibility of a genealogical account, towards a series of 'histories' of sexuality in antiquity.

We cannot stress too much the difficulty of interpreting the evidence of antiquity; indeed, the scarcity and temporal dispersion of the sources makes some generalization necessary if one is to say anything at all. It would seem that Foucault chose to present a particular monolithic version of a highly differentiated and variegated historical moment; we hope to show how this drift into homogenization arose from the way his project became preoccupied with the question of the links between austerity themes in late Hellenistic culture and those of early Christianity. Although his exposition of the development of these themes (HSIII) is often lucid and convincing, his task was made easier by his undifferentiated conceptions of both antiquity and its 'successor', Christianity. In order to look at this drift, we need to continue with an examination of Foucault's treatment of the Greek medical texts.

The problem of austerity: the Greek medical texts

Our contention has been that Foucault's account works on a principle of *eliding* the complexity of sexuality in the ancient world. The same is true of those sections of Foucault's work dealing with dietetics and with the body.[11] These sections rely respectively on the 'Hippocratic corpus' and on the collections of the Greek physicians assembled much later during the Roman and early Christian eras. HSII, Foucault announces, 'is devoted to the manner in which sexual activity was problematized by philosophers and doctors in classical Greek culture of the fourth century B.C.' while HSIII 'deals with the same problematization in the Greek and Latin texts of the first two centuries of our era'.[12]

The 'Hippocratic corpus' draws from the varied practices of numerous Greek physicians from a variety of locations and schools, living between the sixth and the fourth centuries BC. For most of these books or fragments, however, the earliest extant manuscript dates from the tenth century AD. Similarly, Foucault's medical texts of the first and second centuries AD survive only through collections made much later, these Greek manuscript collections being translated into Arabic in the ninth century and thence becoming available in Latin translations from the eleventh century.[13] What seems evident is the protracted time-scale over which these writings were written or assembled, and the variety of social settings involved. The challenge to his project presented by the problem of the sources is, however, never explicitly confronted: on the contrary, Foucault seems to use his text to erode any possibility of differentiating antiquity. We might mention some instances of this erosion, which usually works by juxtaposition. For example, to quote in the same sentence Oribasius and the 'classical age' suggests a monolithic unity spanning antiquity, from the Greek states of the fifth century BC to the fall of Rome in the fifth century AD.[14] While in a single paragraph we have Diocles (fourth century BC) rubbing shoulders not only with Oribasius (fourth century AD), but also with Paulus (seventh century AD): a whole millennium is thus rolled together (HSII: 109; *124*).

If these examples can be characterized as *temporal* homogenizations, then Foucault's examination of the problem of 'epilepsy' in the Greek medical texts is perhaps a *conceptual* homogenization. He selects from the Hippocratic corpus texts dealing with this matter, to which he adds references to Democritus, Diogenes of Apollonia, Plato, Aulus Gellius, Aretaeus, Clement of Alexandria, and Caelius Aurelianus. The implication is that an accord over the nature and treatment of epilepsy can be distilled from these writers whose lives span a period of nine centuries. But neither Greek medicine as a whole in the age of antiquity nor indeed the Hippocratic corpus is a monolithic unity: there were at least forty-five different 'treatments' just for epilepsy. Epilepsy is an interesting problem precisely because of the irregularity of 'attacks' and the lack of effectivity, in modern terms, of these ancient medical interventions. The texts are consequently invaluable sources for any researcher interested in the mutual constitution of the practitioner of the healing art and his noble client: in *The Sacred Disease*, for example, the most celebrated Hippocratic text referring to epilepsy, this is done through a thematic focus on the derogation of 'Temple Medicine'. Interestingly, Foucault does not mention *The Sacred Disease*, and this would seem to be a strategic decision. Selecting references in this way, to mark their similarities rather than their differences, produces a space for a modern conception of epilepsy as some sort of sub-species of another modern conception – disease or pathology in general. Thus epilepsy is read not in relation to the *technē*, but in relation to present-day understandings of epilepsy-as-a-disease. These anachronistic conceptions are crucial because of the analogy made in some of these medical texts between epilepsy and orgasm: Foucault fully exploits this analogy in edging towards a conception of orgasm as verging on the pathological for the ancients. The fact that *The Sacred Disease* does not draw this analogy perhaps explains why Foucault did not make use of that celebrated text.[15]

First of all, then, Foucault is silent on the specificities of epilepsy in the texts he mentions – he fails to locate the theoretical and social contexts into which they are embedded, and is consequently complicit in guiding the reader towards an anachronistic understanding of epilepsy in antiquity. The combination of Foucault's silence here (invoking anachronism) with his accentuation of the analogy made in the texts, implies that the notion of orgasm held in antiquity was as something akin to a diseased state, or at least a condition dangerous for the body, where the person might do harm to the self. The thoughtful reader is thus invited to infer that in antiquity such a condition might with justification be avoided, but such an idea is difficult to reconcile with the predominant opinion of the medical texts that sexual activity is natural, benign, and generally beneficial.[16] Instead, Foucault tells another story, and is therefore able through the strategy of his writing and through his rhetoric to prepare the reader for the notion of an antiquity preoccupied with sexual austerity.

If we look at the medical writings that Foucault examines and the way he deals with them, again we find the story of austerity to be a major principle of selection and emphasis. One of the passages from Rufus which Foucault uses concerns the relation of sexual activity to health:[17] though Rufus begins with a brief warning of the dangers of excess, the bulk of his discussion concerns the various benefits of sexual activity. Foucault quotes directly every word of warning in the Rufus text, and further down the page he repeats this warning in an extended paraphrase which suggests to the reader another Rufus passage from which Foucault had sampled: but there is no such passage. The rest of the Rufus text is compressed by Foucault into a grudging recognition of the possibility of benefit. Thus, through his selection, not only of texts, but also from within his sources, he is able in his discussion of matters of sexuality to reverse the emphasis as regards benefit and danger.

We need to be quite clear about this: if sexual relations were a danger to the economy of the body so that they should be indulged in as infrequently as possible (as the idea of a regime of austerity would imply) then we might expect the Greek medical texts to reflect this: but no, their overwhelming emphasis was that since the sexual act is natural, it cannot be other than beneficial. On this they concurred, however much they might have disagreed on other matters, and Foucault himself admitted as much (HSII: 48; 58; cf. HSIII: 112; 134). Yet Foucault persisted with another story in his text. His sexuality project thereby became increasingly embroiled in the question of sexuality-as-an-austere-economy. This course was facilitated by his erosion of the important difference between *moderation* and *austerity*, an erosion exemplified by the way he persistently employed the terms interchangeably (for example, HSII: 249–50; 273–4).

What is taken by the Greek physicians to be dangerous and what is not becomes clear if we look at an example apparently unconnected with sexuality – the question of 'exercise'. Consider, for example, a passage taken from Galen in the compendium of Oribasius,[18] one of Foucault's favourite sources for Greek medicine in Rome. The writer begins by drawing attention to the specificity of 'exercise': what counts is not the same for one man as for another. Nevertheless, its benefits derive from three of its essential character-istics: as the organs rub against each other, they are made hard; there is an increase in the 'innate heat'; and the 'humours' become more violently agitated. Every form of 'exercise' should be indulged in to ensure a long and healthy life – the danger is to those who do not take 'exercise' (for example, those with sedentary occupations). A variety of Greek physicians, despite differences over some medical questions, are found to share an important general feature here: not only was there no attempt to mark a difference between 'exercise' and sexual activity, but there are obvious parallels in the way these types of activity were viewed. Foucault, by contrast, writes as though sexual activity was something separate and different in the Greek medical texts. The modern day separation of sex and exercise seems to have contributed to an anachronistic reading of those ancients for whom the two elements were part of a common 'regimen'.

Similarly, in the field of dietetics, the other important aspect of Greek medical practice, there is no special treatment of sexuality as such. Foucault was aware of this,[19] yet this is not the emphasis of his own text: he became increasingly involved with the question of sexual ethics in antiquity even though this was a comparatively minor aspect of the contemporaneous regimen of self-care. By contrast Pigeaud (1981), for example, whom Foucault acknowledged as a major source for his section on the body in HSIII,[20] devotes little space to sexuality as such.

It is clear, then, that concern over sexual ethics *per se* was not separable from dietary considerations for the physicians of classical Greece or post-Augustan Rome. Sexual behaviour should be read as a rather minor aspect of a regimen primarily concerned with balancing diet on the one hand and effluxions on the other (what goes into the body and what comes out). But Foucault chose to adjust the emphasis of his primary sources. If in one of the worlds of antiquity there was a concern with the *act* in the abstract, and if the act were considered dangerous, then Foucault's emphasis would perhaps have been justified. However, in the medical sources he uses, it is precisely the specificities of the act, in terms of the auspiciousness of the conditions under which it was to be performed, which determined the balance of danger and benefit (the notion of χρῆσις, chrēsis). Foucault is aware enough of this axis of judgement to devote a whole section of HSII to it, but he takes for granted the separability of sexuality and diet in a way that the sources cannot justify.[21]

The specificities of the sexual act were recognized in the Greek writings in another way, however: a Rufus fragment in Oribasius[22] leaves the reader in no doubt that if special care was required over the exercise of sexual relations, then this was in connection not with heterosexual sexuality, and least of all with conjugal acts, but rather with pederasty. Foucault cited Rufus a number of times and made great play of the 'dangers' attached to sexual relations but he made no mention of the specificity of these hazards. This revealing silence serves to foster the idea of an economy of austerity yet again because of the implication that the 'dangers' attached to the act of pederasty suffused the whole field of sexual relations.

Foucault was aware, then, that the emphasis of the Greek medical texts was a concern over moderation rather than austerity, over diet rather than sexuality, and over special care in regard to pederasty rather than to matrimonial sexuality. Yet the selectivity of his account, with its elision of contradictions and ambiguities, allows for a quite different reading of Greek medicine, one which draws the reader into a story of austerity. Foucault is therefore himself drawn into producing not so much a history of the present of sexuality, an examination of the space for manoeuvre, as a sort of backwards genealogy of continence, a history of the progress of constrictions which, he implies, still have their effectivity in modern technologies of the desiring subject. In his story of antiquity, Foucault is able to trace an over-arching continuity, the concern for austerity – a theme that serves as the harbinger of the confessional, the harbinger of an ascetic Christianity.

Christianity: an austere economy

We have been concerned so far with Foucault's tactical decisions in selecting between and within primary texts to present a story of sexuality in antiquity. What is at stake here, however, is Foucault's whole strategy.[23] We hope to make this clear by examining the developing role of Christianity in each of the three published volumes of Foucault's *History of Sexuality*.

First, in HSI there are three discrete passages where there is a substantial discussion of Christianity,[24] these passages are integral to the overall argument and are, moreover, points to which Foucault returns in his conclusion. In HSII, having set the scene with a discussion of Christian austerity in the earlier part of the book, Foucault can thereafter rely on the reader's tacit understanding of the significance it has for his project, an understanding evoked and maintained by sporadic and occasional references to Christianity scattered throughout the rest of the volume. In HSIII, finally, there are occasional (mostly isolated) pages where Christianity is mentioned, but in the main it is an absent presence, constantly taken-for-granted; it is this taken-for-granted which enables Foucault to make antiquity understandable through its difference. 'It is not that there is an obligation to practise sexual intercourse only in order to have children,' Foucault says (HSIII: 128; *151*). The absence Foucault here exploits is instantly recognizable as the orthodoxy of the Church of Rome. Similarly, from time to time, features of antiquity are taken as prototypical of ascetic Christianity. For instance, when Foucault has extracted the three principles of the ethics of conjugality, he unveils their purpose thus: 'We shall find them again in a later period, in what the Church demanded of a good Christian married couple' (HSIII: 183; *214*). On the other hand, Foucault identifies features of antiquity which are *not* prototypical of ascetic Christianity. For instance, discussing the principles governing the timing of intercourse for the wife, Foucault remarks 'it does not seem that there was, despite the identity of principle, the kind of interrogation that will be encountered in Christian teaching concerning the lawfulness of sexual relations' (HSIII: 179; *209*). Similarities and differences are made according to a yardstick of ascetic Christianity, and this holds whether the yardstick is mentioned explicitly or left implicit. A monolithic idea of ascetic Christianity is the basis for understanding antiquity and this still holds even when it is not necessary for Foucault to mention Christianity as such. Or rather it is precisely because Christianity is largely absent that the notion of it that the text suggests can be at once conflationary and monolithic. When Foucault has completed his account of the philosophers and physicians of the first two centuries or so, the stage is already set for a discussion in terms of 'a future ethics, the ethics that one will find in Christianity' (HSIII: 235; *269*). In his concluding discussion the same subject crops up: it is the monolithic notion of an ascetic Christianity that is once more confirmed as the unspoken authorization which has called the entire opus to order. Just as in our discussion of antiquity, we would like again to argue that this homogeneous picture of Christianity which Foucault draws is by no means a foregone conclusion. We are particularly concerned with the way in which his characterization underlines an exclusively ascetic Christianity, one which is dominated by those austerity themes which he shows to have emerged from pagan discourses.[25]

However, there is another story to be told from our sources. It is possible to unfold a map of Christianity quite different in its contours from the linear tale of austerity. There has been a seemingly endless stream of little-known, mostly small, often secret and sometimes isolated, sectarian or heretical movements, a number of which were explicitly committed in some degree to Eros as part of their practices of worship. In such groups sexual intercourse verged on the sacramental, so that far from being some unfortunate necessity, a means to a higher end, sexuality itself took its place alongside the eucharist as a central feature of the life of a good Christian. If such beliefs seem exotic, then it should not be forgotten that the ascetic followers of, for example, Montanus were very much a minority within second-century Christianity. The obvious point remains that it is the erotic that goes uncelebrated in the (hi)story traditionally highlighted both by the official record of the Church and by its critics.[26]

Our suggestion is, then, that Foucault's characterization of Christianity as monolithically austere is wide of the mark. In addition, an account that makes the austerity themes of pagan antiquity the sole discursive resource for those of Christianity is similarly problematic. One might look at the fragmented and contradictory practices of fifth-century Christian nobles centering around marriage and sexuality: in developing a rhetoric of austerity, these Christian nobles seem to have appealed to what they saw as an example in the behaviour of the lower orders (Shaw 1987): the new ideas were theorized and glossed to be sure, but the practices raised up pre-existed as a derogated discourse of the pagan poor. Here,then, is a non-classical, non-Christian discursive resource related to an emergent asceticism in the early Church. There are other examples: in the period Foucault looks at, the case for a new strictness might have been an easier one to make by examining the role of the Mishnah in the development of Judaism, rather than that of Greek medical writings in the emergence of a Christian identity. The Mishnaic collection was assembled over a considerable period (30 BC to AD 210), its redaction associated with Judah he-Nasi. The commentaries of Raba (299–352) and Abaye (280–338) are particularly important. Restrictions on sexual practices are elaborated in a way which has no counterpart in Christianity until at least several centuries later.[27] For austerity themes, then, there are discursive resources other than pagan antiquity which would bear examination. Foucault, however, avoids even those important collections of the Greek medical texts which were assembled by Arab and Jewish physicians, restricting his story to the question of balancing the 'influence' of two alternatives – an homogeneous pagan antiquity on the one hand, and a monolithic Christianity on the other. In effect he chooses not to confront the complexity of austerity themes just as he 'reduces' the complexities of antiquity, of Christianity and of sexuality. The question which immediately arises is why Foucault chose to proceed in this way. It is clearly beyond the scope of this paper to rehearse all these arguments, but we should like to develop some thoughts concerning Foucault's strategic decision to make a commitment to the idea of a monolithically ascetic Christianity, an investment that became pivotally important for his developing work – pivotally important because of its status as a discursive resource for psychoanalysis.

Psychoanalysis and the pilgrimage to the past

Although we have been concerned so far in the main with HSII and HSIII, we cannot simply pass over HSI, which in Hurley's translation announces itself as 'An Introduction', and which has in any case been seen as the key orienting document for the project of a *History of Sexuality* and which, after all, does contain within it a section which bears a remarkable resemblance to an author's methodological introduction.[28] In relation to this initial document, we would like to pose three questions:

First, can we legitimately take HSI as this introduction or key orienting document to a larger project which has an internal logic and coherence?

Second, what is the nature of this project to which HSI might be viewed as introductory, and to what extent is any thematic maintained?

Third, how far does the project remain within the confines of a 'history of the present', or rather, when does it start to stray from that objective?

We would like to demonstrate that one way of getting to grips with these three interlocking questions is through considering the subtle shifts of problematizations that emerged as Foucault's project was pursued. What seems clear is that however it was initially conceived (and from at least 1960, Foucault was concerned with the possibility of writing a particular type of *History of Sexuality*, one predicated on the assumption of an opposition between repression and liberation which was made explicit in HSI), by the time of the publication of HSII, a whole new series of problematics were under examination. It would seem that the project underwent a total transformation in subject matter,[29] and we hope to suggest some possibilities as to how and why this happened.

We can see even from the title of the first part of HSI that Foucault becomes embroiled in a debate over We/Other Victorians. He entitled this section 'Nous autres, victoriens' (literally, '*We* Victorians'): this punning reference to Steven Marcus's book (which Foucault does not actually name in his text) is completely lost in the American translation.[30] Foucault's French title plays upon the notion that we too are Victorians; yet it is clear, also, that the reader will be able to erase the comma to refer to Marcus's notion of an 'other Victorian', a notion which had contemporary currency and with which Foucault was clearly familiar.[31] Foucault's heading signifies that *we* are Victorians (rather than 'Other Victorians') and simultaneously that we are '*Other Victorians*', like the self-confessed anonymous author who makes public his secret life.[32] The juxtaposition of ourselves and the Victorians sets up an opposition between liberation and repression,[33] an opposition which Foucault is able to exploit even though he is determined to turn conventional wisdom on its head. Although he is concerned to deny the 'fact' of the liberation of modernity just as much as the 'fact' of the repression of the Victorian Age, he is none the less able to point the finger at an older discursive resource, a repressive (because assumed to be ascetic) Christianity.

Yet what this amounts to is a deconstruction in name only: Foucault's strategy is to retain the dichotomy (implicit in the repression/liberation process) as a grid through which to understand the history of sexuality. Our contention is that this followed from his decision as to what was the most obvious modern technology of the self, that which might most clearly claim to speak the truth about the self, a truth spoken through sex and sexuality: psychoanalysis. Foucault himself said: 'The history of the *dispositif* of sexuality, as it has developed since the classical age, amounts to an archeologizing of psychoanalysis'.[34] By virtue of the strategic importance thus invested in it, psychoanalysis, with its peculiarities and specificities, comes to shape the development of Foucault's expanding project. Foucault clearly saw the repressive character of psychoanalysis (while pointing up its productivity as a technology of the self);[35] it is also clear that psychoanalysis cannibalizes Christianity's obligation to confession and privileges sex and sexuality; all these peculiarities bear on the way the *History of Sexuality* project developed: sexuality thus came to be regarded as that which speaks the truth about the self throughout a variety of historical periods. However, what came to be important to Foucault was not sexuality as such but the 'technologies of the self': genealogizing technologies of the self came to mean looking for a history of sexuality, and doing it through a grille of repression/austerity. Certainly it seems clear from our discussion of the Greeks that this was how Foucault, in HSI, II and III, conceptualized the relation between sexuality and truth in antiquity, though the sources could be used to suggest quite another story.

HSI, then, concerns itself in effect with a genealogy of psychoanalysis, centering on the way in which sex has been put into discourse and characterizing psychoanalysis as of a piece with de Sade on the one hand and Victorian proscriptive texts on the other. That is, Foucault is concerned to deny the claim that Freud innovates a new technology of the self, and lines him up as a descendant of those medical and other men from whose 'sexualization' of the body emerges a new anatomo-politics, whose other pole, incidentally, is a new bio-politics of the population (HSI: 139–45; *183–91*). Foucault is not concerned to deny psychoanalysis its truth effects by this demotion, but rather to argue that its conditions of possibility lay in those Christian discourses of the pre-Freudian era, specifically the 'pastoral', as well as in the existing technologies of the flesh whose reification was the confessional. So Foucault's first step is to set up psychoanalysis as the most important technology of the self in modernity, and to situate the 'talking cure' as a descendant of the Christian confessional.

Thus Christianity becomes established as the parent of psychoanalysis through an emphasis on the continuity of the confession. Indeed it is

Christianity that comes to play a determining role throughout Foucault's project, as the 'silent presence', the omnipresent spectre which constrains his conceptual categories, governs his choice of sources, and dictates the form that his developing work will take. HSI might form a suitable introduction to a genealogy which concerns itself with modern formations of subjectivity as implicated in post-Christian discourse; within the developing project, however, with its subtly altered concerns and points of departure, HSI also becomes the thumb-nail sketch which sets the agenda for a series of archaeological slices, slices which are positioned to project the emergence of modern austerity themes. What we cannot afford to take for granted is the identification of this story of austerity with the genealogical task.

A question that arises at this point, then, is why HSI was selected for this determining role. After all, the possibility existed for Foucault to have made it clear that the subsequent volumes formed part of a different project. Indeed there is a hint of this in an interview that appeared just before the publication of the second volume: 'I must confess that I am much more interested in problems about techniques of the self and things like that than sex . . . sex is boring' (Foucault 1983). Yet despite his avowed interest in this *terra nova*, Foucault remained committed to that conceptualization of Christianity that was a feature of HSI. The legacy of Nietzsche and Weber of an ascetic Christianity must not be underestimated: if it underlies western Social Sciences and Humanities, it also pervades the modern age and is formative of its problematics. Weber's essentialization of Christianity cannot be examined here, but one might note in passing the irony of his (that is, Weber's) selection (to exemplify Christian asceticism) of Zinzendorf, with his 'outrageously sensual' cult of the Five Sacred Wounds. Foucault, too, takes on board this essentialization of Christianity, the more so because of his determination to locate it in the genealogy of psychoanalysis: what followed was less a genealogy than a Genesis story, linking the repressive modern compulsion inherent in the psychoanalytical confession to the repression inherited from its Christian progenitor.[36]

The traces of this strategy continued to have their truth effects even in the radically revised project signalled by HSII. Initially, at least, a supposed contrast between the pessimism engendered by an examination of modernity which seemed to turn up nothing but a series of false dawns for liberation, and the prospect of a golden age of (homo)sexual freedom in antiquity propelled Foucault into an analysis of the sort of texts we discussed earlier. However, once Foucault had embarked upon his analysis of Greek and Latin texts after his process of familiarization with the Classical languages, he discovered that homosexuality was just as much a 'problem' and a 'danger' then as it is now. Foucault's presumed 'Golden Age' rapidly disappeared, leaving in its stead a series of austerity themes whose deployment is discussed above. One is tempted to read Foucault's state of *ennui* as regards sex as a deliberate attempt to recast his project in the light of his failure to uncover a deployment of sexuality to which he might be politically sympathetic. At this point, HSI becomes the 'fatal' thumbnail sketch: Foucault was only too ready to see in those austerity themes a continuity with the austerity of a (Weberian) ascetic Christianity; that is, his analysis became preoccupied[37] with explanations producing a given Christianity out of a continuity of austerity themes which christ-alize into austerity rules from their dispersions in antiquity. The next step had already been taken – HSI had located psychoanalysis as an emergent technology of the self, which could now take its place as descendant not only from Christianity but also from antiquity. The vast dispersion of austerity themes from the fifth century BC up until the present could now be characterized as of a piece.

Conclusion

To sum up our position: we maintain that Foucault's project of a *History of Sexuality* came to be pivoted on a series of monolithic conceptions; we have tried to highlight the importance of antiquity and Christianity, austerity and confession; we have tried to show how Foucault's project relied upon the 'austere economy' as he developed the arguments of HSI, even though it is clear from interviews and lectures that he was fully aware of the heterogeneity of sexuality in Christianity and in antiquity.[38] We should like to point out a series of documentable dislocations. First, there is a gap between the primary source material and the story we find in Foucault's *History of Sexuality*: we find that he chooses to avoid fully confronting the dispersions and heterogeneity of the evidence in his account of antiquity in HSII and HSIII. Secondly, there is therefore arguably a gap between the genealogical promise of HSI and the archaeological slices that make up HSII and HSIII. Thirdly, as we have indicated briefly, a gap emerges between the arguments of *The History of Sexuality* and the views Foucault put forward contemporaneously in other work. In short, there would seem to be a series of problems in Foucault's genealogical work *in its own terms*.

Our contention is that these 'gaps' are the conditions of possibility for a particular type of *History of Sexuality*, which, we argue, constrains itself in the process of its own development. Consequently, what emerges from his account is a metonymous, monolithic antiquity which is tailored to the possibility of critical intervention in a country like France, where psychoanalysis is pivotally important as *the* modern technology of the self. It is not, however, clear that this strategy is appropriate for another country (like Britain) where the positioning of psychoanalysis within the structuration of discursive domains is not prioritized in the same way. We need to seriously question whether, from the viewpoint of British readers, *The History of Sexuality* provides the appropriate perspectives for a history of the present, for (say) deconstructing homosexualities in particular, or taking account of gender to look at the positionings of women (we take for granted that these are two of the most pressing aims of a genealogy of sexuality).

We have argued that it is evident from the way Foucault dealt with the writings of the Greek physicians in HSII and HSIII that his account becomes critically detached from 'the slice' (that is to say, the archaeological slice) to float free into an overarching stream of continuity, preoccupied in the interrogation of source materials by an ascetic Christianity absent from the text. We are not suggesting that Foucault did not realize the heterogeneity of sexuality, of Christianity, or of antiquity or that he was unaware, for example, of the difference between the notion of Christian ascesticism we inherit from Nietzsche and Max Weber and askesis (ἄσκησις) in the Rome of the second century AD or the Athens of the fifth and fourth centuries BC.[39] Our claim is rather that a series of apparently external factors made a narrow channel into which Foucault's project was forced.

We are faced, therefore, with a new problem: the genealogical method presents itself as the only way out of what one might characterize as the *impasse* of socio-history,[40] as well as providing an explicitly political approach to problems around sexuality with a pay-off for future action; yet there is such a gap between the promise of Foucault's work and what is accessible to the anglophone reader, that the entire venture might seem just a brilliant failure. His project became enmeshed in a concern with austerity to the extent that it was this theme which came to be the managing principle, the economy, for Foucault's story of antiquity and Christianity.

Foucault has been identified as the *bête noire* of the Marxist left, who has delivered the intellectual life of France into the hands of 'reactionary Prussianism'; he is charged with holding out too pessimistic a view of the present, betraying the ameliorative venture of the forces of progress. It seems clear from our analysis that precisely the opposite might be the case: his uncritical acceptance of a whole series of givens resurrects a whole series of ghosts of the present to people the paths of the past, and betrays a lack of that profound suspicion over what can be taken for granted which characterizes the deconstructive principle, a principle we insist on as fundamental to any genealogy. For example, Foucault could have gone on deconstructing psychoanalysis, but he chose to stop when he reached an ascetic (Weberian/ Nietzschean) Christianity, with a double consequence both for the level of reality at which Foucault's story finally arrives and for the resilience of his work in the face of homogenizing tendencies which bear on the way we can read this work. He 'forgets' to deconstruct. While we note the final pages of HSI where Foucault does voice suspicions over the stories of ascetic Christianity and prudery, psychoanalysis and liberation, this interpellation[41] of the comfortable amnesia of the trilogy as a whole (where his suspicions are forgotten) becomes a voice crying in the wilderness.

Paradoxically, at this point, it is still possible, we would argue, to reaffirm the radical potential for intervention which Foucault's work offers us. It seems clear that Foucault shifted his emphasis in his last works from the analysis of power that characterized *Discipline and Punish* and HSI, to as greater concern with ethics and the self, and the games of truth through which the subject enters into its own formation. This was not at the cost of downgrading his earlier work (see Foucault 1987): he was thinking differently, escaping from himself, just as he had made clear that this, for him, was the point of thinking, of 'philosophy'. A critique of Foucault's project has served as our way in to understanding the problematics it engages; while dubious of the value to us of an archaeology of antiquity or a (backward) genealogy of austerity, we are inspired by Foucault's recapitulation of the relation between self, truth, and sexuality. After Foucault, the whole terrain of the history of sexuality is unmistakably altered. He has mapped out a new terrain for investigation and developed the toolkits for this work. But his investigations give us not so much a finished account as a basis for thinking otherwise about the problem of sexuality and the self. After Foucault, therefore, the possibilities for *penser autrement* are greater than ever: an epitaph he might have wished for.

P.B.
South Bank University
M.C.
Department of Humanities
Richmond International College
1 St Albans Grove
London W8 SPN
G.K.
Department of Psychology,
University of Lancaster

Notes

1   See Foucault 1976, 1984a, 1984b, with the corresponding English translations 1978a, 1985a, 1986. These three volumes will henceforth be referred to as HSI, HSII, and HSIII. For page references to *The History of Sexuality*, the first figure refers to the English edition while the second refers to the French. Page references to Foucault in French editions are given in italics.

2   Throughout this piece we take for granted a certain familiarity with Foucauldian terminology, but for those unfamiliar with it, see Sheridan 1980, Henriques *et al.* 1984, Rabinow 1984.

3   Foucault (1978b: 16) comments that 'En parlant d'archéologie, de stratégie et de généalogie ... [il s'agit ...] plutôt de caractériser trois dimensions nécessairement simultanées de la même analyse.'

4   Our usage of the term 'discursive formations' is based on but not identical to that set out in Foucault's earlier 'methodological' work (1969: *44–54, 94–101* 1972: 31–9, 71–6); cf. Kremer-Marietti 1985: 141–63.

5   Gary Wickham (pers. comm.) has suggested to us that a whole series of problems arise from using Foucault if one looks for radical potential *in the work itself.* Wickham's position is that Foucault's work has no intrinsic revolutionary value but must be used in conjunction with other theoretical tools.

6   See Plutarch's Cleomenes, Xenophon's Lacedaemonian Constitution. Cf. HSII 122–4, *138–40*; 141–84, *157–203* for Foucault's account of women in ancient Greece. Also important on the role of women in Sparta is Kunstler 1987.

7   See particularly Plutarch, Pelopidas 18–19 where there is mention of the Theban 'Sacred Band', the pride of the Theban army, composed of one hundred and fifty homosexual pair-bonds. It is important to note that Plutarch, our best source on Sparta, is writing nearly seven hundred years later, and perhaps portrayed Sparta as somewhat exotic.

8   Lycurgus 16–17.

9   Diodorus Siculus, xvi.80.4 and xx.10.6, reports how the Carthaginians formed a Sacred Band in the image of the Theban one.

10   It should be pointed out that our use of Cohen here relates solely to the evidence he marshalls that suggests a heterogeneity of sexual practice; despite his evidence, Cohen is unconcerned with the discursive dispersion of sexualities, preferring instead to push a story of heterosexual conjugal domesticity. His concern seems to lie in recasting the 'patterned chaos' as a naturalised 'normality' of sexual practice; he is able to do this through the notion that homosexual relations are an inferior substitute for a 'healthy' heterosexuality which is for some reason unavailable. While we cannot rehearse Cohen's argument and our critique of it here, it seems clear that his story is not only essentialistic but also veers towards a politically suspect homophobia.

11   See 'Dietetics' (HSII: 95–139, *109–56*), and 'The Body' (HSIII: 96–144, *119–69*) respectively.

12   HSII: 12, *18*. Cf. Smart 1985: 109.

13   See A. Lesky 1963 for a general introduction with short annotated bibliographies; on the Hippocratic corpus see Hall 1975, vol. 1: 66–82 and Lloyd (ed.) 1983: 'Der enkaphalomyogene Samenlehre', 1233–54 in E. Lesky 1950 gives an account of the importance of 'seed stuff' for Plato and his contemporaries; on the transmission of texts for the later works see Bowersock 1969. Note that Foucault himself cites the last two works.

14   The classical period of Greece normally refers to C5 and C4 BC; Oribasius was an important physician of the C4 AD who assembled a vast collection of medical texts dating from Hippocratic times, through the first century (Aëtius) the second century (the Ephesian eclectics, Rufus and Soranus) through to the great Galen who died in about AD 200. Only a comparatively small proportion of these texts have survived. A number of these figures were, like Oribasius himself, physicians to the Roman Imperial court.

15   See HSII: 126–30, *142–6* and HSIII: 109–10, *132–3*; 113–14, *135–6*.

16   See, for example, Rufus of Ephesus in the edition of C. Daremberg and E. Ruelle, Paris, 1879: Fragment 60 ('Sur les Rapports Sexuels') in 'Fragments extraits d'Aétius' Livre III, Chapitre VIII (pp. 318–23), which is typical: 'L'acte vénérien est un acte naturel. Aucune des choses naturelles n'est nuisible.' ('The sex act is a natural act. No harm can come from anything natural.' Our translation.) Similarly, the advantages of sexual relations are pointed out in other passages: 'Fragments extraits d'Oribase' Livre VI, Ch. XXXVIII, Frag. 16 (p. 299); 'Oribase Livres Incertains' Ch. IX, Frag. 26 (p. 302); 'Extraits Analytiques de la Synopsis' Livre I, Ch. VI, Frag. 41 (p. 306); in the book 'Sur la Satyriasis et sur la Gonorrhée' we find 'Il était également pénible à cet individu de se livrer au coït et de s'en abstenir' (p. 66), i.e. that continence and licenciousness were equally dangerous. Only in one passage concerning the treatment of those suffering from loss of memory do we find moderation reaffirmed as austerity: 'Fragments extraits d'Aétius' Livre VI, Ch. XXIII, Frag. 75 (pp. 370–1).

17   Compare HSIII: 136–7, *160–1* with Rufus of Ephesus, Sur les Rapports Sexuels (περι ἀφροδισίων) in *Oeuvres* [Fragments extraits d'Aétius]: 318ff., ed. C. Daremberg and E. Ruelle, Paris, 1879. Foucault's quotations come from Daremberg and Ruelle: 370–1, and not from the passage on the dietary treatment of satyriasis cited in his footnotes.

18   Cf. Oribasius [I.6.11], *Œuvres (Collection des médecins grecs et latins)* eds U. C. Bussemaker and C. Daremberg, 1851–76, 6 vols. (vol. 1: 464–67; cf. 2: 368). Foucault discusses Rufus on exercise and health in HSIII: 130, *154* and Galen on the effects of sexual activity in HSIII: 118, *141*.

19   Cf. HSIII: 101, *115*; Foucault 1983.

20   Pigeaud devotes less than five pages of her very extensive study to sexuality.

21   Foucault has to admit that one of his two chosen treatises on dietetics 'does not say a word on the subject of the *aphrodisia*' HSII: 109, *124*.

22   See the opening remarks of Oribasius VI (Des Exercises), §38 'Du Coït (Tiré de Rufus)' (Bussemaker and Daremberg, *op. cit.* Vol. 1: 540).

23   For Foucault's own avowal of his method and strategy, see HSII: 31, *38*.

24   HSI: 18–23, *27–33*; 58–63, *78–85*; 119–23, *157–63*; minor references occur on pp. 35, *48*; 37, *51*; 39, *54*; 41, *56*; 67–8, *90–1*; 70, *93–5*; 113–14, *149–50*; 115–17, *153–5*; 156, *206*; 158–9, *209–11*. About 23% of the text is concerned with Christianity. The corresponding figures for HSII and HSIII are 17% and 9% respectively. Of those pages of HSI where the subject is discussed, 53% comprise the three main passages but there are no passages of comparable length in HSIII; on the other hand, 19% relate to isolated references on singleton pages of HSI, but for HSIII singletons make up 57% of the pages where Christianity is discussed. Something of the contrasting distribution of the discussion of Christianity in HSI, HSII and HSIII can be seen from the following table which shows for each volume the number of passages of each type. Parenthetically we show the pages for the category as a percentage of all pages mentioning Christianity in the text:

	HSI	HSII	HSIII
singleton passages	6 (19%)	12 (30%)	12 (57%)
doubleton passages	3 (19%)	02 (10%)	03 (29%)
passage-length 3–4 pp.	1 (09%)	06 (48%)	01 (14%)
passage-length 5+ pp.	3 (53%)	01 (12%)	00 (00%)
TOTAL PASSAGES	13 (100%)	21 (100%)	16 (100%)

It should be noted that we have used the Hurley translations to compile this table and that the length of HSII and HSIII is 237 and 230 pages respectively, diverging from HSI's 141.

25   This, of course, is hardly a new proposition: see, for example, Swain 1916, Leipoldt 1961: especially 31ff., 60ff. Also of interest in this regard is von Harnack 1886–90. There is, of course, a long line of Christian apologists for the ethics of antiquity, as we can see from the pseudo-Seneca texts of the tenth and eleventh centuries and the (unsuccessful) moves to have Seneca canonised (though it was he who wrote Nero's speech justifying the killing of his mother, Agrippina).

26   We cannot attempt a full-scale discussion of Christianity here, and content ourselves with suggesting that Foucault's evidential basis for an austere Christianity is problematic. An anonymous reader has suggested that this uncritical acceptance of a particular notion of Christianity may well relate to Foucault's own personal history as the 'bad boy' at school, and his subsequent transfer to a strict Catholic school. See also Megill 1984.

27   For example, in the case of a man, masturbation was highly punishable: the hand ought to be cut off. There was thus a strictness in the Talmudic teachings well before Christianity became concerned with this issue. See Epstein (ed.) 1948: Niddah Ch. II, Comm. 13.

28   See, for example, Smart's (1985: 94) interpretation of HSI as 'introductory', and Rubin 1984: 276 where it is an 'emblematic text'.

29   The first written commitment to the importance of this future project is in Foucault 1961: 3–4, a preface written in Hamburg in 1960. The changing nature of

the project can be clearly seen from the fly-sheets inserted in the *History of Sexuality* series. With HSI was promised a six-volume series viz:–

Vol I: La Volonté de Savoir
Vol II: La Chair et le Corps
Vol III: La Croisade des Enfants
Vol IV: La Femme, la Mère et l'Hystérique
Vol V: Les Pervers
Vol VI: Population et Races

but by the time HSII appeared the project had been completely revised into a four-volume series, of which the last volume may or may not appear posthumously:

Vol I: La Volonté de Savoir
Vol II: L'Usage des Plaisirs
Vol III: Le Souci de Soi
Vol IV: Les Aveux de la Chair.

However, even this new plan was not the end of the story: there were other projected versions, as is clear from the earlier preface (Foucault 1984c) to HSII which was eventually omitted from the published work, as well as from frequent references to a book based around Plato's *Alcibiades*. He seems to have had another project in mind in 1983, when he claimed (Foucault 1983) that *L'Usage des Plaisirs* would be the first volume (a disregarding of HSI was presumably still on the agenda), *Les Aveux de la Chair* would be the second, and then *Le Souci de Soi* would be a book separate from the sex series, and include, for example, a commentary on *Alcibiades*. This last venture seems to have surfaced as Foucault 1988. Foucault's (1982, 1985b) commentary on Cassian claimed to be an excerpt from HSIII but is not to be found in that volume. In addition, Defert (1985) reports that in 1983 Foucault prepared a work entitled 'Gouvernement de soi et des autres', which presumably was an early draft of HSIII.

30   Marcus 1966. See HSI: 4, *11*.

31   We can see this clearly from his editorial remarks in the preface (Foucault 1977g) to a French edition of *My Secret Life* where Foucault compares the anonymous author and Freud. Discussion of *My Secret Life* takes up the heart of Marcus's book, the middle 122 out of the 268 pages constituting the substance of his study. Popular reviews of Marcus tended to stress his psycho-analytical interpretation. *Nova* noted 'The passages quoted here reveal an appalling crudity and inhumanity, by-products of the prevalent fear of sex.'

32   Perhaps this is because 'Other Victorians' were more central figures for Victorian sexuality than 'Victorians' (HSI: 22, *31–2*).

33   Foucault is thus able to embark on a discussion of the 'Repressive Hypothesis' which, as we shall try to show, continually circles around a double 'genealogy' linking the emergence of psychoanalysis to the Christian 'pastoral'. There are echoes here of Nietzsche's attack on Christianity.

34   HSI *172*: 'L'histoire du dispositif de sexualité, tel qu'il s'est développé depuis l'âge classique, peut valoir comme archéologie de la psychanalyse.' We have used our own translation. Hurley translates this: 'The history of the deployment of sexuality, as it has evolved since the classical age, serves as an archaeology of psychoanalysis' (HSI: 130).

35   Foucault devotes a large section of HSI to an attack on the Lacanian reading of Freud, even though he does not mention Lacan by name. See HSI: 81–91, *107–20*.

36   This notion of asceticism derives perhaps equally from Nietzsche and Weber, the latter providing something of a social science veneer on the former.

37   There is some evidence in interviews and elsewhere that the ancient classics held a fascination for Foucault. Certainly his decision to delay his project while he learnt Latin and Greek is evidence of the importance he attached to these texts.

38   That is, the corpus of work where Foucault was free from the constraints of his *magnum opus* – see, for example, Foucault 1983, 1988.

39   In his Berkeley lectures, Fall 1983, Foucault dealt explicitly with the ἄσχησιζ (askēsis) point: 'Although our word "asceticism" derives from the Greek word ἄσχησιζ . . . the meaning of the word changes as it becomes associated with various Christian practices . . . [Thus,] for the Greeks the word does not mean "ascetic" but has a very broad sense denoting any kind of practical training or exercise. For example it was a commonplace to say that *any* kind of art or technique had to be learned by *mathēsis* and *askēsis* – by theoretical knowledge and practical training' (Foucault 1985c: 95–6). Foucault's argument in this lecture is that ἄσχησιζ is concerned with the production of the self (for the self) while the Christian notion of asceticism implies a denial of the self.

40   This *impasse* is discussed in, for example, *Social History* 1976, White 1978, Megill 1979, Attridge *et al.* 1987.

41   HSI: 122–3, *162–3*; 158–9, *209–11*.

References

Allbutt, Rt. Hon. Sir T. C. (1921) *Greek Medicine in Rome* [The Fitzpatrick Lectures, 1909–1910], Macmillan & Co.

Attridge, D., Bennington, G. and **Young, R.** (1987) *Post-Structuralism and The Question of History*, Cambridge University Press.

Boswell, J. (1980) *Christianity, Social Tolerance and Homosexuality*, University of Chicago Press.

Bouchard, D. F. (ed.) (1977) *Michel Foucault: Language, Counter-Memory, Practice: Selected Essays and Interviews*, Cornell University Press.

Bowersock, G. W. (1969) *Greek Sophists in the Roman Empire*, Clarendon Press.

Cohen, D. (1987) 'Law, Society and Homosexuality in Classical Athens', *Past and Present*, 117: 3–21.

Defert, D. (1985) 'Quelques Repères Chronologiques', in R. Badinter, P. Bourdieu, J. Daniel, F. Ewald, A. Farge, B. Kouchner, E. Maire, C. Mauriac, M. Perrot (eds), *Michel Foucault: une Histoire de la Vérité*, Syros.

Dover, K. (1978) *Greek Homosexuality*, Harvard University Press.

Epstein, I. (ed.) (1948) *The Babylonian Talmud, Seder Tohoroth*, Soncino Press.

Foucault, M. (1961) *Folie et Déraison: Histoire de la Folie à l'Age Classique*, first edn, Plon.

Foucault, M. (1963) 'Une Préface à la Transgression', *Critique*, 195–6: 751–70.

Foucault, M. (1969) *L'Archéologie du Savoir*, Gallimard.

Foucault, M. (1971a) 'Nietzsche, la Généalogie, l'Histoire', in *Hommage à Jean Hyppolite*, Presses Universitaires de France.

Foucault, M. (1971b) *L'Ordre du Discours*, Gallimard.

Foucault, M. (1972) *The Archaeology of Knowledge*, Tavistock.

Foucault, M. (1975) *Surveiller et Punir: Naissance de la Prison*, Gallimard.

Foucault, M. (1976) *Histoire de la Sexualité I: la Volonté de Savoir*, Gallimard.

Foucault, M. (1977a) *Discipline and Punish: the Birth of the Prison*, Allen Lane.

Foucault, M. (1977b) 'Nietzsche, Genealogy, History', in D. F. Bouchard (ed.).

Foucault, M. (1977c) 'Corso del 7 Gennaio 1976', in M. Foucault *et al.* (eds).

Foucault, M. (1977d) 'Les Rapports de

Pouvoir Passent à l'Intérieur des Corps', *Quinzaine Littéraire*, 247: 1–15.

Foucault, M. (1977e) 'Le Jeu de Michel Foucault', *Ornicar?*, 10 (July).

Foucault, M. (1977f) 'A Preface to Transgression', in D. F. Bouchard (ed.).

Foucault, M. (1977g) [Preface] *My Secret Life: Récit de la Vie Sexuelle d'un Anglais de l'Époque Victorienne*, Les Formes du Secret.

Foucault, M. (1977h) 'Intervista a Michel Foucault', in M. Foucault *et al.* (eds).

Foucault, M. (1977i) 'The Political Function of the Intellectual', *Radical Philosophy*, 17: 12–14.

Foucault, M. (1978a) *The History of Sexuality Volume I: an Introduction*, Random House.

Foucault, M. (1978b) 'Conférence Inédite à la Société Française de Philosophie', mai 1978. Bibliothèque du Saulchoir, Paris.

Foucault, M. (1979a) 'Interview with Lucette Finas', in M. Morris and P. Patton (eds).

Foucault, M. (1979b) 'Truth and Power', in M. Morris and P. Patton (eds).

Foucault, M. (1980a) 'Two Lectures', in C. Gordon (ed.).

Foucault, M. (1980b) 'The Confession of the Flesh', in C. Gordon (ed.).

Foucault, M. (1981) 'The Order of Discourse', in R. Young (ed.), *Untying the Text: A Post-Structuralist Reader*, Routledge and Kegan Paul.

Foucault, M. (1982) 'Le Combat de la Chasteté', in P. Ariès and A. Béjin (eds), Sexualités Occidentales, *Communications*, 35: 15–25.

Foucault, M. (1983) 'On the Genealogy of Ethics: an Overview of Work in Progress', in H. L. Dreyfus and P. Rabinow (eds), *Michel Foucault: Beyond Structuralism and Hermeneutics*, second edn, University of Chicago Press.

Foucault, M. (1984a) *Histoire de la Sexualité II: l'Usage des Plaisirs*, Gallimard.

Foucault, M. (1984b) *Histoire de la Sexualité III: le Souci de Soi*, Gallimard.

Foucault, M. (1984c) 'Preface to The History of Sexuality, Volume II', in P. Rabinow (ed.).

Foucault, M. (1985a) *The History of Sexuality Volume II: the Use of Pleasure*, Random House.

Foucault, M. (1985b) 'The Battle for Chastity', in P. Ariès and A. Béjin (eds), *Western Sexuality: Practice and Precept in Past and Present Times*, Basil Blackwell.

Foucault, M. (1985c) 'Discourse and Truth: the Problematization of ΠΑΡΡΗΣΙΑ', notes to the Seminar given by Foucault at University of California at Berkeley, 1983, edited by Joseph Pearson, Dept of Philosophy Offprint, Northwestern University, Evanston, Illinois.

Foucault, M. (1986) *The History of Sexuality Volume III: the Care of the Self*, Random House.

Foucault, M. (1987) 'The Ethics of Care of the Self as a Practice of Freedom', *Philosophy and Social Criticism*, XII, 2–3: 112–31.

Foucault, M. (1988) 'Technologies of the Self', in L. H. Martin, H. Gutman and P. H. Hutton (eds), *Technologies of the Self: a Seminar with Michel Foucault*, University of Massachusetts Press.

Foucault, M., Fontana, A. and Pasquino, P. (eds) (1977) *Microfisica del Potere*, Einaudi.

Gordon, C. (ed.) (1980) *Michel Foucault: Power/Knowledge: Selected Interviews and Other Writings 1972–1977*, Harvester.

Hall, T. S. (1975) *History of General Physiology 600 B.C. to A.D. 1900, 2 vols*, University of Chicago Press.

Harnack, C. G. A. von (1886–1890) *Lehrbuch der Dogmengeschichte*, 3 vols, Sammlung theologischer Lehrbücher.

Henriques, J., Hollway, W., Urwin, C., Venn, C. and Walkerdine, V. (1984) *Changing the Subject: Psychology, Social Regulation and Subjectivity*, Methuen.

Kremer-Marietti, A. (1985) *Michel Foucault: Archéologie et Généalogie*, Libraire Générale Française.

Kunstler, B. (1987) 'Family Dynamics and Female Power in Ancient Sparta', *Helios* n.s. 13, 2: 31–48.

Leipoldt, J. (1961) *Griechische Philosophie und Frühchristliche Askese*

[Berichte über Verhandlungen der Sächsischen Akademie der Wissenschaften zu Leipzig-Phil.-Hist. Klasse], Akademie Verlag.

Lesky, A. (1963) *Geschichte der Griechischen Literatur*, Fracke Verlag.

Lesky, E. (1950) *Die Zeugungs- und Vererbungslehren der Antike und ihr Nachwirken, Abhandlungen der geistes- und sozialwissenschaftlichen Klasse*, Akademie der Wissenschaften und der Literatur in Mainz.

Lloyd, G. E. R. (ed.) (1983) *Hippocratic Writings*, Penguin.

Lloyd, G. E. R. (1986) 'The Mind on Sex', *The New York Review of Books*, March 13: 24–8.

Marcus, S. (1966) *The Other Victorians*, Weidenfeld and Nicolson.

Megill, A. (1979) 'Foucault, Structuralism, and the Ends of History', *Journal of Modern History*, 51: 451–503.

Megill, A. (1984) 'Looking Back: Philosophy and Myth', *University Publishing*, 13: 13.

Morris, M. and Patton, P. (eds) (1979) *Michel Foucault: Power, Truth, Strategy*, Feral, Sydney.

Pigeaud, J. (1981) *La Maladie de l'Ame: Etude sur la Relation de l'Ame et du Corps dans la Tradition Médico-Philosophique Antique*, Les Belles Lettres.

Pomeroy, S. B. (1975) *Goddesses, Whores, Wives, and Slaves: Women in Classical Antiquity*, Schocken.

Pomeroy, S. B. (1984) *Women in Hellenistic Egypt: From Alexander to Cleopatra*, Schocken.

Rabinow, P. (ed.) (1984) *The Foucault Reader*, Pantheon.

Rubin, G. (1984) 'Thinking Sex: Notes for a Radical Theory of the Politics of Sexuality', in C. S. Vance (ed.), *Pleasure and Danger: Exploring Female Sexuality*, Routledge and Kegan Paul.

Shaw, B. D. (1987) 'The Family in Late Antiquity: the Experience of Augustine', *Past and Present*, 115: 3–51.

Sheridan, A. (1980) *Michel Foucault: the Will to Truth*, Tavistock.

Smart, B. (1985) *Michel Foucault*, Ellis Horwood.

Social History (1976) 'Social History Today . . . and Tomorrow?' [Tenth Anniversary Issue] (Winter) 10 (2).

Swain, J. W. (1916) *The Hellenic Origins of Christian Asceticism*, privately published PhD thesis, Columbia University.

White, H. (1978) *Tropics of Discourse: Essays in Cultural Criticism*, Johns Hopkins University Press.

Name index

Abbott, A. 143
Adorno, T. 25
Althusser, L. 1
Appleby, J.O. 60–1, 62
Arnold, M. 159
Aron, R. 131, 137n.
Aurelius, M. 176

Bachelard, G. 20
Badiou, A. 3
Baldwin, T.W. 162
Balibar, E. 3
Barry, A. 143
Baudelaire, C.P. 30–1
Benjamin, W. 25, 31–2
Bismarck, O. von 109, 110
Boisguilbert, P. de 60, 61, 62–3, 67, 73n.
Boulainvilliers, H. de 59–60, 61
Braudel, F. 50, 51, 71, 72n.
Brett, J. 156, 158, 159, 160
Brown, J.A.C. 95
Brown, W. 97
Burchell, S. 79, 80
Bureau, P. 121

Callon, M. 83, 84
Canguilhem, G. 2, 19, 20, 40, 45, 48
Cassirer, E. 23, 25
Chatelet, F. 3
Cheysson, É. 113, 115
Clark, M. 1
Cleland, J. 163
Coady, C.A.J. 160
Cohen, D. 196, 210
Cohen, S. 143
Colbert, J.B. 58
Coleman, J.S. 185

Connelly, W. 79

Dandieu, A. 130, 131, 137n.
Davenant, C. 59
Davis, D.J. 190n.
Dawkins, J.S. 153, 155
Déat, M. 130, 137n.
Defert, D. 2, 4
Descartes, R. 10, 11
Diocles 198
Donzelot, J. 177
Dover, K. 196, 197
Dubreuil, H. 127, 137n.
Dumézil, G. 40
Dumont, L. 54
Durkheim, E. 109, 112

Elias, N. 167
Emery, F. 97
Eribon, D. 1, 2, 3, 4, 6
Ewald, F. 19

Facarello, G. 60
Fletcher, A. 59, 68
Fourquet, F. 86, 87
Friedson, E. 7–8

Galen 200, 210
Gide, C. 109
Gordon, C. 78, 98
Grafton, A. 162, 163
Guichard, O. 4
Gurvitch, G. 2, 127
Guyot, Y. 121

Habermas, J. 20, 48
Hacking, I. 24, 81
Hasbach, M. 54

Hayek, F. 25, 26
Hazard, P. 55
Hegel, G.W.F. 165
Hennis, W. 32, 33
Hobbes, T. 37–8, 67
Hopwood, A.G. 79, 80
Horkheimer, M. 25

Immergut, E. 148, 149, 150

Jacques, E. 97
Jannet, C. 113
Jouhaux, L. 126, 127, 129

Kant, I.: 'Conflict between the
    faculties' 13–14; and culture of
    person 165; on Enlightenment
    10–11, 13, 16, 17–18; Foucault on
    20–33; on French Revolution
    14–15, 16, 17
Koselleck, R. 58, 73n.
Kouchner, B. 6

Laertius, D. 44
Larson, M.S. 144
Lash, S. 177
Latour, B. 76, 83, 84
Laveleye, É. de 109
Lefort, C. 52–3
Le Goff, J. 41
Leinster-Mackay, D.P. 160
Le Play, F. 112
Leroy, M. 127, 137n.
Leruez, J. 89
Lesky, A. 210
Light, A. 156
Lingren, J.R. 65
Lipsius, J. 163
Lloyd, G.E.R. 196
Locke, J. 62, 66, 67, 70
Loft, A. 79
Luftalla, M. 54

MacIntyre, A. 78, 82
Man, H. de 130, 137n.
Marcus, S. 204, 212
Marx, K. 71
Mauss, M. 165–6, 176
Mendelssohn, M. 20
Meyer, J. 98
Miller, J. 3
Miller, P. 78, 80, 82, 86, 87, 90, 93,
    95, 96, 99, 102, 144, 182, 183

Minogue, K. 160
Molinari, G. de 121, 137n.
Monnet, J. 86
Montchrétien, A. de 57, 58, 72
Montesquieu, C. 66, 69
Mun, T. 57, 58, 72n.
Myers, C. 94

Newman, J.H. 160, 161
Nietzsche, F.W. 30, 31

Oestreich, G. 37, 162, 177
O'Leary, T. 78, 80, 82, 93
Oribasius 198, 210

Pasquino, P. 27
Paulus 198
Perroux, F. 130, 137n.
Peters, T.J. 100
Petty, W. 57, 58, 73
Pigeaud, J. 200
Plutarch, 196, 210
Polanyi, K. 25
Pomeroy, S.B. 196, 197

Quesnay, F. 66, 67

Rancière, J. 3
Raulet, G. 19, 29
Regnault, F. 3
Rose, N. 78, 80, 81, 82, 93, 94, 95,
    96, 98, 99, 144, 182, 183
Rostand, E. 113
Rothblatt, S. 161–2, 168, 169, 170
Rousseau, J.J. 66, 69
Rufus 199–200, 201, 210
Rustow, A. 25, 29

Salamatian, A. 5
Savary, J. 57, 58
Schumpeter, J.A. 26, 28, 42, 73n.
Scull, A.T. 143
Serres, M. 3
Sfez, L. 70
Shapiro, M. 79
Shaw, B.D. 203
Small, A. 181
Smith, A. 50, 53, 55, 56, 62, 63,
    64–70
Sombart, W. 28, 29
Soranus 196
Sorel, G. 106
Spinoza, B. 38

Starr, P. 148, 149, 150

Taylor, C. 79
Taylor, F.W. 128
Taylor, G.R. 94, 95, 97, 122–3
Thevenot, L. 94
Thomas, A. 127, 128, 137n.
Thompson, G. 78, 79, 84, 99
Thorsrud, E. 97
Tocqueville, A. de 26
Tomlinson, J. 79
Tribe, K. 79
Trist, E.L. 97

Valleroux, H. 120
Vauban, S. 59

Veyne, P. 40

Waterman, R.H. 100
Weber, H. 3
Weber, M. 26, 27, 32–3, 45, 159,
    180, 188, 189, 206; on 'cultivated
    man' 157, 164, 190–1; Foucault on
    27–8; and Protestant ethic 37,
    38–9; on science as vocation
    170–7, 178
Whimster, S. 177
Williams, B. 158, 159, 161
Williams, K. 78

Zinzendorf, N.L. 206

Subject index

absolutism 55, 56; economics of 56–8, 63; end of 59
academic career structure, Weber on 171
'action at a distance' 76, 83, 88
aesthetics of existence 31, 32
Agence de Presse-Libération (APL) 5
antiquity: and ascetic Christianity 202; sexuality in 195–201
archaeology, Foucault and 194–5
asylums 143
austerity: in ancient sexuality 196, 198–200, 201; and Christianity 201–4
Australia, reform of higher education in 153–6, 187
Australian Historical Association 155
authoritarian democracy 129–31
autonomy: of humanities 156, 161; of the professions 145–6; and security 32

balance of trade theory 62
bodily arts 164, 167
Broadcasting in the '90s 140

capitalism 28, 29, 50, 51, 65, 66–7; Industrial Revolution and 71; Smith and 66–8
catastrophe 25–6, 27
cause, for progress 13–14
change, Foucault on 21
Christianity: austerity of 202–4; Foucault on 202–4, 208, 211; and psychoanalysis 205–7; and sexuality 202, 203
circular mechanism 132
citizenship 97–8, 99

civility, as a goal of liberal education 167–8, 169
Collège de France 4, 5
commerce: domestication of 64–6; and economics of absolutism 57–8; and society 68–70; and the state 55–6, 59–60
community of labour 130–1
confession 205–6
consumption 99–100
contract 37–8; for hire of a service 117, 121–2, 125; and oppression of working class 116–17
Courts and Legal Services Act, 1990 149
criticism, Foucault and 23–4
cultivation, as a goal of liberal education 157, 159, 163–4, 168–9, 180, 181; ethical character of 174
culture 158; Arnold and 159

deregulation 139–40; and the professions 144–50
dietetics, and sexuality 200–1
discipline, and Taylorism 123–4
disciplines: Foucault on 37, 39; Weber and 174, 176
discontinuity 45–6
Discounted Cash Flow Analysis (DCF) 90–2
dissidents 27
drug use 6

economic growth 89–91; language of 92
economic policy 79
economic rationality 123–4, 126, 127,

128; link with social 129, 130, 131, 132

economy: national 85–6, 88–92; political 49–72; representations of 50–2; social 108–9, 110, 112–14

education 183–4; administration of 186–7; analysis of 186, 187; goals of 156, 157; and governmental objectives 186, 187; see also higher education; liberal education

Education Reform Bill, 1988 140

employers: complaints of 117–18; powers and responsibilities of 119–20, 121–2, 134; Taylorism and 122–3, 124

employment conditions, normalization of 123, 124

Enlightenment 12–13, 16; Foucault on 19–20, 22–3; Kant on 10, 11, 17–18

enterprise 98, 99, 100, 101; government of 93–7

entrepreneurship 100

epilepsy 198–9

equilibrium, in the economy 57, 58, 60, 62–3

ethics, history of 41, 43–4

evaluation, of policy 78

exercise, sex and 200

experience 176

expert, Weber and 157

expertise 82, 84, 88–9, 93; of enterprise 100, 101; state and 139–52

factory regulations 118, 119; debates on 120–2

family 112–13

fidelity 46

Foucault, Michel 40, 83, 177, 208–9; academic career of 1–4; action on human rights in Iran 5; on Baudelaire 30–1; at Collège de France 4–5; and drugs 6; on the Enlightenment 19–20, 25; and genealogy 24–5, 26–7, 30, 194–5, 197; and GIP 5; on governmentality 76, 101, 140–4, 149–50, 178, 181; and history of thought 41–7; and neoliberalism 28, 29; as philosopher of discontinuity 45–6; on the professions 142–4, 145; on Smith

67; use of sources in HS 197, 198–201; **Works**: *Discipline and Punish* 5, 27, 36–7, 42; *History of Sexuality* 39–40, 42, 44, 46, 194–207, 211, 212; 'Kant on Enlightenment and revolution' 10–18, 19–33; *Madness and Civilization* 27, 46; 'On governmentality' 6

France: development of national accounting in 86–8; employment conditions in 116–21; Third Republic in 106–8, 133

Frankfurt School 19–20, 25, 28

free exchange 59

freedom, and knowledge 24

Freiburg School 28–9

French Revolution, Kant on 13, 14–15

genealogy 24–5; and the Enlightenment 25; Foucault and 25, 26–7, 30, 194–5, 197; of political economy 49–72

general practitioners 147, 148

government 38, 39, 46, 178, 181; in ancient Greece 43–4; 'at a distance' 83–4; Foucault on 6, 7, 8–9, 75–6, 141; higher education and 186–8; language and 80–1, 82, 84, 98; and liberal education 183–5; and political economy 51; and power 43, 177, 182–3; and the professions 145–6, 149–50, 151; programmes of 80, 84, 88, 92, 98–9, 102, 182–3; techniques of 81–5, 188; see also governmentality; state

government of variables 132–3

governmentality 8–9, 76–8, 102, 177–8; discursive character of 78–81; economy and 85–92; Foucault on 76, 101, 140–4, 149–50, 178, 181; and mechanisms of rule 84; and rise of the professions 142–4, 150–1

Greece, ancient: government in 43–4; sexual practice in 195–8

group relations 96

Groupe d'Information sur les Prisons (GIP) 5

health service, reform of 147–8, 149

higher education: goals of 154–6; and
    government 186–8; reform of in
    Australia 153–6, 187
Hippocratic corpus 198–9
homosexuality 6, 196–7, 206
human relations, management of
    95–6, 100
humanism 162–3, 180
humanities 175, 180–1; governing of
    179–89; and liberal education
    158–61, 173; response to reform of
    higher education in Australia 154,
    155, 156, 157–8

imprisonment 36
individualism 54
industrial accidents 96, 110–11
industrial democracy 127–8, 129
industrial rationality 128, 129
Industrial Revolution 71
industrial tribunals (*conseils de
    prud'hommes*) 117, 118, 119
input–output table 87
insurance technique 110–12, 113–14,
    120; state and 115
interests, allied (*interessement*) 84
intervention 81, 82; at a distance 92;
    in economy 89, 90; in the
    professions 145; in society 106–8,
    109, 113, 114, 133–6
interview, technology of 97
'inventory of differences' 45
investment decisions 69, 90, 91
Iran, Foucault on 5
irrationality 123, 124

Judaism 203

Keynesian economics 79, 127, 132–3
knowledge 24, 80–1, 174; government
    and 80–1; and higher education
    155–6, 158–9; as a vocation
    170–1, 172; Weber and 171, 172,
    175

laissez-faire 62, 63, 69
language: economy and 86, 88, 92; of
    enterprise 98–9, 100; of expertise
    84; of government 80–1, 82, 84,
    98; of management 94, 96; politics
    and 79–81; of right 133–4
law 146–7, 149

leadership 96
Lebensführung (lifestyle) 32, 42,
    43–4, 164
Le Chapelier law, 1792 116–17
liberal education 156, 158–61, 180;
    aims of 167–8; in
    eighteenth-century Britain 169;
    ethical claims for 163–7;
    governmentalizing of 183–5;
    historical claims for 161–3; social
    claims for 167–70; vocational
    character of 168, 170
liberalism 59, 60–1, 83, 109; failure of
    28–9, 61–2, 63; and insurance
    technique 110, 112; and the
    professions 146
Libération 5
liberation/repression 204–5
livret ouvrier (workers' passbook)
    117, 118, 119
Louis XIV 59

madness 46, 143
management 90–2, 94–6; scientific
    93–4
Marxism, F. and 2, 3
mechanisms of rule 83
medical audit 149
medical texts, Greek 198–201
medicine 146, 147–8, 149
merchants 58, 61, 65, 66
modernity 12, 30–1, 36, 37
monasticism, as origin of liberal
    education 160
monopolies 126, 134
Monopoly and Mergers Commission,
    report on professional advertising
    140
mutual aid societies 112, 113

national accounting 86–8
National Economic Development
    Council 90
national economy: at a distance
    88–92; governing of 85–6, 88
National Health Service 145, 146, 149
National Institute of Industrial
    Psychology 94
nationalized industries 91–2
neo-corporatism 129–31
neoliberalism 28–9
networks, in government 84–5
New Left 20–1, 24, 32

'new school', of social economy 109,
    110, 113, 114
1968, political consciousness of 22, 28
nobility, criticism of 60
normalization 9, 37, 39, 123, 124–5,
    143, 149

occupational risk 111–12
OECD, education policy analysis 154
Ordoliberalen (Freiburg School) 28–9
Ordre Nouveau 130, 137n.

party politics 179
Patients' Charter 147
personality, as a vocation 170–9, 180,
    184
personhood 165–6, 180
philosophical anthropology 24, 33,
    165
philosophical journalism 20
philosophy 11; and law 13
planning 139
Poland, Foucault and 6
policy 77–8, 79
political economy, genealogy of 49–72
political power 75, 102, 177, 182–3;
    redistribution of 129–30; state and
    77, 129
political rationalities 79–80, 82, 86,
    89, 98; historical character of
    178–9; of humanities 189
politicization, and deregulation
    139–40
politics 43; and expertise 148–50; and
    science 175, 177–8, 180; teaching
    of 177
population, and government 141,
    184–5
power: Foucault on 9, 42–3, 142–3;
    legitimation of 38; see also political
    power
present 12, 24–5, 30; Kant on 10–11;
    in philosophy 11, 18; see also
    genealogy
prison 36–7
prisoners, action on behalf of 5
problematizations 186, 187
production, and national economy 87
productivity 50, 90–1; workers and
    95, 96, 100, 122–4
professionalism 144, 145; public
    opinion and 146; state and 150–1
professions 7–8; disestablishment of

139–40, 144–50; governmentality
    and 142–4
profit motive 124, 128
programmes of government 80, 84,
    88, 92, 98–9, 102, 182–3
progress 13–14; and commerce 59,
    65, 69; Kant on 14–15, 16; of
    society, state and 106–8, 127,
    128–9, 131–2, 133–6
protectionism 60–1
Protestant ethic 38–9
psychoanalysis, genealogy of 205–7,
    208, 212
psychology 94; of the workplace 96,
    97, 100
public, government and 52, 63, 93
Puritanism 166

Regional Planning Councils 139
Renaissance scholarship 162–3
representation 80
responsibility, in social relations 135–6
revolution 21–2; see also French
    Revolution
right to work 115, 116, 134
risk, socialization of 111, 115–16, 120

Sacred Disease, The 199
salvation 39
science: and politics 175–6, 177–8,
    180; vocation for 171, 172–3, 174
scientific management 93–4
self: Foucault on 6–7; person as
    166–7
self-discipline 38–9
self-government 43–4
sexuality: in antiquity 195–8, 200–1,
    203, 205; Christianity and 202,
    203; Foucault on history of 40–1,
    43–4
social control 37, 39, 143
social discipline 37, 38, 39
social economy 108–9; new school of
    109, 110, 113, 114; traditional
    school of 112–13, 114
social rationality 124–5, 126, 127,
    128; links with economic 129, 130,
    131, 132
social right: employment and 120–5,
    134; in the Third Republic 107–16
socialism 109; and insurance system
    114
society: and social right 128; state and

106–8, 109–10, 127, 131–2, 133–6
solidarity 106, 107; and insurance
    technique 110–12, 114; and social
    right 107–8, 109
Sombart's thesis 29
sovereignty, Foucault and 141
specificity 44–5
state 50, 51–2, 65, 77; authority of
    130, 131; and capitalism 67; and
    commerce 55–6, 59–60;
    domestication of 68–70; and
    economic equilibrium 62–3; and
    employment problems 125, 126;
    and exercise of power 182–3;
    governmentalization of 182–3; and
    insurance system 115; intervention
    of in society 106–8, 109, 113, 114,
    133–6; neutrality of 132; and
    professionalism 150–2; Smith and
    68–70; and social progress 106–8,
    127, 128–9, 131–2, 133–6; theory
    of 38; and wealth 61
statistics 133–4, 141
status 115, 125
'subject of desire' 44–5
subjectivity 41, 42
supervision 123

Taylorism 93–4, 122–4
technologies of government 81–5,
    102, 182, 184, 188, 189
trade unions 124–5, 126, 134

traditional school, of social economy
    112–13, 114
trust hospitals 147–8
truth 41–2, 49, 51

United Kingdom: economic regulation
    in 89–92; eighteenth-century
    education in 162, 169
universities: functions of 161; and
    government objectives 186–7; and
    governmentality 156, 159–60,
    185–6; in history 162–3; role of in
    liberal education 156, 160, 161–2,
    184–5

Vincennes, University of 3–4

wealth 60, 61; desire of 64; and state
    61
welfare state 32; genealogy of 108,
    125–36
William III 59
women 196
workers: demands of 126;
    management of 93–6; and means
    of production 129; and
    neo-corporatism 130; psychology
    of 94–5, 96–7, 100; rights of 129,
    130
working class, oppression of 116–17
Working for Patients 140, 147